23085

D

WITHDRAWN

BUSINESS DECISION MAKING

BUSINESS DECISION MAKING

ALAN J. BAKER

CROOM HELM LONDON

© 1981 Alan J. Baker
Croom Helm Ltd, 2-10 St John's Road, London SW11

British Library Cataloguing in Publication Data

Baker, Alan John
  Business decision making.
  1. Decision-making
  I. Title
  658.4'03   HD30.23

  ISBN 0-85664-871-X
  ISBN 0-85664-872-8 Pbk

Typeset by Leaper & Gard Ltd, Bristol
Printed and bound in Great Britain
by Billing and Sons Limited
Guildford, London, Oxford, Worcester

To Ann Bannon and Sarah Ann

CONTENTS

PREFACE

This book provides an introduction to the analysis of business decision making in relation to a firm's deployment of its existing resources and its selection of new investments. The unifying theme of the book is a recognition of the crucial importance of risk in business decisions, and this recognition is reflected in two ways. First, theoretical models of decision making in the face of risk are considered in the light of conditions likely to prevail within firms. Second, attention is focused on the potential of decision techniques for providing decision makers with useful information about the implications of the choices open to them.

The model of the firm adopted is the familiar one of a management-controlled business with equity capital widely held and traded on a stock exchange. Management is represented as a unified decision making 'personality' with a well-defined utility function. Discretionary behaviour in both product and capital markets is assumed, in the sense that managers have the freedom, and are in fact obliged by their position, to determine the goals of the firm and the criteria by which their decisions will be guided. Resources are sufficiently large and diverse, and the firm's activities sufficiently numerous, to create within the firm the classic resource allocation problems of which goods to produce and how to produce them. In addition, the firm relies heavily on internally generated funds for investment finance; so in this area of choice too, management must determine which set of principles to apply in selecting projects involving risky returns.

Although it is useful to categorise decision making in the way indicated, it is also true that policies for the short period have implications for the longer term. This intrusion of long-term considerations into short-term policy making is particularly true of pricing, which is not considered in depth in this book. Short-period price decisions are seen as part of a general policy which is not itself in question in the context of other short-period decisions, e.g. output, though it may of course be part of general policy to respond in planned ways to prevailing market conditions. On this interpretation, price policy is perhaps best seen as an ongoing aspect of an investment decision, evaluated along with other conditional policies in management's *ex ante* probabilistic view of the investment's lifetime profitability. This is far from being a completely satisfactory treatment of an important and complex area of decision, but in a book of moderate length which concentrates on resource allocation decisions, it will serve as a workable background for discussing both short-period policies and long-term investment choice.

The plan of the book can be summarised briefly. As a preliminary to the consideration of specific decision contexts, Chapter 1 discusses the objectives of the firm with the modest intention of establishing a general presumption about managerial motivation. Chapter 2 introduces elements of probability theory which will be applied in later chapters, and questions the value to decision makers of probability information which, realistically, is acknowledged to be imperfect. This latter theme, namely the interpretation of decision making in conditions of risk and uncertainty, is developed in Chapter 3.

Chapters 4-6 deal with various aspects of linear programming (LP). After a detailed treatment in Chapter 4 of the simplex solution method as applied to a simple business problem, Chapter 5 develops the LP theory of the firm, discusses the representation of various 'managerial' policies and shows how different attitudes towards risk might be reflected in models of the firm's short-period decision. Chapter 6 applies LP to a variety of business problems, laying stress on the derivation of indications of shadow value and shadow cost, and on the sensitivity of solutions to the assumption employed. In this latter sense, too, the LP framework is helpful in understanding decisions involving risk.

Chapter 7 explores decisions on expenditures designed to obtain information about risks, with a view to understanding the nature of optimising behaviour in this area and the different types of strategy that are possible.

Finally, Chapters 8-10 explain rival interpretations of the market valuation of risky prospects and their implications for theoretical models of optimal investment choice by firms. A number of operational applications of investment choice theory are also discussed. Risk figures prominently in these chapters not simply as a factor to be borne in mind by decision makers, but also as a concept whose definition in investment choice theory is itself a matter of controversy.

The book is intended as an advanced undergraduate text for students taking business economics as part of a degree in economics or business studies, as an introductory text for postgraduate courses in business economics, and as supplementary reading for advanced undergraduate courses in microeconomics and the theory of the firm. A familiarity with microeconomics and the theory of the firm is assumed, together with a basic grounding in probability theory and statistics. No previous experience of linear programming is assumed, beyond the essentials of simultaneous equation theory. The reader is assumed to be familiar with the basic concepts of cash flow discounting, and for those whose knowledge extends no further than this an appendix to Chapter 9 will be helpful.

I am glad of the opportunity to record my appreciation of the help I have received from my colleague Derek Deadman, who read the great bulk of the draft chapters, and whose comments on major matters of content and exposition and on minor points of style have almost invariably led to improvements in the final text. All remaining errors of omission or commission are of course my own responsibility.

Thanks are also due to the secretarial staff of the Economics Department at Leicester University — Joan Cook, Jeanne Cretney, Heather Hopper, Mavis Johnson and Dorothy Logsdon. Their helpful co-operation has been extended to me in much greater measure than duty dictated, throughout the drafting and final typing of the book.

Lastly, it is no exaggeration to claim that without the understanding and support of my wife this book could not have been written. Much of the writing has been done under the hospitality of my own and my wife's parents, and for the encouragement of our two families I am very grateful.

A.J. Baker
University of Leicester

1 THE OBJECTIVES OF THE FIRM

> Don't put the fate of your business in the
> delusions of economists.
>
> Peter Drucker

1.1 Introduction

This book deals with the economic analysis of a wide range of business
decisions, but its purpose is a wider one than parading an array of
'problem-solving' techniques. Where techniques are involved we shall
show how they can yield operational answers to the sorts of questions
economists would regard as important, e.g. shadow valuations of scarce
resources, shadow costs of constraints and the value of information. And
where the theoretical foundations of decision models are themselves
controversial, for example in the area of capital market valuation
theory, we shall attempt to explain rival theories and their differing
implications for decision making.

Our purpose in this opening chapter is to prepare the way for those
later discussions, both of technique and theory, by establishing a
presumption that the business firm does operate in its owners' interests
— or at least that distortions of this principle do not seriously affect the
nature of decision making in the situations we shall consider. Our plan
is to bring two contrasting themes or traditions in the theory of the
firm (broadly defined to include business finance theory) into a brief
but productive confrontation. The themes chosen for this purpose are
the 'managerial' theory of the firm and what may be termed the
'business finance tradition'. Both of these relate to the standard model
of enterprise adopted throughout this book, namely a model in which
managers effectively control policy making and the distribution of
profit, and equity capital is widely held and traded at prices determined
by market forces.

1.2 Williamson's Managerial Model

1.2 (i) The Background to 'Managerial' Theories of the Firm

'Managerial' theories represent a form of response to a number of long-
established themes in the study of the business environment and

business behaviour. Briefly, these themes relate to the emergence of a managerial class of businessmen who have largely replaced owner-managers in the control of large enterprises; and to the weakening of capital market and product market pressures on such firms. Recognition of these trends dates back at least to the 1930s (see Berle and Means, 1932), a period which also saw important theoretical developments in the shape of new market structure models (Chamberlin, 1933; Robinson, 1933) and the beginnings of doubts about the validity of the profit-maximising concept of business behaviour. On the latter point, doubt was expressed as to the practicability of profit maximisation given the information likely to be available to businessmen (Hall and Hitch, 1939); and it was not long before the implausible implications of an exclusive pursuit of profit – even by the owner–manager – were recognised (Scitovsky, 1943).

Managerial theories spring from a general recognition of all of these points, and the 'empty box' which managerial theorists have attempted to fill is one in which managers, who possess considerable freedom of action in their product market behaviour, as well as independence and security in capital markets, have to determine exactly which objectives to pursue.

Perhaps surprisingly in view of the long prehistory of its component ideas, managerial theorising as a recognised area of the theory of the firm took a considerable time to develop. Much of the early running in the developing critique of out-and-out profit maximisation was made by models which stressed external constraints rather than internal choices as reasons for failure to pursue profit maximisation to the full. Oligopolistic interdependence and entry-preventive pricing are examples of this type of emphasis (see Koutsoyiannis, 1979, for reviews of these developments).

From the late 1950s, theorists began to formulate models in which the emphasis had shifted from external constraints on would-be profit maximisers to the recognition and formal representation of deliberate compromises between profit and more 'managerial' satisfactions. However, in theory the managerial form remains close to the traditional in possessing a unitary or unified decision making 'personality', maximising a fairly restricted 'top-level' utility function (see Machlup, 1967, pp. 5–6). Within this broadly defined common ground managerial theories differ widely in their interpretation of managers' objectives. Our purpose will be adequately served by considering one representative managerial model in some detail – the 'staff and emoluments' model of O.E. Williamson. (For a general introduction to managerial theories of the firm, and detailed treatment of a number of different models, see Wildsmith, 1973. Other useful texts are Koutsoyiannis, 1979, and Crew, 1975.)

1.2 (ii) Williamson's Staff and Emoluments Model

Like the standard theory of the profit-maximising firm, O.E. Williamson's model of managerial choice (Williamson, 1963 and 1964) is presented in the framework of the firm's short-period cost and revenue functions. Williamson's managers do not share the same objective as the firm's owners, who are assumed to prefer maximum profit to all other possible benefits of ownership. In particular, managers derive utility from the various types of expenditure they control. First, expenditures on *staff* (S) yield utility for various reasons: managers' own salaries or promotion chances may be related to the size of organisation they control; and non-pecuniary motives such as prestige, authority and security also play their parts. It is vital to the model that staff outlays, which Williamson alternatively describes as '(approximately) general administrative and selling expense' actually influence demand for the firm's product, at any given price, and as such are an obvious instrument of policy.

Second, *managerial emoluments* (M) require little explanation as a source of utility. They represent the diversion of profit into expenditures which increase managers' enjoyment of their working lives, but which are not strictly necessary for the running of the business or for its ability to attract and retain management personnel. The fact that outlays on luxurious office accommodation, expense accounts, company cars, etc., have the effect of reducing the company's tax burden is only one reason for their widespread use. Another is that in an age of high marginal rates of personal taxation, executives can award themselves untaxed increases in their living (or working) standards in ways which appear innocuously in the company's accounts as 'costs' rather than 'executive remuneration'.

Finally, *discretionary investment* (I_d) is defined as the level of after-tax profit remaining for managers to allocate as they wish once the firm's minimum profit constraint has been met:

$$I_d = (1 - t)(R - C - S - M) - \Pi_0 \qquad \text{(i)}$$

where R is the firm's total revenue from sales, C is production cost (a function of output), Π_0 is the minimum profit constraint, S and M are staff and emoluments outlays respectively and t is the corporate tax rate. We exclude lump-sum taxes on firms, though these are included on Williamson's model. (Note that *all* expenditures, including M, are tax deductible.) The minimum profit constraint is seen as the minimum after tax return necessary to satisfy shareholders' dividend expectations and prevent any threat of a takeover bid in which another firm might try to enlist the support of disgruntled shareholders.

The full managerial utility function, with U denoting managerial ability, can now be given.

$$U = U(S, M, [(1 - t)(R - C - S - M) - \Pi_0])$$ (ii)

Demand for the firm's product is a function of price and staff expenditures (advertising, etc.) such that at any level of S the firm's demand curve is downward-sloping in the normal way; and the outlay on staff affects the level of demand at any given price. Since output, denoted by X, staff outlays and emoluments can all be varied independently, maximisation of U in equation (ii) requires the following three first conditions to be satisfied simultaneously:

$$\frac{\partial U}{\partial X} = 0, \quad \text{implying} \quad \frac{\partial R}{\partial X} = \frac{\partial C}{\partial X}$$ (iii)

$$\frac{\partial U}{\partial S} = 0, \quad \text{implying} \quad \frac{\partial R}{\partial S} = \frac{-\frac{\partial U}{\partial S} + (1 - t)\frac{\partial U}{\partial I_d}}{(1 - t)\frac{\partial U}{\partial I_d}}$$ (iv)

$$\frac{\partial U}{\partial M} = 0, \quad \text{implying} \quad \frac{\partial U}{\partial M} = (1 - t)\frac{\partial U}{\partial I_d}$$ (v)

We shall assume that all second-order conditions for the maximisation of U are satisfied. An important assumption Williamson makes is that managerial indifference surfaces in dimensions S, M and I_d do not touch the axes of the space in which they are drawn: this ensures that positive solution values of all three variables will be obtained.

From condition (iii) we can see that in his output decision at least, Williamson's manager remains a profit maximiser, equating marginal production cost and marginal revenue. Condition (iv), however, marks a departure from full profit maximisation: given that all marginal utilities are positive, $\partial R/\partial S$ (the increase in revenue resulting from a unit increase in staff outlays) must be less than unity; whereas a profit maximiser would set S to achieve $\partial R/\partial S = 1$. Spending on S is excessive because staff outlays yield utility to managers apart from their contribution to the firm's revenue. Finally, condition (v) suggests that managers achieve a balance between M and I_d that depends on the corporate tax rate: a higher rate of tax effectively cheapens emoluments, which are tax-deductible, and managers respond by increasing M (lowering $\partial U/\partial M$) and reducing I_d (raising $\partial U/\partial I_d$) to restore condition (v).

Whereas staff outlays influence demand and hence the level of output (and price) at which marginal cost equals marginal revenue, the balance struck between M and I_d in condition (v) does not directly influence output or price. However, if management's appetite for M were to be expressed differently, as a target level of expenditure, a change in that target *would* affect the firm's policy. This view of M is appropriate, for example, where as seems likely in many cases, managers feel obliged to follow a 'going market rate' for emoluments. Recognising that a change in the target for M is akin to a change in the firm's fixed costs, the relevant analysis is Williamson's own comparative static analysis of a change in lump-sum taxation in his 'staff only' model (Williamson, 1964, p. 49). In effect, an increase in *any* component of fixed costs reduces the firm's ability to support an 'excessive' level of S, with the result that the price and output combination generated under condition (iii) moves closer to that at which profit would be maximised. Thus it is possible that management's emoluments policy, as well as its staff policy, has an influence on price and output in Williamson's framework.

1.2 (iii) An Evaluation of the Staff and Emoluments Model

The essence of Williamson's model is that managers actually allow their expense preferences to influence the firm's price and output policy. This is obviously a more radical interpretation than one in which managers maximise profit and then merely divert some of that profit into favoured uses.

The crucial dual role played by staff expenditures — as an element of cost which simultaneously influences demand and yields managerial utility in its own right — seems doubtful as a general proposition. Williamson equates staff outlays with general administration and sales expenditures, and the obvious questions are (1) whether outlays in this category which raise the level of demand actually contribute to managerial utility, and (2) whether outlays which contribute to managerial utility actually influence demand. While money spent outside the firm on advertising, or inside the firm on an unglamorous sales force remote from head office, may influence demand, it seems unlikely to yield much utility of the kind envisaged by Williamson (authority, prestige, etc.). On the other hand, money spent on a large sales department in the company's head office will yield considerable utility but may have little real influence on demand — especially under static demand conditions, when the firm's sales performance must surely depend on the size of its sales force in the field, rather than on the size of a sales planning team (however grandiosely titled) at head office. (No doubt this sceptical generalisation has its exceptions: an excellent illustration of demand creating and utility yielding outlays might be found in building societies, which are frequently accused of excessive branch office proliferation.)

The relevance of the model for the analysis of either long-term equilibrium or short-term decision making is also open to question. In the context of long-term static equilibrium we must assume that the purpose of Π_0 is 'keeping shareholders happy', while I_d is employed in ways which do not alter future cost and revenue prospects in any way. This seems unlikely in itself, and in any case it is most improbable that the capital market would indefinitely tolerate the obvious diversion of profit into purely managerial purposes.

On the other hand, if the context of the model is intended to be short-period decision making under dynamic conditions, two different criticisms seem applicable. First, it is unlikely that firms actually co-ordinate their price, output and staff policies as fully as the model implies. For example, if S is determined independently of X — perhaps because it is a lagged function of the firm's *past* performance — maximising managerial utility coincides with the maximisation of profit for the prevailing level of S. Second, if managers derive utility from the prospective growth of the firm through the retention and reinvestment of profit (because growth is desirable *per se*, or because of the prospect of higher managerial-type outlays in the future), the tension between the profit goal and expense preferences should be less pronounced than in the static context. This is not to imply that management's preferred growth programme is necessarily in the best interests of the firm's shareholders: in effect the debate about managerialism simply shifts from the short period to the firm's goals and decision making for the long term.

1.3 Reactions Against Managerialism

1.3 (i) Profit Maximisation and X-Inefficiency Theory

One possible reaction to Williamson's staff and emoluments model is that while it undoubtedly identifies believable managerial preferences, it pictures management as indulging those preferences to an unbelievable degree. An alternative model of short-term managerial behaviour is suggested by Leibenstein's concept of 'X-inefficiency' (Leibenstein, 1966) as adapted by Crew, Jones-Lee and Rowley (Crew *et al.*, 1971, and Crew, 1975, Ch. 5). Leibenstein recognised that in the absence of strong competitive conditions in product markets there is scope for groups within the firm to pursue their own interests at the expense of the interests of owners. The resulting loss of efficiency − 'X-inefficiency' − can be countered by top-level management, but only by incurring additional costs of a 'policing' nature. This adds an extra dimension to traditional profit maximisation, the optimal amount of policing being identified simultaneously with optimum output.

The model suggested by Crew, Jones-Lee and Rowley, like that of Williamson, is basically one of short-period equilibrium under static conditions. Total costs are made up of policing costs, G, and non-policing costs, M. The level of G is a separate policy decision, while M is a more complex function:

$$M = M(Q, G, \Pi) \tag{vi}$$

in which M depends *positively* on output (Q), *negatively* on policing costs (given the level of output) and *positively* on the level of profit (Π). The first and second of these relationships are obvious, but the third requires further explanation. The relationship Crew *et al.* are trying to convey is an inverse one between the firm's freedom from competitive pressures in its product market and its general efficiency and cost-consciousness; thus actual profit serves as an admittedly unsatisfactory proxy for the security of the firm's market position.

A profit-maximising manager will wish to maximise the difference between revenue and *all* costs, by maximising profit with respect to both Q and G. In this model the firm's demand curve is given, and revenue (R) is determined by the area under the firm's demand curve once output is chosen. The maximising problem is as follows:

maximise: $\Pi = R - M - G$, with respect to Q and G

The two first-order conditions which must be satisfied simultaneously are

$$\frac{\partial \Pi}{\partial Q} = 0, \quad \text{implying} \quad \frac{\partial R}{\partial Q} = \frac{\partial M}{\partial Q} \tag{vii}$$

$$\frac{\partial \Pi}{\partial G} = 0, \quad \text{implying} \quad \frac{-\partial M}{\partial G} = 1 \tag{viii}$$

(again we assume that the appropriate second-order conditions for a maximum are satisfied).

Condition (vii) is the familiar one of equality between marginal revenue and marginal production cost. Condition (viii) defines the optimum level of policing in terms of equality between the marginal cost and marginal return to policing outlays.

Two aspects of this model are important in our present discussion. First, X-inefficiency is undoubtedly a many-sided problem, and we should expect to find a separate condition such as (viii) for each area of policing that can be separately treated in this way. This raises the question of whether managers will be as dutiful in policing 'managerial' X-inefficiency as they are in policing 'shop-floor' X-inefficiency. Whatever the answer to this question, it is probable that elements of X-inefficiency will survive even within a profit-maximising solution. However, if cost reductions achieved through policing in the managerial area take the form of savings in fixed costs, as seems likely, the firm's output and price policy determined by condition (vii) will *not* be affected by the degree of managerially-motivated slippage from the observance of condition (viii). This likelihood contrasts strongly with the role of S (and possibly M) outlays in Williamson's model.

A second aspect of policing relates to one of this chapter's recurring themes, namely the importance of the horizon against which management is assumed to frame its policy. Outlays on policing, e.g. management consultancy fees and new incentive schemes, may produce benefits which are both uncertain in amount and distributed over time. For both reasons it is doubtful whether the optimisation of such outlays can in fact be co-ordinated with a decision on current output and price as suggested by conditions (vii) and (viii).

1.3 (ii) O.E. Williamson's M-Form of Business Organisation

Some years after the publication of his managerial discretion models discussed in 1.2, Williamson modified the stance implicit in those models on the relative importance of internal and external pressures on managers (Williamson, 1970). In identifying the significance of the 'M-form' (multidivisional) company structure, Williamson recognised that certain emerging forms of business organisation embody the potential for creating pressures on managers similar in effect to those which would operate in fully competitive capital markets.

An M-form company is one having a number of more or less separately managed operating divisions or subsidiaries, each of which might in earlier times have existed as a separate business entity — a

'U-form' (unitary) company — perhaps large enough in relation to its markets to qualify as a 'managerial' firm of the kind we have been discussing. But the fact that each member firm or operating division now has to satisfy the group's top-level management instead of the capital market in general may make a profound difference to the pressures it experiences and the objectives it feels obliged to pursue.

The capital market advantages enjoyed by the U-form of business organisation in managerial models are the comparative security of the supply of internally generated investment funds, the market's weakness in imposing minimum profitability standards and the relative security of managers against threats of takeover or shareholder revolt (see Wildsmith, 1973, Ch. 1). However, as part of an M-form organisation, much of this managerial independence and security is undermined. Standards of financial performance set by the group's top management are likely to be more demanding, access to funds is no longer automatic or unquestioned, and divisional managers are conscious of the comparative ease with which they can be replaced.

Such marked differences in the pressures under which an operating division of an M-form company exists, compared to those it would experience as an independent firm, can hardly fail to affect the 'managerial' aspects of its behaviour. It is even possible that a new competitive spirit will be communicated downwards through the division, transforming it into something much more akin to a cost-conscious profit maximiser.

1.4 Financial Decision Making in the Firm

1.4 (i) The Financial Objective of the Firm

A student of the theory of the firm and a student of business finance might each be forgiven for expressing astonishment, on first encountering the literature of the other's field of study, at the assumptions they would find relating to the firm's objective. In contrast to managerial theories, the objective prescribed by the great majority of business finance theorists, and apparently accepted as a guiding principle by firms (see Mao, 1970), is the maximisation of the market value of the owners' wealth (generally, the ex dividend stock exchange value of equity capital plus whatever dividend is to be paid in the near future).

The breadth of theoretical support for this interpretation of the firm's objective must be due to its almost unarguable appropriateness, as well as to its overriding simplicity. What could be more fitting than that managers should direct their efforts to making shareholders as wealthy as possible, within the prevailing moral code and the existing legal framework? An added attraction, at least to economists, is the suggestion that in maximising the wealth of investors, managers are also tending to promote the general good of society (e.g. Solomon, 1963, pp. 23-4).

The inevitability of a multi-period interpretation of the firm's financial objective is obvious. Profit maximisation as a view of the firm's objective suffers from three kinds of difficulty: profits accrue at different points in time; profit prospects in later years may be affected by the firm's price and output policies in earlier years; and profit is generally subject to risk. These factors all suggest the need for a valuation model to enable a decision maker, whatever his motivation, to compare policy options with uncertain consequences extending beyond the current period.

1.4 (ii) The Instruments of Financial Policy

No prescriptive criterion, however obvious as a general principle, can hope to carry conviction unless it can be made operational. Nor can we hope to bypass the issue of the firm's short-period objective and behaviour simply by shifting our focus to the level of the firm's overall objective. There is obviously a need to achieve an integrated view of long-term objectives and short-term policy in the firm, and we shall return to this issue after further discussion of the implications of value maximising as an overall financial objective.

The major policy areas in which, in principle, the value-maximising objective is pursued are: (1) investment choice; (2) capital structure (in broad terms, the choice between risk capital and fixed-interest debt in financing an investment programme); and (3) dividend policy (Van Horne, 1977, Ch. 1).

Maximising the value of shareholders' wealth with respect to all three policies simultaneously and continuously must surely appear to managers an impossibly ambitious exercise. Indeed, it will seem obvious to them that *constancy* in capital structure and dividend policies is above all what the capital market requires if it is to perform its task at all reliably. The firm must be able to undertake investments on some understanding of how the market values their prospects *now* and how it will value them *in the future*; and to these ends its general policies on capital structure and dividend payout will take the form of fairly permanent commitments which the market can interpret and rely on. Thus we are likely to find at the heart of the structure of financial decision making a large and almost inevitable component of discretionary choice.

Notwithstanding general agreement on the nature of the firm's financial objective, the literature of business finance is no more free of controversy than is that of the theory of the firm. The nature of the valuation process itself remains in dispute — hardly a surprising state of affairs in view of the fact that the capital market itself is constantly in a state of flux, in which speculative forces and 'underlying reality' are extremely difficult to disentangle, and the fact that the expectations which form the basis of valuation are also constantly being revised and are in any case not directly observable. Valuation therefore remains an imperfectly understood phenomenon, and this has the obvious consequence that when rival theories yield contradictory prescriptions for optimal policy, managerial discretion is unavoidable.

1.4 (iii) Managerial Discretion in Value-Maximising Investment Choice

Our main concern remains the same as in earlier sections of this chapter, namely to try to throw light on the role of 'managerialism' in business decision making. This task is made more difficult by the inevitability of discretionary decision making over wide areas of financial policy, for the reasons referred to in the preceding sub-section. Discretionary choices may be well-intentioned towards shareholders, or they may be managerially motivated, and in the areas of capital structure choice and dividend policy it is probably impossible for us to tell the difference. However, in the crucial area of investment choice managers are obliged *repeatedly* to make choices which might reveal their purposes.

In principle it might seem that an objective capital market test of acceptability can be applied to any investment proposal regardless of whether the entrepreneur in question comprehends the underlying market valuation process. All that matters is whether the securities he offers can be sold in the market for a sum at least as great as the cost of undertaking the project. Even in this simple situation, however, the entrepreneur has to decide on the mixture of securities he wishes to offer the market (capital structure choice): he has little opportunity to learn by experimentation, and if the project is dissimilar to others he has undertaken in the past he will only achieve the value-maximising financing plan by coincidence. (Helliwell, 1968, pp. 9-37, develops a useful model of financial decision making starting from a 'basic' model of the firm and its investment and financing opportunities.) In practice, of course, matters are far more complex than our simple model suggests. It would be totally impracticable for established firms to refer all investment/financing proposals to a direct market test, one at a time; indeed, such a system would be quite out of keeping with the nature of the business firm as an institution that exists in its own right, is expected to outlast the lifetimes of the individual investments it undertakes and intends to finance itself largely out of retained earnings.

Even so, the possibility of a quasi-objective test of the value of an investment to a firm's shareholders is not to be summarily dismissed. An obviously appropriate criterion for the retention of equity earnings in a business is whether the investment of funds withheld from shareholders adds a greater amount to the market value of the firm's equity capital, because of the new earnings prospects it generates. We should consider how far the usefulness of this criterion is likely to extend.

If, for each period of its lifetime, an investment proposal has a pattern of risky earnings prospects which the investing firm's management believes would make no significant difference to the overall risk of the firm's earnings prospects in that period, as seen from the present day; and if the investment would be financed in a way which more or less maintained the firm's existing balance between debt and equity capital, then management may feel reasonably confident in predicting the change in the firm's equilibrium market value that would occur if the proposal were accepted. If this predicted change exceeds the cost of the project, the proposal should be accepted. This heavily qualified criterion reflects a 'traditional' approach to an objective test for an investment's acceptability, and it will be discussed at length in Chapter 8.

Of course, not all internally financed investments have earnings prospects which can fit comfortably into the highly convenient 'constant risk' mould just defined. And the resulting complexities of project evaluation in the absence of a direct market test of acceptability are compounded if, as implied by our suggested criterion, managers believe that the market values the firm *as a whole*. Under this approach, by definition, an investment's future earnings prospect has no unique market value which managers might hope, in principle, to be able to infer: the change in the equilibrium value of the firm depends on a 'portfolio' effect, namely the way in which the firm's overall risk is affected by the investment in question, as well as on the investment's expected returns.

More encouragingly, the modern theory of capital market valuation has been used to demonstrate that in principle an investment proposal should be evaluated as a separate prospect, and not for its effect on the risk of the investing firm. Capital market theory is therefore moving towards providing firms with a market value investment criterion. But the gaps between theory and practice in this area are still very wide, as Chapter 10 will argue, and for the foreseeable future managerial discretion will continue to dominate the firm's attempts to maximise the market value of shareholders' wealth.

1.5 Conclusion

In spite of the acknowledged gaps between principle and practicability, value maximisation as a general objective attracts widespread theoretical support and is not strongly or coherently opposed among managers. Of equal significance is the growing use of discounted cash flow techniques in investment decision making, which can be interpreted as practical managerial support for value maximisation (see Gitman and Forrester, 1977). Can we reconcile these impressions of the firm's long-term objective with contradictory impressions of 'managerialism' in short period behaviour?

The most logically satisfactory models of the firm are those in which the firm's long-term objective and short-period decision making are consistent with each other. Among managerial models, those of Baumol (1967), Ch. 10, and Marris (1964) meet this criterion, albeit in different ways. Much less satisfactory would be a model in which short-period behaviour was described in managerial terms, that is in terms of a conscious sacrifice of profit in favour of other goals, but the long-term objective was assumed to be the maximisation of shareholders' wealth. To see why we cannot simply assume that different sets of preferences operate in different 'compartments' of decision making, we only have to compare the way investments are appraised by a value maximiser with, for example, the way they might be appraised by a Williamson-type manager. In attempting to maximise the firm's value to its shareholders, managers discount future profit (revenue minus cost) expectations; whereas in an expense preference model some parts of a project's future costs would be valued along with that part of its profits managers believed they could retain for their own purposes.

The most promising starting point for an attempt to achieve consistency between our views of long-term objective and short-period behaviour is the X-inefficiency–profit maximisation model discussed in 1.3 (i). This model allows realistically for the presence of residual elements of excess cost, including managerial excesses, even under optimal policing; and it suggests that if managerial X-inefficiency is reflected in higher fixed costs, the precise degree to which management masters its managerial instincts should have no influence on the firm's price and output decision. In any case, as managers themselves have to make the often difficult distinction between justifiable and excessive outlays, we cannot realistically hope to detect a failure on their part to optimise the policing of such outlays. (We argued in 1.3 (i) that some policing outlays are comparable to investments with uncertain payoffs; and the same might be said of some managerially determined outlays, e.g. various aspects of research.)

A blurred picture of the objectives of managers is something we should have anticipated. The impression we carry forward is one of a profit/value maximising intention, overlaid by residual managerial instincts and sustained by the inevitability of discretionary choice in areas where objective criteria are unavailable. This model of the firm's objectives, indistinct in so many respects, will nonetheless form a sufficient basis for our analysis of specific areas of decision making in later chapters.

2 PROBABILITY AND DECISION MAKING

> Probabilities direct the conduct of the wise man.
>
> Cicero

2.1 The Concept of Probability

2.1 (i) Introduction

In this chapter we discuss the nature of probability statements in real-life situations before reviewing some basic probability concepts and relationships. Our theoretical treatment of probability is not intended as a rigorous and comprehensive introduction to the subject: indeed the coverage of 2.2–2.5 is deliberately selective, focusing on the processes by which probability judgements can be modified in the light of additional relevant information. Readers with little previous experience in the subject should therefore be able to follow the argument undistracted by material that is, for our immediate purpose, superfluous. Most readers, however, will be familiar with the concepts and relationships covered in 2.2–2.4, and for them the emphasis given to probability revision and the illustrative examples in 2.5 should demonstrate the relevance of theory to practical decision making. Texts which will be found useful in conjunction with this chapter include Hamburg (1970), Moore (1972) and Yamane (1967). Weaver (1963) provides an entertaining yet effective introduction to probability concepts.

2.1 (ii) Objective and Subjective Probability

The Relative Frequency Concept. In many situations it is possible to define the probability of an event objectively, in terms of the value towards which the relative frequency of that event will converge in the course of a very large number of identically conducted 'trials'. Textbooks on probability abound with examples of coin tossing, card drawing, dice rolling, etc.; these are the hardy perennials of probability theory, and there is no need to dwell on the definition here. It is worth emphasising, however, the 'long-run tendency' connotation of the relative frequency concept; we would be rather surprised, for example, on tossing an unbiased coin 100 times to obtain *exactly* 50 heads and 50 tails.

The Subjective Probability Concept. On moving away from textbook
situations of chance we may be pardoned for questioning the relevance
and usefulness of the relative frequency concept. If a businessman
states that in his opinion the probability of sales in the range 40,000–
50,000 units in a certain month is 0.40, we may be fairly sure that he
does *not* mean, 'If the month in question could somehow be repeated
a very large number of times, the level of sales achieved would lie in
the range 40,000–50,000 units in approximately 40 per cent of all
months observed.' The businessman recognises that a relative frequency
forecast of this type could only be based on knowledge of the objective
probabilities relating to the many and complex factors that will
determine sales in the month in question, and that such objective
information is simply unattainable. His probability statement, therefore,
must be seen as an expression of a personal, subjective, assessment of
the underlying objective risk situation. As such, it will of course reflect
his experience of similar situations in the past, his knowledge of current
and recent developments relating to sales prospects, not to mention
his intuition or 'feel' for the market situation. But all of these data and
feelings are imperfect substitutes for hard, objective probability data;
and our business-sales forecaster is no doubt aware of the subjective
nature of the probability statements he makes.

Being forced into a second-best situation as far as probability
measurement is concerned is regrettable, no doubt, but very far from
fatal to the relevance of the probability concept in decision making.
A subjective probability estimate is often described as an indicator
of the strength of the assessor's belief in the outcome in question; but
it is equally correct to interpret it as a personal assessment of the
underlying, invisible, objective risk situation. The assessor recognises
the fallibility of his own judgement, but, for the moment at least, he
can do no better. Therein, paradoxically, lies the strength and the
relevance of subjective probability.

Our main concern in this chapter is the property of 'recognised
fallibility' implicit in any subjective probability estimate. Decision
makers will often feel that their probability judgements are capable
of improvement through the acquisition and processing of further
relevant information; and the existence of this possibility helps to
sustain our belief that decision makers, who must surely wish to be as
well informed about risks as is economically sensible, will not simply
abandon the concept of probability because of its essentially subjective
nature. This chapter focuses on some of the more widely applicable
and precise techniques for the 'improvement' of probability estimates,

but it must be stressed that the ultimate criterion for the acceptability of any estimate is simply whether the decision maker in question is satisfied with it.

In the earliest stage of probability assessment the decision maker forms preliminary estimates of the probabilities of the various possible outcomes of the decision or action he is considering. The subject of the initial formulation and expression of probability judgements is itself extremely large, and we shall assume that the decision maker has already made his initial probability judgements, *prior probabilities* as they are generally called, in a process which we do not explore in detail, but of which some brief mention is required. (A much fuller discussion is provided by Moore, 1972, Ch. 9, and by Moore and Thomas, 1967, Chs. 7 and 8.)

However it is conducted, the basic objective at the preliminary stage of probability estimation should be to arrive at mutually consistent numerical statements of the decision maker's sentiments about the risks confronting him. Estimates of probability relating to complex and perhaps unfamiliar risk situations do not spring readily to mind; the process requires careful introspection and perhaps the use of techniques for eliciting probabilistic sentiments and giving them numerical expression. The fact that decision makers may experience difficulty in translating their feelings about risk into a set of mutually consistent values is hardly surprising, and in no way does it condemn subjective probability as a chimera or an unworkable tool. How many of us could set down *precisely* our views on any subject at all, even one in which we take a close interest, without giving serious thought to what we wished to say, and perhaps even submitting ourselves to an interviewer skilled in the art of helping people to clarify and organise their own opinions? For the present we rest our defence of the importance of probability in a study of decision making on the observation that thinking and expressing ourselves in probabilistic terms does seem to 'come naturally' to us all, even if our thoughts and expressions are sometimes less than crystal-clear.

2.2 Probability Concepts Relating to a Single 'Event'

Decision makers are often interested in a number of aspects of the outcome of an 'event', rather than, or as well as, a single qualitative or quantitative value. In market research, for example, an investigator may be interested in a potential customer's age, sex, income, home neighbourhood, size of family, previous 'brand' experience, etc. The 'event' in this case is simply the interview with the potential customer, and for more complex 'events' the multiplicity of aspects is equally obvious.

Our task in this section is to review the basic probability concepts relating to multiple characteristics of an event, and we can do this most effectively by working with an example in which a fairly simple event has two aspects of immediate interest to an observer. Table 2.1 presents the results of an imaginary random sample of 1,000 members conducted by a motoring organisation, with a view to improving the marketing of its various consumer products and services. In discussing this example we shall refer to the 1,000 members as 'the population'. This means that the probabilities we identify will be objective ones for that particular population; but if, as seems likely, the investigator should wish to make probability statements about the total membership of the organisation, the sample results would only have the status of reasonably reliable indicators of the underlying objective probabilities.

Table 2.1: Two-Way Classification of 1,000 Motorist-Members

		Classification by social status			
		A	B	C	Total
Classification	High (H)	25	200	75	300
by annual	Moderate (M)	70	280	150	500
car mileage	Low (L)	25	100	75	200
	Total	120	580	300	1,000

Table 2.1 is fairly self-explanatory, but before defining the basic probability concepts it illustrates, the notation that will be employed must be introduced. We shall use A, B and C to denote the numbers of members in social classes A, B and C, respectively; similarly, H, M and L will represent the numbers of members with high, moderate and low annual car mileages, respectively. We shall use P to denote the population in the sample (P = 1,000). Single lower case letters a, b, c, h, m, l denote the occurrence of a single characteristic, e.g. class A, class C or moderate mileage, in a random selection of one member from the population. Lower case letter combinations such as ha or mb

denote the numbers of 'high mileage – class A' or 'moderate mileage – class B' members in the population. Using Table 2.1 for frequent reference, we define four basic probability concepts.

Marginal Probability. This term is used to define formally the most obvious of probability concepts – for example, the probability that a high mileage member will be selected when a random drawing is made from the population of 1,000 members. As its name suggests, a marginal probability value can be read from the margins of a classification table such as Table 2.1, where we can see that the probability (i.e. relative frequency) of obtaining the characteristic 'high mileage' in a single random selection, denoted by $p(h)$, is given by

$$p(h) = \frac{H}{P} = \frac{300}{1,000} = 0.30$$

The marginal probabilities for all other single characteristics are obtained in exactly analogous fashion.

Joint Probability. The meaning of this concept is intuitively obvious, and a tabular classification of observations such as Table 2.1 makes its value in any case easy to identify. We are now interested in two characteristics of a randomly chosen member: social class and annual car mileage. In particular, suppose we wish to know the probability that a randomly chosen member will belong to the 'moderate mileage – class B' category. The total of such individuals, denoted by mb, is 280, and since we are sampling from the full population of 1,000 members we can state

$$p(m, b) = \frac{mb}{P} = \frac{280}{1,000} = 0.28$$

in which $p(m, b)$ is the probability (i.e. relative frequency) of the joint occurrence of the characteristics 'moderate mileage' and 'class B' in a randomly chosen member. It is useful to remember that when expressing joint probability the order in which we deal with the characteristics is immaterial. The group 'moderate mileage – class B' is identical to the group 'class B – moderate mileage': mb = bm = 280. Hence it makes no difference whether we write $p(m, b)$ or $p(b, m)$; both versions mean exactly the same thing. The remaining joint probabilities are obtained in exactly analogous fashion, and the sum of all possible joint probabilities (nine in this case) must obviously be unity.

Another important result is that the sum of the joint probabilities obtained along any row (or down any column) of Table 2.1 must obviously equal the marginal probability obtained at the end of that row (or foot of that column); e.g.

$$p(b) = p(h, b) + p(m, b) + p(l, b)$$
$$0.58 = 0.20 + 0.28 + 0.10$$

This illustrates the general proposition that the probability of an event (b) can be defined as the sum of the probabilities of the mutually exclusive ways ((h, b), (m, b) and (l, b)) in which that event may occur. (This is an application of the rule known as the *addition rule* in probability theory; see Moore, 1972, pp. 17-19, 23-4; Hamburg, 1970, pp. 29-31; or Yamane, 1967, pp. 97-9.)

Conditional Probability. This concept, too, is practically self-explanatory, but it is most important to realise that we are now in effect redefining (i.e. reducing) the population from which an imaginary random choice will be made. As with joint probability, we are interested in two characteristics of a randomly chosen member, but in the case of one characteristic we specify in advance the 'value' that characteristic must have. For example, if we are concerned only with members in class B, the relevant population is 580. Within this reduced population it would be surprising if the probabilities p(h), p(m) and p(l) had exactly the same values as they do in the population as a whole, and we must therefore recognise an appropriate new probability concept and extend our notation accordingly. As an example, the expression p(h/b) means 'the probability of selecting a high mileage member at random, given that the selection is made from among class B members only'. Apart from this precondition our probability definition proceeds exactly as before. Thus

$$p(h/b) = \frac{hb}{B} = \frac{200}{580} = 0.345$$

By analogous calculations we also obtain p(m/b) = 0.043 and p(l/b) = 0.172.

Obviously, there are as many ways of narrowing the population as there are categories within the two characteristics considered. In this case we have six such sub-populations, each with its conditional probabilities for the categories in the non-specified characteristic. Once again, the remaining sets of conditional probabilities can be obtained in analogous fashion to those illustrated here. One further point deserves emphasis: the order in which we place the characteristics in our conditional probability notation is *not* immaterial. Thus $p(c/m)$ has a completely different meaning from $p(m/c)$, and, except by coincidence, a different value too.

'And/Or' Probability. Although it may at first glance suggest something less precise than the three concepts already discussed, the concept $p(m \text{ } and/or \text{ } c)$ does have an equally precise meaning. In Table 2.1 the total of 500 moderate mileage members is made up of 70 class A, 280 class B and 150 class C members:

$$M = ma + mb + mc$$
$$500 = 70 + 280 + 150$$

Similarly, the total of 300 class C members is made up of 75 high mileage, 150 moderate mileage and 75 low mileage members:

$$C = hc + mc + lc$$
$$300 = 75 + 150 + 75$$

The group of 150 class C members in the moderate mileage sub-population is identical to the group of 150 moderate mileage members in the class C sub-population. Clearly, the number of members satisfying the description 'moderate mileage and/or class C' is given by the total of moderate mileage members *plus* the total of class C members *minus* the total of any overlap between the two ways of classifying: that is $500 + 300 - 150 = 650$. The probability of randomly selecting from the whole population a member who is *either* a moderate mileage member, *or* a class C member, *or* both, is given by

$$p(m \text{ } and/or \text{ } c) = \frac{M + C - mc}{P} = \frac{650}{1,000} = 0.65$$

(The reader can confirm from Table 2.1 that there are 350 members who are *neither* moderate mileage *nor* class C.) By slightly modifying the algebraic presentation of this definition we obtain a more operational statement in terms of the marginal and joint probability concepts already discussed:

$$p(m \text{ } and/or \text{ } c) = \frac{M}{P} + \frac{C}{P} - \frac{mc}{P} = p(m) + p(c) - p(m, c)$$

2.3 The Revision of Probabilities: Bayes' Theorem

In the section just concluded it may have seemed that the probability statements we were able to make added little to the knowledge actually contained in Table 2.1. Now we begin to shift our interest away from the kinds of situation in which all probability values are readily accessible to the investigator or decision maker. For the present, however, we continue with the same example, that is Table 2.1, in order to illustrate a fundamental relationship involving three of the four probability concepts discussed in 2.2.

Recall the definition of conditional probability, illustrated by

$$p(m/c) = \frac{mc}{C}$$

and the definition of marginal probability, illustrated by

$$p(c) = \frac{C}{P}$$

Taking the product of these two probabilities and simplifying our result, we obtain:

$$p(m/c)\,p(c) = \frac{mc}{C}\,\frac{C}{P} = \frac{mc}{P}$$

Following our earlier discussion, the final expression of the product of the two probabilities, mc ÷ P, can be recognised as the definition of another probability, $p(m, c)$. In other words:

$$p(m/c)\,p(c) = p(m, c)$$

This three-cornered relationship between conditional, marginal and joint probabilities is important enough to deserve repetition through another example from the same source:

$$p(a/h)\,p(h) = \frac{ah}{H}\,\frac{H}{P} = \frac{ah}{P} = p(a, h)$$

The general relationship illustrated by these examples can now be given. For a two-way classification in which each characteristic may take a number of values (quantitative or qualitative):

$$p(x_i/y_j)\,p(y_j) = p(x_i, y_j) \tag{i}$$

where x_i is the ith value of the x-characteristic and y_j is the jth value of the y-characteristic.

To complete the basic relationship, known as Bayes' theorem[1] we need only recognise that any three-cornered relationship has its 'opposite' or 'reverse' three-cornered relationship, sharing one term with the original. Thus, taking as our original

$$p(m/c)\, p(c) = p(m, c)$$

we can readily construct its 'opposite':

$$p(c/m)\, p(m) = p(c, m)$$

Recalling that $p(c, m)$ is the same as $p(m, c)$, we can see that the left-hand sides of original and 'opposite' are equal:

$$p(m/c)\, p(c) = p(c/m)\, p(m)$$

Applying this principle to (i) above, we obtain a general expression of Bayes' theorem:

$$p(x_i/y_j)\, p(y_j) = p(y_j/x_i)\, p(x_i) \tag{ii}$$

The symmetry of this result should prove helpful in committing it to memory. As we shall see, its importance lies in the fact that any one of the four probabilities contained in the relationship can be expressed and often identified in terms of the other three. At this point the reader should return to Table 2.1 to confirm the validity of Bayes' theorem on any properly matched pairs of conditional and marginal probabilities.

The full potential of Bayes' theorem is hardly evident from the example we have been using so far, in which all probability information can be read directly from a table. Reality is usually less generous to probability estimators and decision makers, and it is against the comparatively unpromising background of gaps and imperfections in probability information that Bayes' theorem comes into its own. A new example is called for.

A company has for some time been conducting inspections of randomly chosen units of its finished product. The inspection results in an A or B grade being awarded to each item inspected. Ideally, an A grade should indicate a fault-free item and a B grade a defective item; but follow-up investigations have shown that only 80 per cent of fault-free items inspected have achieved an A grade and only 60 per cent of defective items inspected have achieved a B grade. The company's experience of production quality has been that 90 per cent of production has been fault-free. This information, while quite detailed, does not tell management what it presumably would most like to know, namely, how worthwhile the inspection procedure is. Here we go no further than to identify the conditional probability estimates that will be required in any full study of the expected cost effectiveness of the inspection procedure.

The information given reveals the following conditional and marginal probability estimates. (We must now use the term 'probability estimate' instead of 'probability' or 'objective probability' because the values are derived from or based upon past conditions which may no longer be completely relevant.) Arrows are used to indicate the sequence of derivation from the information given.

$$p(A/F) = 0.80 \longrightarrow p(B/F) = 0.20$$

$$p(B/D) = 0.60 \longrightarrow p(A/D) = 0.40$$

$$p(F) = 0.90 \longrightarrow p(D) = 0.10$$

F represents the occurrence of a fault-free item, D a defective item; A represents the awarding of an A grade, B a B grade.

The probability estimates for fault-free and defective items, 0.90 and 0.10, respectively, are examples of *prior probabilities*; that is, they are estimates about the reliability of the firm's output in general, made in advance of whatever testing may be carried out on particular items of output. In this situation, prior probabilities are likely to be based upon the estimator's experience, his general knowledge of current production conditions, even his intuition in matters that are relevant but difficult to analyse objectively. Prior probabilities are what a decision maker would be obliged to apply to each unit of output in the absence of the additional information provided by the inspection we are discussing, and in the absence of any other relevant information that might be obtained.

It will be obvious that what a quality controller really wants to know are the values of the conditional probabilities $p(F/A)$, $p(F/B)$, $p(D/A)$ and $p(D/B)$, the probabilities of an item being satisfactory or defective, given the result of the inspection. Evidently $p(D/A) = 1 - p(F/A)$ and $p(F/B) = 1 - p(D/B)$, because the item inspected must be either satisfactory or defective. This means that we need identify only two unknowns to complete our knowledge of the indicative powers of the inspection procedure. As an example we concentrate on $p(F/A)$, the probability that an item given an A grade is indeed satisfactory.

Applying the general formula (ii) to this situation gives

$$p(F/A)\,p(A) = p(A/F)\,p(F)$$

from which the required conditional probability is easily isolated:

$$p(F/A) = \frac{p(A/F)\,p(F)}{p(A)} \qquad \text{(iii)}$$

Of the three probability values on the right-hand side of this expression, two were given directly in the paragraph introducing this example. The remaining value on the right-hand side, $p(A)$, is not given directly, but can be calculated indirectly in a way which will be found applicable in a great many situations of probability assessment.

Our earlier discussion of joint probability referred briefly to the proposition that a marginal probability can be expressed as the sum of the probabilities of all of the mutually exclusive ways in which the event in question may occur — i.e. the sum of all of the joint probabilities involving the event in question. Applying this to the problem of identifying $p(A)$ we obtain

$$p(A) = p(A, F) + p(A, D)$$

Event 'A' — the award of an A grade — can occur in conjunction with characteristic F or in conjunction with characteristic D, and in no other way; so adding the joint probabilities $p(A, F)$ and $p(A, D)$ is a correct, if indirect, way of expressing $p(A)$. Further expansion of the two terms on the right-hand side of our expression for $p(A)$ involves the three-cornered relationship between joint, marginal and conditional probabilities already explained. Thus we obtain

$$p(A) = p(A/F)\,p(F) + p(A/D)\,p(D) \qquad \text{(iv)}$$

the right-hand side of which is made up of probabilities whose values were given in, or inferred from, the original statement of the problem. The common sense of this result, which will be found to have a general usefulness, is that $p(A)$ is defined in effect as a weighted average of the probabilities of A in fault-free and defective items, the weights being given by the probabilities of F and D, respectively.

Now we substitute (iv) for $p(A)$ in the denominator of (iii), obtaining

$$p(F/A) = \frac{p(A/F)\,p(F)}{p(A/F)\,p(F) + p(A/D)\,p(D)}$$

The numerical solution is as follows

$$p(F/A) = \frac{0.8 \times 0.9}{0.8 \times 0.9 + 0.4 \times 0.1} = \frac{0.72}{0.76} = 0.9474$$

The *revised* or *posterior* probability of F, conditional upon the achievements of an A grade, is 0.9474; and this represents an increased level of confidence in the item's quality compared to the prior probability, $p(F) = 0.90$, before the inspection is carried out. It follows from this result that $p(D/A) = 0.0526$, a significant drop in the prior defective probability, $p(D) = 0.10$. The A grade is confirmed as effective in the sense that it results in significant modifications to prior probabilities; though whether the inspection procedure as a whole is cost effective is a much larger question.

We can repeat the above process to discover the effectiveness of a B grade in modifying probabilities for the item inspected. Analogously to the expanded formula for $p(F/A)$ above, we have

$$p(F/B) = \frac{p(B/F)\, p(F)}{p(B/F)\, p(F) \,+\, p(B/D)\, p(D)}$$

into which we can insert our numerical information as follows:

$$p(F/B) = \frac{0.2 \times 0.9}{0.2 \times 0.9 \,+\, 0.6 \times 0.1} = \frac{0.18}{0.24} = 0.75$$

From this we can obtain $p(D/B) = 1 - p(F/B) = 0.25$.

The B grade has an even stronger effect on the prior probabilities than does the A grade, but in the opposite directions. However, a quality controller is unlikely to be very happy about the probability revisions that follow for an item given a B grade: ideally, with only two possible grades, a B grade should give a much stronger indication of a defective item.

One final point of general importance can be discerned in our example. A quality controller can predict in advance how his prior probability estimates about an item's quality will be modified by the results of the inspection. This will be useful in assessing the costs and expected benefits of information gathering procedures in general. As a preliminary to that discussion (in Chapter 7) we note that the decision maker is aware of the probabilities of obtaining A and B grades (the denominators of the expanded formulae for $p(F/A)$ and $p(F/B)$, respectively) and presumably of the decisions (and their related cost expectations) he will make in those two eventualities.

2.4 Binomial Theorem and the Importance of Sample Size

In earlier sections we have been considering the concepts relating to a single 'event'; now we focus on the probability characteristics of sets or sequences of events. Textbook examples of multiple events abound: coin tossing and card drawing are an ever-present source of inspiration to teachers. In the real world the enormous subject area of repeated sampling provides ample material for the application of theory. Our interest in sampling is limited to a demonstration of its usefulness in the processes of revising prior probabilities. After the preparatory work of this section, the following section will return to the latter theme.

An important distinction is necessary at the outset, between repeated sampling in situations where the probabilities of different outcomes remain constant, or virtually constant, on each occasion, and situations where the outcomes of earlier sampling affect the probabilities of different outcomes in subsequent samples. Random sampling from an infinite or very large population, with or without replacement of each item sampled, comes into the first category. No matter how many times a coin is tossed, the probabilities of head and tail remain the same at each toss; no matter how many different voters are selected at random in a typical public opinion poll, the sample size falls so far short of the total number of electors that the probabilities of obtaining any particular political allegiance at any stage of the sampling must be practically constant. On the other hand, random sampling from a small population without replacement must affect the probabilities of different outcomes in subsequent samples. Evidently, 'large' and 'small' must be understood in terms of the effects of repeated sampling on probability values.

The pattern of possible results of random sampling with constant probabilities can be anticipated with the aid of the *Binomial theorem*. Generally we are interested simply in whether an 'event' or 'trial' results in 'success' or 'failure', though more complex classifications are easily accommodated in the basic framework. Let the probability of a 'success' in one trial (a 'head' in coin tossing, or an ace in card drawing) be denoted by p, so that the probability of 'failure' (a 'tail' or a non-ace) is equal to $(1 - p)$. Without having to repeat tediously an experiment many hundreds of times, we may wish to know the probability of a particular overall pattern of 'successes' and 'failures' in a given number of trials; and for this purpose a standard formula is available. In introducing and employing this formula we shall assume that the reader is familiar with the proposition that the probability of a

particular pattern of statistically independent events is given by the
product of their separate probabilities. For an explanation of the
multiplication rule of probability theory, from which this well-known
result derives, see Hamburg (1970), pp. 32-42; Yamane (1967), pp.
105-10; or Moore (1972), pp. 20, 24-5.

The formula for the probability of a particular breakdown of results
in a series of independent trials is as follows:

$$p(\tfrac{x}{n}/p) = [\, p^x (1 - p)^{n-x} \,] \,[\, \frac{n!}{x!\,(n-x)!} \,] \tag{v}$$

The notation introduced in (v), and the underlying theory, may need
some clarification before we proceed. The left-hand side of (v),
$p(\tfrac{x}{n}/p)$, is simply a shorthand way of writing 'the probability that n
trials will produce exactly x "successes", given that the probability of
"success" in each separate trial is p'. The expression in the first square
bracket on the right-hand side of (v) gives the probability of any
particular sequence of results having the overall total of x 'successes'
and (n − x) 'failures', given that the probability of 'success' in one trial
is always the same. The factorial expression in the second square
bracket on the right-hand side of (v) gives the number of different
sequences of outcomes by which the assumed overall results pattern
could have been achieved. It is obvious that the probability of the
overall result x 'successes', (n − x) 'failures', is given by the probability
of achieving that pattern in one particular sequence multiplied by the
number of different sequences possible.

Binomial probabilities for small samples are easy to calculate, but
for larger samples we are fortunate that tables of binomial probabilities
are widely available in statistics texts and in compilations of mathematical and statistical tables (e.g. Moore, 1972, pp. 331-6; and
Kmietowicz and Yannoulis, 1976, pp. 12-14).

To illustrate the potential importance of sample size in relation
to population we calculate the probability of drawing any three kings
and any two other cards from a pack of 52 playing cards (a) when each
card drawn is replaced and the pack shuffled before the next card is
drawn, and (b) when the card drawn is not replaced. Situation (a) is
covered by the Binomial theorem, because the probabilities of drawing
a king and a non-king are the same at each drawing. Thus

$$p\!\left(\begin{array}{c}\text{3 kings and 2 non-kings,}\\ \text{with replacement}\end{array}\right) = [(\tfrac{4}{52})^3 \times (\tfrac{48}{52})^2]\,[\tfrac{5!}{3!\,2!}]$$

$$= 0.00388$$

When drawn cards are not replaced (situation (b)) the probability of obtaining a sequence of three kings followed by two non-kings is as follows:

$$\frac{4}{52} \times \frac{3}{51} \times \frac{2}{50} \times \frac{48}{49} \times \frac{47}{48} = 0.000174$$

(The probability of obtaining a king on the first card is $\frac{4}{52}$; then the probability of obtaining a king on the second card is $\frac{3}{51}$; and so on.) But the probability of *any* specified sequence yielding three kings and two non-kings is the same, as the reader should confirm. So the probability we seek is obtained by multiplying 0.000174 by the number of different sequences that are possible. The 'number of possible sequences' component of the calculation is of course obtained in the same way as in the binomial probability formula. Thus

$$\begin{aligned} p\binom{\text{3 kings and 2 non-kings,}}{\text{without replacement}} &= [\frac{4}{52} \times \frac{3}{51} \times \frac{2}{50} \times \frac{48}{49} \times \frac{47}{48}] \, [\frac{5!}{3! \, 2!}] \\ &= 0.000174 \times 10 \\ &= 0.00174 \end{aligned}$$

The general approach to problems of this type is by means of the *hypergeometric distribution* (explained formally in Moore, 1972, pp. 59-61).

2.5 Examples of Probability Revision

We can formalise the steps involved in probability estimation and revision as follows: (i) formulation of prior probabilities, based upon experience, intuition, etc.; (ii) acquisition of additional information about the particular situation in question (usually at some expense); (iii) revision of prior probability estimates for the immediate situation in the light of the additional information acquired. In this section we continue to assume that steps (i)-(iii) are conducted on rigorous lines, and our object is to take the revision of probabilities beyond the level reached in 2.3 above, where the reader may have come to suspect that 'scientific' probability revision is operable only within a narrow range of situations. The two examples discussed here are intended to correct such an impression, by showing Bayes' theorem at work in differing situations, as well as different ways of generating additional information.

Example 1. The first example illustrates the powerfulness of the combination of Bayes' theorem and Binomial theorem. A magazine publisher believes that a planned new publication could achieve regular sales amounting to 10, 15 or 20 per cent of a clearly defined specialist readership. The prior probabilities he estimates for these readership levels are 0.20, 0.50 and 0.30, respectively, and are based on past experience of launching other specialist publications and a 'feel' for the market in question. In principle, the publisher could work with these prior probabilities in reaching a decision about launching the new magazine, but it seems likely that because possible sales levels (and profits) differ widely, he will seek to strengthen the estimated probability of one of the three outcomes before reaching a decision. We assume that he decides to commission in-depth interviews with 15 randomly selected potential readers; in each case the skilled interviewer is assumed able to decide correctly whether or not the interviewee would become a regular reader of the new magazine in the event of its publication. How does this information help the publisher to revise his prior probabilities of the different readership levels?

To illustrate the process of probability revision, assume that three of the 15 interviewees are identified as readers of the new magazine, should it be launched. This result is not incompatible with any of the possible readership levels, but it is obviously least likely to have occurred if the true readership level is at the low end of the range, 10 per cent. This casual impression can be confirmed and quantified by making the fullest use of the sample result. We begin by using the Binomial theorem to calculate the probability of the sample result occurring under each of the three possible readership levels. If potential readership is in fact 20 per cent, the probability that exactly three favourable responses will occur in 15 randomly chosen potential customers is expressed in conditional probability notation as follows:

$$p(\frac{3}{15}/R = 0.2) = 0.2^3 \times 0.8^{12} \times \frac{15!}{3! \times 12!} = 0.2502 \ ,$$

where $\frac{3}{15}$ is shorthand for 'three favourable responses out of fifteen interviews', and $R = 0.2$ expresses the assumed 20 per cent readership level as a probability (the probability of choosing a favourably disposed reader at random is obviously 0.20).

The analogous conditional probabilities for the result $\frac{3}{15}$ given readership levels of 15 and 10 per cent, respectively, are:

$$p(\frac{3}{15}/R = 0.15) = 0.15^3 \times 0.85^{12} \times \frac{15!}{3! \times 12!} = 0.2185$$

$$p(\frac{3}{15}/R=0.1) = 0.1^3 \times 0.9^{12} \times \frac{15!}{3! \times 12!} = 0.1285$$

(These probabilities could of course have been read directly from tables of binomial probabilities.)

Now we need to remind ourselves of how the problem would look to a Bayesian theorist. Consider the revision of the prior probability for a readership level of 20 per cent, which was stated earlier to be 0.30. In the now familiar Bayesian terms, the problem is to solve the equation

$$p(R=0.2/\frac{3}{15}) = \frac{p(\frac{3}{15}/R=0.2)\, p(R=0.2)}{p(\frac{3}{15})}$$

The numerator values on the right-hand side of this equation are already known: the conditional probability has just been calculated, and $p(R = 0.2)$ is given as one of the publisher's prior probabilities. The value of $p(\frac{3}{15})$ is not yet known, but it can be obtained through the process of expansion explained in 2.3 above; thus

$$p(R=0.2/\frac{3}{15}) = \frac{p(\frac{3}{15}/R=0.2)\, p(R=0.2)}{\left[\begin{array}{c} p(\frac{3}{15}/R=0.2)\, p(R=0.2) + p(\frac{3}{15}/R=0.15) \times \\ p(R=0.15) + p(\frac{3}{15}/R=0.1)\, p(R=0.1) \end{array}\right]}$$

In this formula for the probability of a readership level of 20 per cent, conditional upon three favourable responses in 15 interviews, the denominator is a weighted average of the probabilities of obtaining the result $\frac{3}{15}$ under the three possible readership levels, the weight in each case being the prior probability of that readership level. The correspondence with earlier, simpler, expansions of the denominator in the Bayesian formula is exact.

We now possess all the information needed to complete the calculation:

$$p(R=0.2/\frac{3}{15}) = \frac{0.2502 \times 0.30}{0.2502 \times 0.30 + 0.2185 \times 0.50 + 0.1285 \times 0.20}$$

$$= 0.3574$$

In the light of the additional information acquired through interviews, the revised probability that readership is 20 per cent is 0.3574.

With very little extra work we can calculate the remaining revised probabilities conditional upon the same sample result. In each case the appropriate product taken from the denominator of the above expression is used as the numerator, while the denominator itself remains constant. Thus

$$p(R = 0.15 / \frac{3}{15}) = \frac{0.1093}{0.2101} = 0.5202 ;$$

$$p(R = 0.1 / \frac{3}{15}) = \frac{0.0257}{0.2101} = 0.1223$$

The result of the interviews is that the prior probability of $R = 0.10$ has, as expected, been affected most strongly; while the other two readership levels have each achieved a modest gain in probability. In this particular case the publisher may feel that his position remains confused, particularly if the difference between readership levels of 20 per cent and 15 per cent is one of profits on the one hand and losses on the other. But three points of general importance have also emerged.

First, it is obvious that a larger sample size would be likely to produce a greater discrimination in favour of one of the three possible readership levels. Compared to the potential profit or loss involved, the extra expense of achieving greater confidence would probably be trivial. Second, the publisher's prior probabilities obviously have a great influence on the revised probabilities that emerge from the sampling of opinions; a given sample result yields different posterior probabilities depending on the prior probabilities employed. Third, the publisher can predict in advance how his prior probabilities will be revised in the light of *any* sample result; this puts him in a very strong position (as we shall see in Chapter 7) to assess in advance the expected net benefits from information gathering and adjust his policies in that area accordingly.

Example 2. To increase the reader's familiarity with, and confidence in, the technique of probability revision, and at the same time show that binomial probabilities are not always relevant in acquiring and interpreting new information, consider the following problem. A company which manufactures jet engines has reached a stage with one of its new designs at which a decision about production planning must be taken. The sales manager believes that a maximum of three airframe producers might be prepared to use the new engine in their own new airliners, and he suggests the following (prior) probabilities for the number of customers who will actually buy the new engine, should it be produced:

Table 2.2: Prior Probabilities of Numbers of Customers

Number of customers (C)	0	1	2	3
Probability	0.2	0.4	0.3	0.1

The probability distribution of C, the number of customers purchasing the new engine, is certainly not an example of binomial probabilities at work; the sales manager does not assume that the decisions of all three potential customers can be simulated by an identical chance process, but he is unable to assign different independent probabilities to individual customers. One interpretation is that the sales manager, in stating the above probabilities, is trying to allow for 'ripple' effects among customers: a favourable decision by one potential customer might influence the decisions of others, either favourably or unfavourably. Such considerations are obviously very difficult to quantify with any accuracy, and it is scarcely surprising that management wishes to improve its probability estimates before coming to a decision on producing the new engine.

At this stage the company's sales team has only got time to ascertain the intentions of one (randomly chosen) potential customer. It may seem unlikely that the result of a single interview can provide much help in revising the prior probabilities of customer numbers, $p(C = 0)$, $p(C = 1)$, and so on; but we can at least be certain that whether the potential customer's answer is 'yes' or 'no', one possibility will be eliminated ($C = 0$ if the answer is 'yes', $C = 3$ if the answer is 'no'). In fact we can revise *all* prior probabilities; and the process will be demonstrated for the case of $p(C = 1)$, on the assumption that the customer interview produces a favourable result, Y. Using Bayes' theorem,

$$p(C=1/Y) = \frac{p(Y/C=1)\,p(C=1)}{p(Y)}$$

As in previous examples the right-hand side denominator, $p(Y)$, the probability of obtaining a 'yes' in a single interview, is not directly available, and the familiar expansion procedure is required:

$$p(C=1/Y) = \frac{p(Y/C=1)\,p(C=1)}{\left[\begin{array}{c}p(Y/C=0)\,p(C=0) + p(Y/C=1)\,p(C=1) + \\ p(Y/C=2)\,p(C=2) + p(Y/C=3)\,p(C=3)\end{array}\right]}$$

The expanded denominator, as usual, merely sums the separate conditional probabilities of Y in all different demand situations, weighting each one by the prior probability for the situation in question. (The first product in the denominator is of course zero, but it is advisable to include it formally to emphasise the method of expansion.) Each conditional probability, $p(Y/C=0)$, $p(Y/C=1)$, etc., is simply a 'law of averages' probability; for example, $p(Y/C=1) = 0.333$. We now have all the necessary data to calculate the revised probability that $C = 1$, given a single favourable interview result:

$$p(C=1/Y) = \frac{0.333 \times 0.4}{0 \times 0.2 + 0.333 \times 0.4 + 0.667 \times 0.3 + 1.000 \times 0.1}$$
$$= 0.3074$$

As usual, we generate the remaining revised probabilities by using as the numerator the appropriate product from the (unchanged) denominator. Obviously, $p(C = 0/Y)$ is zero. The other results are: $p(C = 2/Y) = 0.4618$ and $p(C = 3/Y) = 0.2308$. Again, we stop short, at this stage, of investigating the company's decision on production of the new engine. The general points made at the end of Example 1 above apply equally here.

2.6 Conclusions on Probability and Decision Making

We have argued that thinking probabilistically 'comes naturally' to all of us, however imperfectly we perform the mental processes involved. But does it follow that decision makers actually take account of probabilities in framing their policies? After all, 'thinking' and 'doing' are different operations.

Two brief comments will suffice here. First, a decision maker will find it an extremely difficult mental exercise to expunge from his consciousness all preconceptions about the probabilities of the different outcomes of the decision under consideration. This is far from being a complete defence of the relevance of probability, given our recognition in 2.1 that in many situations probability estimates require the most careful elucidation. But the rationality of deliberately choosing to reach decisions *without* the aid of probability estimates may also be challenged, quite apart from the issue of the mental gymnastics that might be involved. Is it not likely that decision makers, wishing to be as fully informed about risks as seems sensible and necessary, will seek to improve their estimates and understanding of relevant probabilities rather than eschew probability as a weak and unreliable tool? (As we shall see in Chapter 7, this process of seeking additional information about risks is itself greatly facilitated by the decision maker's willingness to venture probabilistic judgements.)

These preliminary arguments in favour of a probability-based interpretation of decision-making will have to stand comparison with rival theories of decision making in Chapter 3.

Notes

1. Thomas Bayes, who first identified the relationship we are describing, was an eighteenth-century mathematician and nonconformist clergyman.

3 DECISION THEORIES AND BUSINESS DECISION MAKING

He that leaves nothing to Chance will do few things ill,
but he will do very few things.

Lord Halifax

3.1 Introduction

In the course of reviewing some important probability concepts,
Chapter 2 defended the general significance of probability to decision
makers, though not in very rigorous terms. This chapter formally
introduces the subject of decision theory, in both its descriptive and
prescriptive aspects; and although we shall reaffirm a belief in the
relevance of probability in an understanding of most decisions, and
establish a prescriptive role for probability in rational decision making,
we shall have to concede that in the descriptive area at least there is
room for a variety of models. Such an eclectic attitude on the question
of how risky decisions are taken is obviously quite in keeping with the
recognition in modern microeconomic theory of a diversity of
managerial attitudes and objectives.

The structure and approach of this chapter are based on F.H.
Knight's distinction between states of knowledge about risky situations
(Knight, 1921). Knight used the term *risk* in relation to decisions or
forecasts where the decision maker had some knowledge or estimates
of the probabilities of the different results that might occur. The term
uncertainty was used to describe situations in which probabilities could
not be assigned to outcomes, even though the outcomes themselves
might be clearly envisaged. (We ignore the extreme form of uncertainty,
an entirely featureless view of future possibilities; even if his mind is
initially completely blank, a decision maker presumably progresses at
least to the point of picturing a limited number of different things that
might happen!)

Although the state of uncertainty, as defined, may appear implausible
in theory, it does not necessarily follow that decision makers perceive
all future events in probability terms. First, we cannot dogmatically
exclude the possibility of genuine and irreducible uncertainty,
particularly in relation to distant events or unfamiliar risks. Second, a
decision maker may — perhaps deliberately, perhaps through casual

indifference — take no account of relevant probability indicators in some or all of his decisions. Our plan in this chapter is to look at both sides of this question; 3.2 discusses decision making under uncertainty, and 3.3 deals with possible roles for probability.

3.2 Decisions Under Uncertainty

3.2 (i) The Framework of Uncertainty Decision Theories

This section concentrates on decisions whose outcomes are controlled by forces which, following established usage, we shall refer to quaintly but misleadingly as 'states of nature'. To the decision maker the important characteristics of 'nature' are (1) that it is *not* a hostile intelligence, and (2) that although the different possible states of nature are known, their probabilities are unknown. The term 'nature' may seem inappropriate when used outside the traditional context of a farmer trying to allow for the various meteorological possibilities in deciding what crops to sow on his land. Generally we must understand the term to refer to the whole complex of forces that will have a bearing on the outcome of a particular decision, and in business situations some of these forces are obviously intelligent and at least potentially hostile. Is the analogy with nature's 'neutral unpredictability' therefore invalid?

This question can be answered pragmatically, according to the decision context the analyst has in mind. If the decision maker recognises an intelligent opponent, bent on countering his every possible move to maximum effect, the appropriate framework is that of *game theory*, which will not be discussed at length here but which deserves a brief introduction. (See Baumol, 1977, Ch. 18, for a wide-ranging introduction to game theory; Williams, 1966, for an entertaining analysis of some of its applications; and Hawkins, 1973, pp. 56–9, for a view of its relevance in the theory of the firm.)

 In many decision contexts, however, businessmen do not see deliberate counter-moves by their competitors as the predominantly important factor determining the success of their policies, in the way envisaged in game theory. Much uncertainty may be 'internal' in origin, in the sense of factors operating within the firm whose behaviour is difficult to predict; examples are the success of a research programme, the productivity and costs of new technology and the handling of labour relations. There are also many important but essentially impersonal external factors that influence the outcomes of decisions, e.g. trends in the national and international economy and the continuing emergence of new demand patterns and technologies. And in many cases it will be correct to represent the competitive climate in similar terms. This is more likely to be the case, the smaller is the firm in question in relation to its rivals, and the more numerous the latter. Thus the various states of nature correspond to the decision maker's assessments of the possible combinations of actions by other firms and impersonal environmental factors (internal and external); and, as stated earlier, we assume that the decision maker has no information that would help him to assign a probability to any state of nature.

3.2 (ii) Descriptive Criteria

Having examined the general meaning of 'nature' in the context of business decisions, we consider briefly the decision theories that have been suggested to account for observed behaviour patterns. Our purpose is strictly descriptive, and we avoid any prescriptive conclusion. Choice in conditions of uncertainty is best illustrated through the medium of a payoff matrix, which shows the net payoff or return (in cash or 'utility' units) to the decision maker arising from each combination of his own strategy and the state of nature. An example is given in Table 3.1, which lists the decision maker's strategy options, $S_1 \ldots S_3$, downwards, and the possible states of nature, $N_1 \ldots N_3$, along the upper edge. (There is no reason in general for the number of possible states of nature to equal the number of possible strategies.) We shall suppose that the decision situation is unique and of considerable importance to the decision maker.

Table 3.1: Payoffs (£'000) for Combinations of S and N

	N_1	N_2	N_3
S_1	7	10	4
S_2	5	6	9
S_3	3	11	8

Before considering suggestions about the choice between strategies, we should note that all three are actually worth considering: no strategy offers a lower payoff than another under *all* states of nature, and each strategy is the best one for one particular state of nature. Now we enumerate and briefly consider five possible interpretations of the decision maker's thinking (see Baumol, 1977, Ch. 19; and Naylor and Vernon, 1969, pp. 314-18).

Bayes/Laplace Criterion. This criterion represents an attempt to bridge the gap between the states of risk and uncertainty by suggesting that a decision maker simply assigns equal probabilities to all states of nature and then adopts the strategy with the highest probability-weighted average payoff. (The concept of a probability-weighted average payoff is considered in detail in the following section.) This amounts to selecting the strategy with the highest average payoff, even though that average may not be close to any of the actual payoff possibilities and may be strongly influenced by one or two extreme values. In our example, S_3 would be chosen on this criterion, with an average payoff of £7,333.

Hurwicz Criterion. A decision maker acting in accordance with this criterion attaches personal, subjective, coefficients of optimism and pessimism (summing to unity) to the best and worst outcomes of each strategy, regardless of the states of nature under which these outcomes occur. It follows that these coefficients are not to be interpreted as probability estimates. The decision maker then sums the two weighted payoffs for each strategy and chooses that strategy with the highest resulting value; if we suppose that in our example he feels '40 per cent optimistic and 60 per cent pessimistic', his preferred strategy will be S_2 with a weighted average payoff of £6,600 (0.4 × £9,000 + 0.6 × £5,000). This criterion is obviously capable of extension to permit weights to be given to non-extreme outcomes.

Maximin (Profit)/Minimax (Loss). This criterion suggests a more immediately recognisable attitude on the part of the decision maker than the two considered so far. The decision maker chooses that strategy which, if events turn out badly, will leave him least badly affected, i.e. with the highest profit or smallest loss. In other words, he chooses the strategy with the 'best worst' outcome, regardless of the state of nature under which it occurs or the latter's (unknown) probability. In our example the preferred strategy would be S_2, with a minimum payoff of £5,000. The obvious implication of this criterion is that the decision maker is by nature cautious or pessimistic, or both.

Maximax Criterion. This encapsulates the psychology opposite to that of maximin. The decision maker now chooses the strategy which, if things go well, will yield the highest payoff, i.e. the 'best best' payoff. Again, no attention is paid to the values and likelihoods of the various other payoffs that may occur under the chosen strategy. The maximax strategy in Table 3.1 is S_3.

Minimax Regret Criterion. To appreciate this criterion we must first define 'regret' and derive a *regret matrix* from the original payoff matrix of Table 3.1. A decision maker's 'regret' at having chosen a particular strategy, given the state of nature that actually occurs, is measured by the difference between his actual payoff and the payoff he would have achieved had he possessed advance knowledge of the state of nature and chosen the best strategy for it. Regret in this sense can be as low as zero, when the best strategy for the actual state of nature has in fact been chosen. Table 3.2 gives the regret values derived from Table 3.1.

Table 3.2: Regret Values (£'000) Derived from Table 3.1

	N_1	N_2	N_3
S_1	0	1	5
S_2	2	5	0
S_3	4	0	1

The decision maker now chooses that strategy whose *highest* regret is lower than that of any other strategy; in other words, he minimises the extent to which he can be sorry for the choice he makes. Here the lowest maximum regret of any strategy is £4,000 under strategy S_3.

The presentation of this criterion requires some modification if the same set of states of nature does not apply to all strategies. For example, one strategy may be to build a manufacturing plant in Europe to serve the European market; its alternative may be to build a manufacturing plant in South America to serve the South American market. The states of nature relevant to a European plant's success probably overlap very little, if at all, with those affecting the South American option. In such cases, where *any* result under one strategy can be 'paired' (seen as a possible alternative) to *any* result under another strategy, each strategy's maximum possible regret, strictly speaking, is given by the difference between its worst possible outcome and the best outcome possible under *any* other strategy. The objection to this view of regret is that the decision maker knows that he may never be aware of his exact regret; if he invests in Europe he will probably never know how the South American investment would have turned out. So the concept of 'identifiable regret' may be preferred. Often a positive strategy has a 'do-nothing' alternative (e.g. do not invest in manufacturing capacity at all) offering a constant payoff under all states of nature; for any state of nature identifiable regrets for either strategy are calculated in the way explained above.

Under some conditions it may be both possible and sensible to pursue a mixture of the available 'pure' strategies. Numerous examples of strategy mixing can be suggested: farmers may plant a variety of crops which respond differently to each possible climatic state, portfolio managers distribute funds among investments with differing risk characteristics. Whether a mixed strategy, where possible in a once-only decision context, will seem desirable depends on the decision maker's motivation (see Baumol, 1977, pp. 465-6).

3.2 (iii) Comment on Decision Criteria

Our comments are mainly general, but the maximin and minimax regret criteria are so widely discussed that they deserve specific mention. Both have been criticised as implying an excessively cautious approach on the part of the decision maker, and in fact it is relatively easy to make each one yield manifestly absurd 'predictions' about choice. For example, the reader can confirm that a maximin decision maker would still prefer S_2 to S_1 in Table 3.1 even if the S_1, N_2 payoff were increased from £10,000 to £100,000. A minimax regret decision maker would still prefer S_3 to S_2 or S_1 even if the payoffs for S_1, N_2 and S_2, N_3 were each increased by £90,000, to £100,000 and £99,000, respectively; although these changes would suggest that both S_1 and S_2 must appear vastly superior to S_3, the latter still has the lowest maximum regret (now £91,000). In fairness, for a choice between only two strategies the minimax regret criterion is far more convincing; we identify sympathetically with the invited guest who, having mislaid his invitation, finds himself on the day of the party agonising over whether it would be worse to be the only formally dressed guest at an informal party or the only casually attired guest at a banquet!

In their favour, the five descriptive criteria do attempt, with considerable success, to represent psychological attitudes towards risk taking that most of us find familiar and believable. Criticism of the proliferation of criteria is out of order, at least in the uncertainty context, unless one believes that all decision makers will always be identically motivated. Realistically, a decision maker is unlikely to follow any one criterion exclusively; we can readily imagine that after alternative strategies have been ranked according to various criteria a composite ranking exercise is performed, perhaps very impression-istically, to reach a final decision. For example, in Table 3.1 strategy S_3 scores well because its maximum regret is lowest, and it has the highest 'best', 'second best' and average payoffs; but its drawbacks are that it has the lowest minimum payoff and the widest dispersion of payoffs among the three alternatives. A realistic decision model should probably allow for *ad hoc* mixtures of criteria and inconsistency as between different decisions; inelegant and unsatisfactory perhaps, but arguably a fair description of the way most of us function as decision making individuals and groups!

A more important line of criticism questions the assumptions of the typical payoff matrix. 'States of nature' traditionally refer to a relatively small number of clear alternatives (e.g. drought, moderate weather or floods; or rapid growth, stable growth or depression) whose payoff implications are known clearly while probability estimates are completely lacking. But once it is recognised that a state of nature is usually the product of the outcomes of a (possibly large) number of contributory variables, two things become clear. First, the number of possible states of nature (different combinations of the outcomes of contributory variables) multiplies beyond the scope of a manageable payoff matrix. If only five variables influence a decision's payoff, and each one has only three possible outcomes, the number of different states of nature is 243, assuming full independence between the determining variables. Second, in a world where various influences interact to determine a payoff, the importance of probability judgements to the decision maker is strengthened — if only as a means of distinguishing likely from unlikely or impossible combinations of events.

If the concept of a limited number of alternative but unpredictable states of nature is suspect, can uncertainty theory survive? The answer is surely a qualified 'yes'. Where the number of states of nature is small and the relevant probabilities are judged to be indeterminate, the decision maker may feel himself to be in a textbook uncertainty situation. The market's response to a completely new product, the performance of a new production technology, the kinds of products that will be in demand in the future, even the weather — all these *may* belong in the area of pure guesswork rather than that of the more or less scientific or even instinctive probability estimation discussed in Chapter 2. However, having said as much in defence of uncertainty, we may reiterate our belief, first expressed in Chapter 2, that decision makers *do* habitually make judgements of relative likelihoods in matters of importance. They can of course recognise the inadequacy of their judgements, and employ a 'composite' uncertainty criterion of the kind suggested earlier; but it is hard to believe that their impressions of relative likelihoods play no part in their final choice of strategy.

3.3 Decisions Under Risk Conditions

3.3 (i) The Criterion of Expected Utility

Students of economics are familiar with the traditional concept of 'utility' as a fundamental but essentially personal common measure of satisfaction, quite distinct from the variety of goods and services, leisure, etc., that contribute to it. Less familiar perhaps is the idea, first suggested in the pioneering work by Von Neumann and Morgenstern (1944), that an individual's cash-utility transformation can be established in much the same arbitrary yet internally consistent way as a temperature scale is established, and that the product of this exercise can be employed to great effect in understanding and even predicting the individual's economic behaviour in risky conditions. This section illustrates the basic techniques of utility function construction, explains the implied theory of decision making, indicates the kinds of insights offered by the theory, and considers the latter's relevance of an understanding of business decisions. In contrast to 3.2, the main decision criterion discussed here will be shown to have a strong prescriptive content.

Before embarking on this discussion, it will be useful to introduce formally the concept of *expected value*. The expected value of any variable is simply the probability-weighted average of the possible values of that variable:

$$EV(X) = \sum_{i=1}^{n} p_i X_i \tag{i}$$

where $EV(X)$ is the expected value of the variable (X) in question;

X_i is the value X will take should event i occur (i = 1 . . . n); and p_i is the probability that event i will occur.

The basic procedure for identifying an individual's cash-utility transformation is extremely simple — which helps to explain the wide acceptance of utility theory in academic and business writings. Several superficially different approaches can be found in the literature, but ideally all should yield exactly the same result. (An alternative to the approach described here is explained in Moore, 1972, pp. 267-9. The present approach seems marginally preferable in that the form of questioning it envisages is arguably more meaningful to the subject.) In the version we adopt the subject is asked to indicate the *certain* cash amount he would be just willing to accept instead of a risky opportunity with known cash payoffs and probabilities. His answer is taken to establish an equality, or indifference, between the 'utility' of the certain cash amount he indicates and the 'expected utility' of the risky alternative. 'Expected utility' is defined like any other expected value; it is the sum of the probability-weighted *utility* values of the different cash outcomes of the risky alternative.

Identifying a utility function is simple enough in principle, though the subject will find that he needs to consider his preferences and indifferences carefully and be prepared to reconsider some of his statements to resolve obvious inconsistencies. We shall review the basic procedure fairly quickly, leaving questions about its relevance to business decision making for the following sub-section. Arbitrary utility values, usually zero and unity, are assigned to the two cash values at the lower and upper ends, respectively, of the range about which the subject is expected to be able to think clearly. Then the analyst, who may of course be the subject himself, poses a series of questions in a standard form; and this process we can best convey by means of an example. Imagine a university student whose grant income for the term which is about to open is £400, and who is presented with a lottery ticket carrying a one-in-five chance of a £500 prize and a four-in-five chance of no prize. If we now suppose that the student's sense of wellbeing, his utility in other words, is dominated by his current financial position, the range of the relevant cash scale for our purpose is established as running from £400 to £900. To these two cash values we assign arbitrary utility values of zero and unity, respectively.

The student is now asked to indicate how much money he would be just willing to accept in exchange for his lottery ticket. It is important to note that he is *not* being asked how much he would be willing to pay for the ticket out of his £400 grant, but how much he would accept for it. After due consideration, and perhaps some expert prompting, he decides that he would be just willing to sell his ticket for £80, which is below its expected money value (EMV) of £100 (£500 × 0.2 + £0 × 0.8). This brings us to a critical point in the argument. We make the following statement based upon the student's stated indifference between a certain sum of £480 (grant plus sale price) and the risky prospect offered by his retaining the lottery ticket:

$$U(480) = 0.2 \times U(900) + 0.8 \times U(400)$$

in which the term U(480) means 'the utility associated with a certain income of £480', the terms U(900) and U(400) are the analogous utility values for the income levels corresponding to the possible outcomes of the lottery, and the weights 0.2 and 0.8 are the respective probabilities of winning the prize (income = £900) and losing (income = £400). The student's utility value from a prospective income of £480 is equated with his *expected utility value* (EUV) from the risky prospect which, by definition, he finds equally attractive. His utility for a prospective income of £480 can now be given a numerical value based on the predetermined utility values for incomes of £900 and £400:

$$U(480) = 0.2 \times 1.0 + 0.8 \times 0.0$$

$$= 0.2 \text{ utility units}$$

We have now identified a third point in the student's cash-utility transformation, in relation to the two arbitrarily numbered points with which we began. Our information to date is shown by points a, b and c in Figure 3.1, in which utility is measured vertically and cash horizontally.

To fill out the shape of the utility function in the range £400 to £900, different hypothetical risks can be presented to the student, each risk comprising cash outcomes whose utility values have already been determined. For each risk the student is asked to indicate the minimum price, say £X, he would accept in exchange for the risky prospect, and this leads to the identification of the utility value for the income level £(400 + X). If the interviewer wishes to base all his questioning on the two original utility values, U(900) and U(400), he can simply create new risk situations by varying the probabilities in the hypothetical lottery ticket while keeping the original prizes of £500 or nothing; but if he is confident of the consistency of his subject's

Figure 3.1: Student's Utility Function for Term's Income

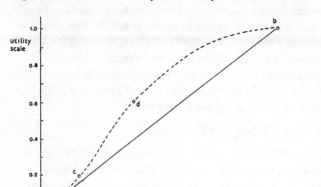

responses he can add extra interest by introducing risks incorporating intermediate cash amounts whose utility values have already been determined. Following the latter approach, imagine a fourth point being generated by having the student indicate the certain cash sum he would just accept in exchange for a fifty-fifty chance of £500 or £80. The EMV of this new risk is £290 (£500 × 0.5 + £80 × 0.5), and we shall again assume that the student would sell his chance for less than its EMV, in fact for £200. This would give him a certain income of £600. As with the first intermediate point identified, we reason as follows:

$$U(600) = 0.5 \times U(900) + 0.5 \times U(480)$$

$$U(600) = 0.5 \times 1.0 + 0.5 \times 0.2$$

$$= 0.6 \text{ utility units}$$

This result, $U(600) = 0.6$ utility units, is shown as point d in Figure 3.1. Evidently this process should continue until the range of cash values between £400 and £900 is represented by utility values at sufficiently frequent intervals to give a clear impression of the function's curvature.

The noteworthy feature of the cash-utility transformation tentatively outlined in Figure 3.1 is its strong suggestion of a diminishing marginal utility of money income, at least in part of the range covered. That is, beyond about £550 successive equal increments of money income appear to yield diminishing increments of utility to the student. It will be argued shortly that this is far from the only utility function shape we might expect to identify; but first it is important to dispose of a possible confusion over the connection between utility function shape and attitude to risk taking arising from the procedure by which the utility function is identified.

Obviously there is a close connection between the student's willingness to sell each lottery ticket for less than its EMV and the fact that in the range considered his utility function lies above the straight line joining its two extreme points (a and b in Figure 3.1). The reader can readily confirm that if every hypothetical gamble is worth *exactly* its EMV to the student, the latter's utility function will be *exactly* linear between £400 and £900; and if he insists on a price in excess of EMV in each case his utility function in that range will be convex to the £ axis. Is it the case therefore that diminishing marginal utility of money income must be seen as a *consequence* of a risk-averting attitude (willingness to accept less than the full EMV of the risky prospect)? This view of causation arises naturally from the order of events in constructing the utility function; the student's attitude to risk (in the shape of his responses to offers) *appears* to dictate the shape of his utility function. However, the construction method is misleading as to causation, and it is more accurate to say that the shape of his underlying utility function determines the student's attitudes to the different risks presented to him. Differently shaped utility functions will then produce different behaviour in the face of risk. (We ignore the possibility that the activity of gambling itself, as distinct from the returns it may yield, gives utility; while this is undoubtedly true for many punters, it seems safe to disregard it in studying business decision making.)

Numerous utility function shapes have been suggested, usually in connection with attempts to explain particular facets of behaviour in the face of risk (Friedman and Savage, 1948). Figure 3.2 is intended as a composite version embodying different attitudes in different cash ranges.

The origin of Figure 3.2 represents an individual's utility from a customary or anticipated weekly income of £100; movements from the origin therefore represent departures from a norm or expectation, and it is important to realise that the utility movements associated with income deviations are those *anticipated* by the individual. This point can be clarified through an explanation of the various curvatures of the utility function shown.

Starting at the origin of Figure 3.2, the first equal increments in

Figure 3.2: Composite Utility Function

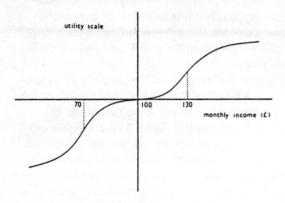

prospective weekly income increase prospective utility at an increasing rate, before diminishing marginal utility sets in beyond an income of £130. We can readily accept that the individual might, in anticipation, place a high value upon the first increments in income, feeling perhaps that certain items of expenditure which are just beyond his reach when income is at its expected level could now be afforded. Beyond a prospective £130 per week the individual may, at present, have less clear ideas of how additional income would be spent once his immediate or 'high priority' desires for additional consumption were being satisfied. Still in Figure 3.2, when prospective income falls below £100 per week we can again suggest different attitudes towards different amounts of income shortfall. Utility is first shown as declining at an accelerating rate as income falls to £70; in this range the individual may see a small decline in income as depriving him of the cherished 'extras' that make life worth living. But when prospective income falls below £70 the decline in utility decelerates, the individual perhaps making little attempt to distinguish between degrees of anticipated misery. 'Without colour television, car and foreign holiday', he might reason, 'it will make little difference whether I can afford a new tie and a new pair of shoes, or only a new tie!'

  Doubtless the reader will be able to suggest different psychological insights for the construction of different utility function shapes. In doing this it is important to bear in mind that the subject is anticipating the effects of income variations in relation to a particular norm or expected level. He is unlikely to be familiar with all of the income levels whose utility equivalents he has indicated; and even if he were, his utility values for those income levels are not absolutes, but 'relatives', to the utility of the income he expected to enjoy. Utility theory in the present sense does not pretend to be able to identify any absolute scale of valuations; indeed the limitations of the theory are implicit in its 'movable origin' aspect.

Some of the insights into business decision making that can be gained through utility function theory can best be shown numerically. In the following two-part example a businessman's (previously identified) utility function is used to explore two types of decision. To show that a utility scale can be expressed in any numerical terms, as long as internal consistency is maintained, the scale in the example extends well outside the conventional limits of zero and unity.

Example 1 (a). A building contractor's utility function for profit in a particular year has been identified as follows

profit (£'000)	−20	−10	0	10	20	30	40	50
utility	−34	−19	−9	0	9	18	26	34

If the contractor accepts no further business for the year in question his profit from existing business will be £10,000 for certain. However, he has an opportunity to tender for one additional contract. He estimates the cost of completing this additional work to be £45,000 with probability 0.2, £38,000 (0.5) or £33,000 (0.3). The different prices at which he considers tendering are £40,000, at which he estimates the probability of securing the contract to be unity, £50,000 (0.6) and £55,000 (0.3). Should the contractor tender for the additional contract, and if so at what price? We shall calculate the contractor's expected utility value (EUV) for the highest tender price (£55,000), leaving the reader to do likewise for the alternatives of £50,000 and £40,000. For convenience we employ a monetary unit of £1000 in our calculations.

When the tender price is £55,000 the contractor's expected utility value, EUV(55), is given by

$$EUV(55) = [0.7 \times U(10)] + 0.3[U(10+55-45) \times 0.2 + U(10+55-38) \times 0.5 + U(10+55-33) \times 0.3]$$

The first product on the right-hand side of this statement covers the eventuality that the contractor's tender is unsuccessful and his profit remains at £10,000; the probability weight for this is 0.7. The large square bracketed expression that follows covers all of the possible cost outcomes of a successful tender — the probability of which, 0.3, weights all three expressions within the square brackets. In the event that the tender is accepted, profit for the year will be (£10,000 + £55,000 − £45,000) with probability 0.2, (£10,000 + £55,000 − £38,000) with probability 0.5 or (£10,000 + £55,000 − £33,000) with probability 0.3. The utility values of these conditional profits, and their probabilities, are contained in the large square bracket; the summation within that bracket is the expected utility value conditional upon a successful tender at the price £55,000. The whole cumbersome expression reduces to

$$EUV(55) = [0.7 \times U(10)] + 0.3[U(20) \times 0.2 + U(27) \times 0.5 + U(32) \times 0.3]$$

Now we solve for EUV(55) by inserting the utility values for the cash amounts in the simplified expression, making linear interpolations where necessary between the stated points on the contractor's utility function:

$$EUV(55) = [0.7 \times 0] + 0.3[9 \times 0.2 + 15.3 \times 0.5 + 19.6 \times 0.3]$$

$$= 4.599 \text{ utility units}$$

This EUV is higher than the utility of a certain profit of £10,000. The reader should now determine whether either of the alternative tender prices offers a still higher EUV.

Example 1 (b). Instead of the choices described in Example 1 (a), suppose that this year, in addition to a certain profit of £10,000 from other business, the contractor is due to complete work on a fixed-price contract which has the following estimated probability distribution of profit outcomes:

profit on contract (£'000)	−12	1	5
probability	0.30	0.50	0.20

This contract allows the contractor to withdraw on payment of a penalty charge. How much money, if any, would the contractor be willing to pay to obtain a release from the contract?

The contractor's EUV for continuing with the fixed-price contract is obtained from the following

$$EUV(continue) = U(10 - 12) \times 0.3 + U(10 + 1) \times 0.5 +$$
$$U(10 + 5) \times 0.2$$

The right-hand side of this expression refers to the utility values of the three possible overall profit levels, each having the relevant probability weight. Simplifying and transforming as before, we obtain

$$EUV(continue) = U(-2) \times 0.3 + U(11) \times 0.5 + U(15) \times 0.2$$
$$= -11 \times 0.3 + 0.9 \times 0.5 + 4.5 \times 0.2$$
$$= -1.95 \text{ utility units}$$

Now let £X be the amount the contractor would be just willing to pay for release from the fixed-price contract, leaving himself with a secure profit of $£(10 - X)$ for the year (a monetary unit of £1,000 is assumed). By definition, £X has the property that

$$U(10 - X) = -1.95 \text{ utility units}$$

Again using a linear interpolation between points on the stated utility function, this time to find the cash equivalent of a utility value, we find that the profit of £7,833 yields a utility value of -1.95. The maximum amount the contractor would be willing to pay for a release from his contract is thus identified as £2,167. The two parts of this example have shown how manipulations with utility functions are performed. Now we must consider some of the issues that arise in applying utility theory to business decision making.

3.3 (ii) Utility Theory and Business Decisions

An important preliminary question is whether utility theory should be seen as descriptive or prescriptive; does it describe how decision makers instinctively behave, or how they ought to behave? A formal proof exists to show that on the basis of a few simple and eminently plausible axioms of preference and indifference in risk situations, a decision maker is behaving rationally in choosing a course of action to maximise his expected utility (Baumol, 1977, pp. 429-35; Naylor and Vernon, 1969, pp. 28-9). However, we have admitted that constructing a subject's utility function is rarely a straightforward exercise, even for a skilled interviewer. Furthermore, lacking skilled guidance, decision makers may instinctively resort to 'irrational' but quite believable attitudes and modes of thought in making risky choices. (For reviews of such criticisms of the expected utility model see Edwards, 1954, and Bromwich, 1976, pp. 276-80.) Yet we cannot ignore the insights into particular decisions gained through the medium of the expected utility maximising hypothesis and an appreciation of realistic utility function shapes. So our answer is a compromise; the hypothesis of expected utility maximisation does help to explain many choices in risk situations, but *strictly* 'rational' behaviour is both time-consuming and mentally taxing, even for an individual. When we add to this impression the special characteristics of business decision making – the mixture of collective, representative and scattered decision making, the bewildering variety and quantity of decisions and the likelihood of substantial shifts in the 'origin' of the utility function as the business experiences profit fluctuations – it becomes clear that the main useful-ness of utility theory is to provide both a means of clarifying a firm's scale of values and a powerful aid to consistency in its subsequent decisions.

Some of the practical problems for the utility function approach deserve elaboration. The most obvious are the linked questions of whose utility function is, or should be, consulted (a) when management acts on behalf of a wide and disparate ownership, and (b) when decision making within the enterprise is decentralised. We recognise that product and capital market imperfections confer on management wide measures of freedom in many areas, including risk taking; but from the managerial side these freedoms may appear as 'empty boxes' which can only be filled by managerial choice made on behalf of an inarticulate and fragmented ownership. Ultimately, market forces may align managerial risk taking with what 'the market' expects, but in practical terms we have to assume that managers follows their own instincts in this area of decision.

With decentralised decision making the obvious concern is that a divisional or subsidiary manager's personal utility function may bear little resemblance to that of the business as a whole (Swalm, 1966; Hammond, 1967). He may feel that his career prospects will be jeopardised if his decisions lead to losses, or even if profits are some-what delayed. This would make his own utility function turn steeply downwards below some 'acceptable' level (or immediacy) of profit from a risky project – even though the range of possible cash outcomes from that project may be quite narrow from the standpoint of the firm as a whole, with the implication that the firm's utility function in that range could be assumed nearly linear. This potential lack of consistency and rationality in corporate decisions can be countered in a number of ways without unduly curtailing the valuable principle of divisional autonomy. Larger investment proposals are generally referred to top management level for final decision, while procedures are often specified for the standard appraisal of smaller proposals. A target for profit can be set, which, in effect, will operate as the 'norm' or origin in the divisional manager's utility function — even if the *shape* of his function remains highly personal. Most ambitiously, managers can participate in communal discussions aimed at harmonising the spirit of decision making throughout the organisation. The need for such measures will be greater the more variable the firm's overall financial performance; fluctuating profits bring the need for frequent modification of the firm's relative valuations of different profit levels.

In addition to the problems posed by a divided business 'personality' and an uncertain and shifting profit base, an attempt to impose consistency and rationality on business decision making through the utility function approach faces two further difficulties. First, it is unrealistic to picture decisions being made singly, as in our example in 3.3 (i). In effect, the firm maximises expected utility through the choice of an optimal 'portfolio' of risks; and this necessarily involves estimating correlations between the performance of all possible pairs of risky projects — in addition to their individual risk characteristics (see 9.5 (i)).

Second, the financial dimension of a firm's utility function may vary between decision contexts. In our earlier example the determinant of utility was the level of profit in a particular year, but for investment decision making the businessman's horizon would presumably be more distant and net present value (see Appendix to Chapter 9) would be a more appropriate measure of prospective performance and determinant of utility. In principle, all decision making might be analysed in terms of a standard measure of prospective performance, net present value being the obviously appropriate concept. But if accounting periods are seen by decision makers as standing on their own, as in our example, this simplification is ruled out. The firm then faces the problem of harmonising utility functions for decisions with differing time horizons.

Finally, we can forestall possible criticism from the standpoint of managerial theories (see Chapter 1), to the effect that a utility function based exclusively on profit (or value) represents at best a disappointingly short step from the suspect postulate of out-and-out profit (value) maximising behaviour. It is conceded that the only insight that can be gained into business motivations and behaviour through the utility function approach is in the area of risk taking — but this is of course extremely worthwhile. Neither the way in which the firm is managed, nor the nature of the businessman's desire for profit, can be inferred from the existence or shape of his cash-utility transformation.

3.3 (iii) An Extreme Risk Criterion

In order to emphasise our eclecticism on descriptive decision models, let us look briefly at a criterion which stands at the opposite end of the spectrum from the uncertainty criteria of 3.2, with their deliberate avoidance of probability and concentration on payoffs. In a criterion which we shall call the *most probable winner criterion*, the decision maker chooses the strategy with the highest chance of out-performing the other strategies. In its simplest application, a straightforward choice between two strategies, the decision maker simply chooses the strategy with the greater chance of achieving superiority over its rival — just as if the two strategies were rival football teams about to play a series of matches. He is not interested in the margin(s) by which the chosen strategy 'defeats' the rejected one, or in the margin(s) by which it from time to time 'loses'. It follows that the rejected strategy *may* have a higher expected money value (better goal record) than the one chosen. To illustrate this, Table 3.3 gives the payoff probability distributions for strategies X and Y, and we assume that the two probability distributions are statistically independent, i.e. the probability of any outcome under strategy X is not affected by the outcome that occurs under strategy Y, and vice versa — assuming for the moment that both strategies *can* operate simultaneously. This means that the joint probability of any pair of X, Y outcomes is given by the product of their probabilities, just as the probability of two 'sixes' on simultaneous throws of two fair dice is given by

$$\frac{1}{6} \times \frac{1}{6} = \frac{1}{36}$$

(Moore, 1972, pp. 24–5).

The probability that the X outcome will be equal to or greater than the Y outcome is given by the sum of the probabilities of all of the mutually exclusive ways in which the result 'X greater than or equal to Y' $(X \geqslant Y)$ can occur. This total probability, $p(X \geqslant Y)$, is 0.63, as shown in our calculation. This result contrasts with the fact that EMV(X) is actually less than EMV(Y) (£9.80 against £10.60). Evidently this criterion is not unrelated to that of minimax regret

Table 3.3: Payoff Probability Distributions for Strategies X and Y

X		Y	
Payoff (£)	Probability	Payoff (£)	Probability
7	0.20	8	0.45
9	0.20	10	0.45
11	0.60	25	0.10

The X outcome will equal or exceed the Y outcome in the following 'pairings' of outcomes:

Payoffs (£)		Joint probability
X	Y	p(X) × p(Y)
9	8	0.20 × 0.45 = 0.09
11	8	0.60 × 0.45 = 0.27
11	10	0.60 × 0.45 = 0.27
		0.63

which we examined in 3.2; instead of minimising his *maximum potential regret*, the decision maker now minimises his *probability of regret*.

3.4 Conclusion

This chapter's purpose has been twofold: first, to review theories of decision making as general descriptive accounts, with little attempt until now to compare uncertainty-oriented and risk-oriented theories; second, by contrast, to establish the utility function approach as a basis for achieving consistency in adhering to a deliberately chosen scale of values in business decision making. In the first of these areas we examined criteria as widely separated as the more popular uncertainty models (emphasis all on payoffs, no role for probability) and the 'most probable winner' criterion (emphasis on probability, actual payoffs secondary). Between these extremes stands the criterion of expected utility value which recognises both (utility values of) payoffs *and* probability estimates. The second of our purposes has been substantially achieved, but it remains relevant to pursue our first purpose somewhat further and compare the main uncertainty theories — maximin and minimax regret — with our principal risk theory — the expected utility approach.

An obvious difference between the two approaches is that the uncertainty theories attempt to reflect decision makers' attitudes towards risk directly, while in the expected utility model the decision maker's risk attitude emerges only as a by-product of the shape of his utility function. Two different individuals having identical utility functions *cannot* reach different decisions on any risky proposal when they both adhere to the expected utility criterion.

One of the strengths of the expected utility model is that it can embrace the sentiments underlying both maximin and minimax regret, albeit on the assumption that the decision maker *does* make probability judgements. A maximin-type sentiment can be represented by a utility function that turns steeply downwards below some critical cash value, with the result that the decision maker will almost certainly avoid actions which could lead to outcomes with the prohibitively low utility values ruling below the critical point. The sentiment underlying minimax regret is even more deeply embedded in the expected utility model, again on the assumption that the decision maker thinks probabilistically. A simple proof, to be given in 7.3, demonstrates the intuitively obvious point that the strategy which maximises expected utility value also minimises *expected utility loss*. The latter term is simply the expected value of 'regrets', measured as utility differences instead of cash differences. In maximising EUV the decision maker is automatically minimising the expected value of his regret (expressed in utility, not cash, units).

Our comparison between broad theoretical approaches seems to favour the expected utility model, which can accommodate sentiments akin to those singled out by uncertainty models, but is by no means narrowly confined to such sentiments. We can conclude this discussion very briefly, by considering the effect of accepting two simple propositions: (1) decision makers generally estimate likelihoods for the various possible outcomes of their actions; (2) decision makers are guided by the utility equivalents of the various possible cash outcomes of their actions. Accepting these two uncontroversial propositions seems to take us much of the way towards accepting the expected utility model as a descriptive account of decision making, though we cannot ignore slippages caused by our own obvious failings as fully rational calculators or by the various 'costs' of achieving full consistency in our decisions. Nor should we lose sight of the kind of difficulties discussed in 3.3 (ii), specifically relating to the applicability of the expected utility model in business decision making.

This qualified acceptance of the expected utility model as a descriptive account of decision making is moderately encouraging, in that our descriptive account and prescriptive model appear closer than we might have dared to hope — thereby increasing the latter's chance of general acceptance. One final comforting thought is that businessmen may, for good and obvious reasons, actually desire and pursue rationality and consistency in their risk taking behaviour more determinedly than individuals do.

4 INTRODUCTION TO LINEAR PROGRAMMING

The way to see by Faith is to shut the eye of Reason.

Benjamin Franklin

4.1 Introduction

In the years since their emergence during and after World War II, mathematical programming concepts and techniques — especially linear programming (LP) — have caught the imagination of the economics profession in its broadest sense (Dantzig, 1963, Chs. 1 and 2). In relation to the theory of the firm, linear programming offers a widely applicable and realistic representation of the firm's short-run production function and the constraints limiting and influencing the firm's activities in the short run. From this framework can be obtained an understanding of the short-run behaviour of the firm — its choice of products and production processes and its utilisation of inputs — which can be seen as enriching and making more 'operational' the more traditional theory of the firm. Operational researchers have seized on LP as a technique that cries out for application to the many practical problems that can be expressed in the appropriate form.

Our treatment of LP in this and the following two chapters will try to do justice to both of these reasons for its wide acceptance. The three chapters will explain the general mathematical structure of linear programming problems and the basic simplex solution method, the linear programming theory of the firm and applications of LP in operational research.

As we begin, the newcomer to the subject can take comfort from the fact that, in mathematical terms at least, our discussion is about nothing more daunting than the solution of a set of simultaneous linear equations having the awkward but not insurmountable handicap of possessing more unknowns than equations. This perhaps unappetising theme is made more palatable through being presented in the form of a simple business problem.

4.2 The Nature of Linear Programming Problems

4.2 (i) A Simple Linear Programming Problem

The long-established and prestigious grocery firm of Fortran & Muzak prepares and sells two blends of coffee beans under its own label. Only two grades of bean are used, but the proportions in which they are mixed to make each blend vary. The blend marketed under the name 'Cubano' contains one fifth by weight of highly aromatic 'alpha' beans and four fifths of rather undistinguished 'beta' beans. The blend sold as 'Mexicano' contains alpha and beta beans in the proportions three fifths and two fifths, respectively. For the one-month planning period we are considering, F & M have been informed by their suppliers that they will be able to purchase no more than 180 pounds of alpha beans and 320 pounds of beta beans. The prices per pound paid by F & M are £4.00 for alpha beans and £1.50 for beta beans. Cubano coffee sells for £2.60 per pound package, and Mexicano for £4.10. Mixing and packaging one pound of each blend costs £0.10. F & M assume that at the prices stated they will be able to sell within the month all the coffee they prepare, of either blend. An order must be placed immediately for the month's supply of coffee beans. How much coffee of each type should be ordered, and how many one pound packages of each blend should be prepared?

The above information is a mixture of (i) cost and price data, from which we can calculate unit profit margins for the two blends of coffee, (ii) supply or scarcity data, from which we can establish the limitations on the firm's combined outputs, and (iii) input–output information, from which we shall be able to construct a working model of F & M's coffee blending 'technology'. Having completed these three stages, which are fairly standard aspects of many linear programming problems, we shall be ready to consider alternative solution methods.

(i) Costs and Price Data. For every pound package of Cubano blend sold, F & M's gross profit margin is £0.50 (sale price = £2.60; cost of beans = 0.2 × £4.00 plus 0.8 × £1.50; cost of packaging = £0.10). Similarly, the gross profit on a pound of Mexicano blend is £1.00. On the assumption that F & M's objective is to maximise the profit from its coffee sales, we state the following *linear objective function*:

maximise: £(0.50C + 1.00M)   (i)

where C and M are the numbers of one pound packages of Cubano and Mexicano blends, respectively, prepared from the supplies of beans purchased. (We shall see in due course how easy it is to dilute or circumscribe the desire for maximum profit without having to change the stated objective function at all.)

(ii) and (iii) Scarcity and Technology. We can take the second and third data types together. How many packages of coffee can be prepared without breaking the limitation on the supply of alpha beans? A package of Cubano requires 0.2 pounds, and a package of Mexicano 0.6 pounds, of alpha beans. Given that the maximum possible supply of alpha beans is 180 pounds, we can state:

$$0.2C + 0.6M \leqslant 180 \tag{ii}$$

The implied units on both sides of this *constraint expression* are pounds weight. The analogous statement for beta beans is obtained in the same way:

$$0.8C + 0.4M \leqslant 320 \tag{iii}$$

Like the objective function (i), these constraint expressions are linear in both C and M.

Our statement of F & M's problem is all but complete. Because our solution method cannot think for itself, we need to specify that any solution to the problem must be based upon non-negative values of both C and M. Thus we state:

$$C \geqslant 0, \qquad M \geqslant 0 \tag{iv}$$

4.2 (ii) Solution by Graphical Analysis

Although a graphical solution approach is obviously limited to problems that can be expressed in terms of two, or possibly three, variables, there are great advantages in being able first of all to visualise the linear programming problem and solution process and then to follow a non-graphical solution method on a graphical 'visual display'. The constraint expressions of our coffee blending problem are represented in a two-dimensional diagram, Figure 4.1, in which the two axes are the variables C and M.

When the supply constraint for alpha beans is fully effective, we evidently have in operation the strict equation

$$0.2C + 0.6M = 180 \tag{iia}$$

and this is shown as the 'alpha limit line' in Figure 4.1. Similarly, when the beta bean constraint is fully effective we have

Figure 4.1: Graphical Representation of Coffee Blending Problem

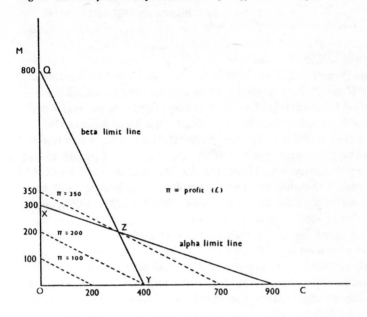

$$0.8C + 0.4M = 320 \qquad\qquad\qquad \text{(iiia)}$$

shown as the 'beta limit line'. The reader should confirm that the points
on each line agree with the relevant equation. (To locate a linear
equation graphically, identify the two intercepts and then join them
with a straight line. Thus the vertical intercept of (iia), with $C = 0$, is
given by $M = 180 \div 0.6 = 300$; and the horizontal intercept, with $M = 0$,
is given by $C = 180 \div 0.2 = 900$.)

Note that in Figure 4.1 we have not allowed our limit lines to extend
into the forbidden territory where either C or M becomes negative.

Having located the strict equalities derived from the two supply
constraints, we can identify the combinations of C and M satisfying
each original 'less than or equal to' condition; then we can identify the
combinations satisfying both conditions simultaneously. Confining our
interest to the quadrant in which both C and M are non-negative, all
points below the alpha limit line satisfy the condition $0.2C + 0.6M <$
180. (From any point on the limit line a slight movement to the left or
downwards reduces the value of one variable and leaves the other
unchanged; so the value of the function $0.2C + 0.6M$ falls below 180.)
Similarly, all points below the beta limit line satisfy the condition

0.8C + 0.4M < 320. The points satisfying each 'less than or equal to' condition are those on or below the limit line for that condition; so the points satisfying *both* conditions are those lying on or below *both* limit lines — the area bounded by, and including all points on, the perimeter OXZY in Figure 4.1.

But the area OXZY contains an infinite number of combinations of C and M values. How far then have we advanced our search for the optimum (profit maximising) combination? To narrow our search still further we introduce into the same diagram the linear function the firm seeks to maximise: £(0.50C + 1.00M). This is done in Figure 4.1 by showing just three members of an infinite 'family' of parallel dashed lines, each representing a different value of the function 0.50C + 1.00M. The method of construction is very simple; for any level of profit, say £200, we simply draw the linear equation 0.50C + 1.00M = 200, just as we earlier located the limit lines for the two constraints. Three of these 'isoprofit lines' are shown; their parallel slopes reflect the fact that no matter what level of profit we consider, the profit on two packages of C is always equal to the profit on one package of M. The most significant isoprofit line is that for £350, which just touches one corner, Z, of the 'bounded space' of feasible C and M combinations. The isoprofit line for any higher profit level would fail to touch OXZY at all, so £350 is the highest profit attainable, and evidently it can only be achieved by a unique combination of C and M: 300 pounds of C and 200 pounds of M. As point Z is the point at which both limit lines intersect, F & M should purchase all of the available supplies of coffee beans (180 pounds of alpha beans and 320 pounds of beta beans) and mix them in the way indicated by the solution.

Before moving on to a mechanical, non-graphical, solution method, we can learn a little more from our graphical result. First, the solution lies at Z rather than at X or Y because the slope of the typical isoprofit line is between that of the alpha limit line and that of the beta limit line. In fact, the optimal output combination is insensitive to the relative profitabilities of the two blends within wide limits; these limits are, at one extreme, a per unit profit on Mexicano three times that on Cubano (the alpha limit line), and at the other extreme a per unit profit on Mexicano only half that on Cubano (the beta limit line). Once the ratio of profit margins moves outside these limits the highest isoprofit line will just touch the bounded space OXZY at either X (if the isoprofit line is shallower than the alpha limit line), or Y (if the isoprofit line is steeper than the beta limit line). It is visually obvious that the optimal solution will never lie *inside* the perimeter OZXY; generally it will lie at one of the corners on the perimeter, but if the isoprofit lines happen to be parallel to one of the limit lines the same (maximum) profit can be attained at any point on that edge of the bounded space formed by the limit line in question. From an infinite number of feasible solutions the graphical approach is able to identify, in most cases, a unique optimum; or, unusually, a range of equally optimal policies.

Only at point Z in Figure 4.1 are both constraints effective simultaneously. Had the solution lain at point X only the alpha constraint would have been effective, together with the non-negativity condition for C; ample 'slack' in the beta constraint would have been available (200 pounds in fact). At Y the picture would have been reversed; the beta constraint would have been fully effective, along with the non-negativity condition for M, and 100 pounds of 'slack' in the alpha constraint would have remained.

It is obvious that even in a two-product problem the number of constraint expressions increases as we introduce further examples of scarcity or managerial decisions about the product mix or input usage. Some of the additional constraint expressions may be 'redundant' in the sense of lying outside the feasible solution space, but even so it is likely that a realistic linear programming problem in two dimensions would have the space containing feasible solutions bounded by more than just four straight lines as with OZXY in Figure 4.1. This would imply a greater number of possible solution points, though in two dimensions the graphical solution method would work just as effectively. But the potential headaches in seeking solutions to problems in more than two dimensions and with more numerous constraints will be obvious. In n dimensions a corner point on the outer edge of the bounded space containing all feasible solutions is defined by the simultaneous solution to n of the equations formed from the constraints of the problem, just as point Z in Figure 4.1 represents the solution to the equations formed from the alpha and beta constraints. Our need is for a systematic and economical way of proceeding from corner point to corner point on the outer surface of a problem's feasible solution space, in search of the highest possible value of the problem's objective function (or the lowest if the problem is one of minimising cost rather than maximising profit). The simplex solution method, to which we now turn, does exactly that.

4.3 The Simplex Solution Method

4.3 (i) Mathematical Background, Layout and Procedure

The simplex solution method proceeds by stages. At each stage the solution rests for the time being at one of the corner points of the problem's angular feasible solution space, and the value of the problem's linear objective function at that point is measured and recorded. Next, the method indicates whether there is at least one move in the direction of a new corner point that would improve the value of the objective function. If more than one such move is possible, the method makes a sensible but perhaps not completely economical choice between the different directions open to it, and the solution comes to rest on a new corner point. This process is repeated until no further move in any direction will improve the value of the objective function. The method is thus mechanical but purposeful; the shortest route to the optimum solution is not guaranteed, but the method will not lose sight of its ultimate objective along the way. In identifying each new corner point solution the simplex method is doing something readily understandable to anyone casually acquainted with simultaneous equation theory; it is simply solving a set of simultaneous equations, in which the number of variables exceeds the number of equations, using a different combination of the available variables as the basis of the solution. To avoid having to find all possible solutions on this basis, which could be a very lengthy process (for example, with five equations in ten variables there are 252 different ways of choosing five variables as the basis for a solution!), the simplex method is able to tell, before fully identifying any new solution, whether the change will represent an improvement over the present solution's objective function value.

We continue to work with our coffee blending problem, to allow the progress of our mechanical solution to be followed visually. The problem can be stated very compactly:

$$\text{\textit{maximise:}} \quad \pounds(0.50C + 1.00M) \qquad \text{(objective function)}$$

$$\text{\textit{subject to:}} \quad 0.2C + 0.6M \leqslant 180 \qquad \text{(alpha constraint)}$$

$$0.8\,C + 0.4M \leqslant 320 \qquad \text{(beta constraint)} \qquad \text{(v)}$$

$$C, M \geqslant 0 \qquad \text{(non-negativity constraints)}$$

First, each constraint expression is stated as an equation by introducing into it a variable to represent 'slack', that is the amount of the available supply of coffee beans *not* purchased by the firm. Thus we have

$$0.2C + 0.6M + S_a = 180 \qquad \text{(iib)}$$

$$0.8C + 0.4M + S_b = 320 \qquad \text{(iiib)}$$

in which S_a and S_b are the slack variables for the alpha and beta constraints, respectively. When the value of a slack variable is zero, the constraint in question is fully effective. Like any 'real' variable in the problem, a slack variable must be non-negative in value.

Next the objective function is modified in a trivial way to take account of the new variables introduced into the problem:

maximise: £$(0.50C + 1.00M + 0S_a + 0S_b)$ (ia)

This formulation makes it clear that the presence of either type of slack makes no contribution to profit. Our earlier formal statement of the problem (v), can now be recast as follows:

maximise: $0.50C + 1.00M + 0S_a + 0S_b$

subject to: $0.2C + 0.6M + 1S_a + 0S_b = 180$

             $0.8C + 0.4M + 0S_a + 1S_b = 320$ (va)

             $C, M, S_a, S_b \geqslant 0$

In this formulation the implicit coefficients of S_a and S_b in the constraint equations are shown explicitly as unity or zero as appropriate; only one type of slack can be present in each equation, and its value in that equation obviously absorbs an equal number of units of the constraint — pounds in this case. Another change from the earlier statement (v) is that the £ sign disappears from the objective function; the unit of measurement is the same for all terms in the objective function, and what really matters mathematically are the ratios of the coefficients to each other. As now expressed the problem's structure is obviously that of a set of simultaneous equations in which the variables outnumber the equations (by four to two) and in which no variable is allowed to take a negative value in a solution. It will become clear that the four possible solutions to this system of equations — each obtained by 'dropping' two variables, i.e. giving them a zero solution value, and solving the equations for the values of the remaining two — correspond to the four corner points of the bounded space OXZY in Figure 4.1, the space containing all feasible solutions to the problem. We already know from our earlier graphical analysis that a linear objective function will reach its maximum (or minimum) attainable value at a corner point of the same bounded space; so a suitable 'mechanical' solution method for our linear programming problem is one which will concentrate on identifying solutions to the set of simultaneous equations constructed from the problem's constraints, in such a way that before any new solution is identified in detail its objective function value is known to represent an improvement over that of the solution it will replace. Such a discriminating and economical search procedure is exactly what the simplex method offers, and we now explain its working in detail.

Different texts explain the basic simplex layout and procedure at differing lengths and levels of mathematical complexity. From the enormous abundance of alternatives, the following (given in an approximate ascending order of difficulty) are chosen to indicate to the newcomer something of the range of textbook treatments available: Battersby (1966); Frazer (1968); Koutsoyiannis (1979), Ch. 20; Sasieni, Yaspan and Friedman (1959), pp. 220–46; Sasaki (1970), Ch. 4; and Horowitz (1972), Ch. 6. Our approach here is to try to maintain the newcomer's consciousness of the development of the underlying algebraic situation, both in the informative layout of each stage in the solution and in the accompanying text. The first step in the simplex method is generally to set up a solution to the programming problem that is trivial, in terms of its obvious inadequacy as a solution to the problem, but algebraically correct and easy to identify. The purpose of this opening move, shown in Table 4.1a, is to provide both stepping stones and signposts towards better solutions.

Along the upper edge of the simplex tableau are listed the four variables in the problem, each headed by its objective function coefficient (vulgar fractions are introduced in place of decimals for computational convenience). To the left of the upper rectangle the details of the solution are presented. On the extreme left we note the two variables on which the solution is currently based — S_a and S_b in the opening tableau. (With two constraint equations, *every* solution will be based on two variables chosen from the four available.) Next we note the respective unit cash values of the solution variables, taken from the objective function. Then, beside the left-hand edge of the upper rectangle we enter the respective solution values of the variables in the solution. It will be obvious that all physical units in the problem are pounds weight. Immediately below these details of the solution stands a box in which is recorded the actual objective function value; here it is £0, i.e. $180 \times £0$ (for S_a) plus $320 \times £0$ (for S_b). Evidently our first solution is trivial and without value, but it has the advantages (i) that it is an *obvious* solution to the two simultaneous

Table 4.1a: Coffee Blending Problem, First Simplex Tableau

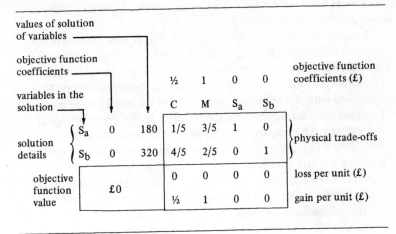

values of solution of variables			½	1	0	0	objective function coefficients (£)
objective function coefficients			C	M	S_a	S_b	
variables in the solution							
S_a	0	180	1/5	3/5	1	0	physical trade-offs
S_b	0	320	4/5	2/5	0	1	
objective function value	£0		0	0	0	0	loss per unit (£)
			½	1	0	0	gain per unit (£)

constraint equations, requiring no effort at all to identify, and (ii) that it represents one of the four corner points of the bounded feasible solution space (point 0 in Figure 4.1), from which moves to more worthwhile corner points are readily identifiable.

Each variable on the upper edge of the tableau has listed below it, in the upper rectangle of the tableau, its coefficients in the two constraint equations of the problem. Vulgar fractions are used instead of decimals, to facilitate the calculations that lie ahead. These coefficients now have a highly significant role: each column shows the physical trade-offs that are possible between the relevant upper-edge variable and the variables presently in the solution without infringing the equations and conditions that define the problem. Taking the first column as an example, to introduce a (one pound) unit of variable C into the solution at this stage would 'cost' one fifth of a unit of the slack variable S_a (of which 180 units are available) plus four fifths of a unit of the slack variable S_b (of which 320 units are available). An analogous statement can be constructed in relation to the introduction into the solution of a one pound unit of variable M. While this interpretation of the coefficients of the original constraints tells us little or nothing new about the trivial opening solution, its usefulness will be crucial later in the solution when trade-offs will otherwise be much less obvious. Moving to the variables already in the solution, S_a and S_b, we expect to find that in each case, with no other change envisaged and with the levels of slack already fully absorbing their respective constraint values, the slack variable exchanges for itself on a 'one-for-one' basis — a trivial exchange.

Now we turn to the financial aspect of the physical trade-offs just identified. Given the linearity of our model this is simply a matter of multiplying the physical opportunity costs of each change by their respective per unit financial costs; the sum of these products is then compared with the financial contribution of the new element now hypothetically introduced into the solution. In the opening stage of the solution this comparison yields an obvious result, but the procedure will prove invaluable as the solution develops. Introducing a unit of C 'costs' one fifth of a unit of S_a plus four fifths of a unit of S_b, and since each type of slack has a zero cash value per unit (shown in the middle column to the left of the tableau's upper rectangle), the formal statement of financial opportunity cost is: $1/5 \times £0 + 4/5 \times £0 = £0$. The gain to the objective function from introducing a unit of C is of course £½. The two elements contributing to the net financial change for each variable are shown separately in the lower rectangle of the tableau.

Evidently the objective function will profit from the introduction of a unit of either C or M into the so far worthless solution; and since the entire structure of the problem is linear we can be confident that further units of either type will be equally worthwhile. However, only one variable at a time can be brought in, and here we choose M with its much higher net financial gain per unit. (This *may* not be the most economical move to make, because we have not considered how many M units will be possible, compared to the number of C units that could be achieved.) The new variable, representing an improvement in the value of the objective function, i.e. profit, will naturally be introduced in the largest possible amount — that is, up to the point at which one or other of the 'slacks' is entirely used up. The profit motive thus dictates that the new solution will again be based on just two variables; to introduce M and retain some of S_a *and* some of S_b would be to fail to take full advantage of the profit opportunities shown in the opening tableau. How much of M can be introduced into the solution? To produce a unit of M requires the sacrifice of three fifths of an S_a unit plus the sacrifice of two fifths of an S_b unit. There are 180 S_a units in the opening solution, so $180 \div 3/5 = 300$ gives the maximum number of M units that could be produced if the scarcity of alpha beans were the only constraint on output. Similarly, the maximum number of M units that could be produced if the scarcity of beta beans were the only consideration is given by $320 \div 2/5 = 800$. The lower of these two quotients obviously establishes the effective constraint on M production; because of the scarcity of alpha beans no more than 300 units of M can be produced, even when output of C is zero. We now know that our new solution is going to contain 300 units of profitable M production, and an as yet unknown residual amount of unprofitable slack, S_b. The variable S_a will disappear, completely squeezed out by a more profitable variable.

Before moving to the second stage of our solution, the procedure for identifying the departing variable can be generalised. Each physical trade-off entry in the column of the entering variable is divided into the corresponding element in the column of solution values (immediately to the left of the upper rectangle), and the row in which the *lowest non-negative quotient* is found indicates the departing variable. (We shall consider shortly the special case where the lowest non-negative quotient is actually zero.) The column of the entering variable is called the *key column*; the row of the departing solution variable is the *key row*; and the intersection of this row and column is the *pivot*. Here the key column is M, the key row is S_a and the pivot is the entry $3/5$. The mechanical transformation of the original to the new solution tableau is facilitated by identifying these important features visually, for example by lightly drawing lines down the column and along the row in question, intersecting on the pivot.

The second tableau, Table 4.1b, is laid out in the same way as the first, though we are dispensing with most of the identifying labels. The physical trade-offs differ from the originals because the solution has moved to a new location on the perimeter of the space containing all feasible solutions, in fact to point X in Figure 4.1. The transformation of the upper rectangle was performed 'mechanically' according to the following rules:

(i)   The trade-off elements and the value of the solution variable in the original key row are divided by the pivot, and the results are entered as the corresponding elements in the new tableau. (Check that the whole of the M-row in Table 4.1b, with the exception of the objective function coefficient of course, has been derived in this way.)

(ii)   The other trade-off element in the column of the entering variable is zero. The column of *every* variable in a solution is constructed in the same way, with a unit coefficient in the row matching its position in the solution and zero in the other trade-off

Table 4.1b: Coffee Blending Tableau, Second Simplex Tableau

			1/2	1	0	0	
			C	M	S_a	S_b	
M	1	300	1/3	1	5/3	0	
S_b	0	200	2/3	0	$-2/3$	1	
		£300	1/3	1	5/3	0	loss per unit (£)
			1/2	1	0	0	gain per unit (£)

position. (Check the S_a and S_b columns in the original tableau, and the M and S_b columns in the new one.) This rule generalises easily for problems of more than two constraints: *all* entries in the column of physical trade-offs for a variable in the solution are zero, except for a unit coefficient matching the position of that variable in the solution.

(iii)   All other entries, including the values of the solution variables immediately to the left of the upper rectangle, are replaced by entries in the corresponding positions in the new tableau obtained as follows:

$$N = 0 - \frac{K_c K_r}{P}$$

in which N is the element in the new tableau, O is the corresponding element in the old tableau, K_c is the entry in the key column horizontally across from O, K_r is the entry in the key row above or below O, and P is the pivot. As an example, the S_b, C entry in the original tableau, 4/5 is transformed as follows:

$$\frac{4}{5} \rightarrow [\frac{4}{5} - \frac{2/5 \times 1/5}{3/5}] = \frac{2}{3}$$

Similarly, the original solution value for S_b is transformed as follows:

$$320 \rightarrow [320 - \frac{2/5 \times 180}{3/5}] = 200$$

These rules look complicated, but they soon become quite automatic; and with practice a number of short cuts will become obvious to the operator. But it is worthwhile warning the newcomer to be very careful to handle minus signs absolutely correctly; a double minus yields a plus here, as elsewhere, and a negative physical trade-off is just as meaningful as a positive one.

We should now confirm that our mechanically generated entries in the new tableaus do indeed represent physical trade-offs in the sense previously defined, and that our new solution is feasible. Preliminary visual confirmation on both aspects is obtained from Figure 4.1 (p. 73). Our new solution, $M = 300$, $S_b = 200$, corresponds to point X, as the reader can confirm by calculating the amount of slack present in the beta constraint at that point. But are the trade-offs involved in moving from point X indeed those given by the entries in the new tableau? Figure 4.1 shows that at X no more M can be produced, and that as C is introduced into the production mix M must be sacrificed at the rate of one M unit for every three units of C (the slope of the perimeter of OZXY, which contains all feasible solutions, is identical in the range XZ to the slope of the alpha limit line). Also obvious in Figure 4.1, though not as numerically clear, is the fact that as C displaces M in the solution some of the slack in the beta constraint is taken up; the solution point moving along XZ is coming closer to the beta limit line. Our new tableau tells us that the precise rate at which this occurs is the loss of two thirds of an S_b unit for every unit increase in the value of C.

We now confirm and summarise these trade-off calculations for the entry of a one pound unit of C into the solution, starting from point X in Figure 4.1.

1. A one pound increase in C requires the removal of one third of a pound of M (the alpha limit line).
2. Each pound of M requires 3/5 pounds of alpha beans, so the amount of alpha beans released by the reduction in M production is $1/3 \times 3/5 = 1/5$ pounds.
3. This release of 1/5 pounds of scarce alpha beans is exactly what is required for the production of one pound of the C mixture (see initial specification for C).
4. The change in the production mix ($\Delta C = 1$, $\Delta M = -1/3$) also changes the total usage of the non-scarce resource, beta beans. A pound of C absorbs 4/5 pounds of beta beans, and a pound of M absorbs 2/5 pounds of beta beans; so the introduction of a

pound of C into the solution at the expense of 1/3 pounds of M has a net effect on beta usage of $1 \times 4/5 - 1/3 \times 2/5 = +2/3$ pounds. This increase in beta bean usage is of course equal to the fall in the value of S_b.

The reader should confirm the other columns of trade-off entries in this way, paying special attention to the minus sign appearing in the S_a column. Our new tableau, generated quite mechanically, gives us the physical trade-offs prevailing at the new solution point much more economically than the diagrammatic approach could do; and the same method will work for problems in more than two dimensions.

Is the new objective function value of £300 the best that can be obtained? According to the loss *versus* gain comparison at the bottom of the second tableau, it is not. Introducing a unit of C now involves a sacrifice of £1/3: one third of a unit of M plus two thirds of a unit of worthless S_b. But this move also brings an increase in revenue of £1/2, and the net improvement in the objective function is £1/6. So we progress to the third tableau, derived from the second in exactly the same way as the latter was derived from the original. C enters the solution by displacing S_b (the quotients are $300 \div 1/3 = 900$ in the M-row, and $200 \div 2/3 = 300$ in the S_b-row).

The third stage of the solution, Table 4.1c, turns out to be optimal. The solution C = 300 and M = 200 corresponds to point Z in Figure 4.1. The loss *versus* gain comparison indicates that no further change can improve the objective function value. The physical trade-offs are now those in force at point Z, where both constraints are fully effective simultaneously. C and M are already present in the solution; neither can be increased, other things being equal, except at its own expense – a

Table 4.1c: Coffee Blending Problem, Third Simplex Tableau

			1/2	1	0	0	
			C	M	S_a	S_b	
M	1	200	0	1	2	-1/2	
C	1/2	300	1	0	-1	3/2	
	£350		1/2	1	3/2	1/4	loss per unit (£)
			1/2	1	0	0	gain per unit (£)

trivial exchange. More interestingly, reintroducing S_a requires the removal of some M but allows an equal *increase* in C; this is equivalent to moving the solution point from Z towards Y (in Figure 4.1) along the beta limit line, opening up a gap between the solution point and the alpha limit line. Alternatively, reintroducing S_b moves the solution point back along XZ, with M increasing and C falling, S_a remaining zero and S_b increasing.

The usefulness of the simplex method is not yet exhausted. Table 4.1c tells us that S_a can be reintroduced into the solution at a net cost of £3/2 for each unit of slack (i.e. pound of unused alpha beans) reintroduced. To maintain deliberately this unit of slack would be pointless, but the detrimental effect on the firm's profit would be exactly equivalent to that of a one unit reduction in the available supply of alpha beans, assuming in the latter case that F & M continued to maximise profit. If the supply of alpha beans was reduced from 180 to 179 pounds, the firm's best possible profit would fall by £3/2 as M output fell by two pounds and C output rose by one pound. This gives us a clue to the answer to a far from pointless question. Reversing the above thinking, we note that if one *extra* pound of alpha beans could be obtained, at the normal price, the firm's profit could *increase* by £3/2, as M *increased* by two pounds and C *fell* by one pound. Evidently we can interpret the net loss-minus-gain values below the slack variable columns in the optimal solution tableau as *net marginal revenue products* for the inputs in question. (In the example above the marginal revenue generated by an extra unit of alpha beans, optimally deployed, would be £8.20 from extra M sales, minus £2.60 from the cutback in sales of C. From this marginal revenue of £5.60 we must subtract the cost of the extra pound of alpha beans, £4.00, and the cost of packaging one extra pound of coffee, £0.10.) This theme of the valuation of marginal units of scarce resources will be developed in 4.4 and in later chapters, but we have shown here that the basic simplex method readily yields exact information that would be extremely difficult to extract from the graphical solution to the problem.

To summarise, our method proceeds systematically around the perimeter or outer surface of the feasible solution space of the linear programming problem. One variable at a time is introduced at the expense of one which departs, always resulting in an improved objective function value until the optimum set of solution variables is found. Each stage of the solution always contains the same number of variables as the number of constraints (equations) in the problem, and it follows that the number of 'real' variables in the solution cannot exceed the number of constraints. Indeed, whenever the number of constraints defining the feasible solution space exceeds the number of 'real' variables it is inevitable that *any* solution to the problem will contain some elements of slack.

4.3 (ii) Extensions and Complications

Still mixing programming theory with its application to the firm, we now consider how the basic procedure may require elaboration to accommodate differently expressed constraints and the computational problems they may entail.

The 'Greater than or Equal to' Constraint. Constraints can express situations other than the scarcity of resources; for example, aspects of demand or managerial policy. Nor are all problems of a maximising nature, as we shall see; and in cost minimising problems constraints may express minimum standards or specifications that constrain the attainment of lower cost levels. In relation to our coffee blending problem a number of quite different 'greater than or equal to' constraints might be suggested, and as an example we shall assume that for the duration of the bean supply shortage already described the F & M management is anxious to ensure that sufficient supplies of its superior blend, Mexicano, will be available for sale to its more esteemed customers. To this end management specifies that the month's output of M must be at least 250 packages. This policy constraint is expressed as

$$M \geqslant 250 \tag{vi}$$

and it might seem logical to form an equation from this constraint, in an analogous fashion to that employed earlier in handling scarcity constraints, for incorporation in the simplex method. This would imply

$$M - W_1 = 250 \tag{via}$$

in which W_1 is a non-negative variable representing any excess of M over its permitted minimum level of 250 pounds. In other words, W_1 takes whatever non-negative value is necessary to balance the two sides of (vi).

Our problem now has three constraint equations, and in solving it by the simplex method we are tempted to look first of all for an easy-to-identify, trivial solution based upon the two slack variables, S_a and S_b, and the balancing variable W_1 — just as in our earlier statement of the problem, we used the trivial solution as a stepping stone and indicator to more interesting possibilities. But each of the variables on which an initial trivial solution is based must be represented in the simultaneous equation statement of the problem by a column in which all entries are zero except for $+1$ in the row matching its position in the solution (see equation system (va), p. 77 and Table 4.1a, p. 79). The coefficient of W_1 in (via) is -1, and the reader will find that an attempted solution based upon S_a, S_b and W_1 is simply nonsensical; whereas $S_a = 180$ and $S_b = 320$ implied $C = 0$ and $M = 0$ in the original trivial solution in Table 4.1a, we now find that $M = 0$ implies $W_1 = -250$ — an impossibility — or alternatively, $W_1 = 250$ implies $M = 500$ — an incompatibility. It should be emphasised that there is nothing logically or mathematically wrong with equation (via), and indeed we shall find that it is fully satisfied by the eventual solution to the problem as now extended. The only trouble with (via) is that *as it stands* it doesn't work in the simplex routine explained earlier, and a simple trick is needed to get the routine started.

The trick is to introduce into the troublesome constraint equation a completely artificial variable with the necessary coefficient of $+1$:

$$M + U_1 - W_1 = 250 \qquad\qquad \text{(vib)}$$

Like S_a and S_b in the scarcity constraints, U_1 has a coefficient of unity and appears in no other equation; therefore in the array of constraint coefficients it too is represented by a column in which all entries are zero except for $+1$ in the row representing the equation it appears in. It should now be possible to construct an initial solution based on the variables S_a, S_b and U_1, from which moves can be made in the usual way to more interesting solutions; but it is of course necessary to make sure that U_1 does not appear in the final solution to the problem. This too is easily accomplished, by giving U_1 an overwhelmingly negative objective function value — in effect causing it to price itself out of the solution. (If the problem is one of minimising subject to constraints, an artificial variable's disappearance can be guaranteed by giving it an overwhelmingly positive objective function value.) We can illustrate the whole treatment of a 'greater than or equal to' constraint by setting out the opening tableau of the extended coffee blending problem.

In Table 4.2 the new constraint in its equation form (vib) has been added as the bottom line of the upper rectangle, which has of course also been extended to the right to accommodate the two new variables. S_a, S_b and U_1 form the basis of the initial solution, as shown on the

Table 4.2: Opening Tableau of Revised Coffee Blending Problem

			1/2	1	0	0	−H	0	
			C	M	S_a	S_b	U_1	W_1	
S_a	0	180	1/5	3/5	1	0	0	0	
S_b	0	320	4/5	2/5	0	1	0	0	
U_1	−H	250	0	1	0	0	1	−1	
	−£250 H		0	−H	0	0	−H	H	loss per unit (£)
			1/2	1	0	0	−H	0	gain per unit (£)

left of the tableau. The objective function recognises the two new variables in different ways. The zero coefficient of W_1 reflects the fact that management derives no extra satisfaction or profit when M exceeds 250 pounds, beyond what is already measured by the objective function value of M. The objective function coefficient of U_1, the artificial variable, is intended to price that variable out of the solution; thus £H represents a very large positive cash amount, which, preceded as it is by a minus sign, will always outweigh any other sums in the loss *versus* gain comparison. For every unit of U_1 remaining in the solution (there are 250 at the beginning) the value of the firm's objective function suffers an imaginary deficit of £H, and an irresistible pressure exists to remove all units of the meaningless but convenient variable.

The solution to the problem now proceeds in the same fashion as the original, with an excluded variable replacing a solution variable at each step until no further improvement in the objective function value can be achieved.

The Strict Equality Requirement. Another constraint type that can be anticipated in various situations is a strict equality, and it is treated similarly to the 'greater than or equal to' constraint just considered. For example, had the F & M management planned to produce exactly 150 packages more of the inferior than of the superior blend, the requirement would have been written first as

$$C - M = 150 \tag{vii}$$

There is no room for a slack or balancing variable in (vii), but the equation does not have the requisite variable with a coefficient of unity that appears in no other equation. So we again employ an artificial variable in the same way as for the 'greater than or equal to' constraint, but without including a balancing variable:

$$C - M + U_2 = 150 \tag{viia}$$

Here the artificiality of the additional variable is even more obvious; but again the solution method, having got itself launched on the basis of U_2, will price the latter out by the time the solution process is complete, through the overwhelming financial penalty incurred by each U_2 unit in the solution.

Computational Problems. Occasionally in switching from one tableau to its successor the 'lowest quotient' rule for identifying the departing variable produces a tie between two or more candidates for removal. This condition is described as degeneracy. Where the tied quotients are all positive the method used to reach a decision is mainly a matter of personal preference. The simplex method can reach the optimum solution by different paths, some longer than others, and there is very little danger that when a tie is broken in an arbitrary way the solution will 'cycle' within a pattern from which no escape to a full optimum is possible (Dorfman, Samuelson and Solow, 1958, pp. 92-3). It is inevitable that in the solution stage following that in which a tie is broken, the retained tied variable will have a zero value in the solution; this in no way precludes its full presence in subsequent solution stages, including the final solution, should that be justified.

Of greater practical concern is the possibility that the lowest non-negative quotient is actually zero, or that several quotients equal to zero are found. This can arise when one or more constraint expressions have constant terms equal to zero instead of positive values. Here we show such a problem in the abstract, first as an objective function and a set of inequalities, then as an expanded objective function and matching constraint equations.

maximise: $4x + y$

subject to: $3x \geqslant 2y$

$x \leqslant 4y$

$x + y \leqslant 5$

maximise: $4x + y + 0W_1 - HU_1 + 0W_2 + 0W_3$

subject to: $3x - 2y - W_1 + U_1 = 0$

$x - 4y + W_2 = 0$

$x + y + W_3 = 5$

Table 4.3: Initial Simplex Tableau

			4	1	0	-H	0	0	
			x	y	W_1	U_1	W_2	W_3	
U_1	-H	i^2	3	-2	-1	1	0	0	
W_2	0	i	1	-4	0	0	1	0	
W_3	0	5	1	1	0	0	0	1	
	$-Hi^2$		-3H	-2H	H	-H	0	0	loss per unit
			4	1	0	-H	0	0	gain per unit

x replaces U ($5/1 > i/1 > i^2/3$)

The expanded version of the problem uses the symbols W and U (with appropriate subscripts) to represent balancing and artificial variables respectively. As in Table 4.2 above, the objective function coefficient of $-H$ for the artificial variable U_1 is intended to ensure the latter's exclusion from the final solution to the problem. Inspection of the constraint equations in the expanded version indicates than an initial feasible solution will be based upon U_1, W_2 and W_3; but that when a move is made to introduce x (the variable with the highest positive objective function coefficient) into the solution, the variables U_1 and W_2 will tie as candidates for removal — each having a zero quotient ($0 \div 3$ and $0 \div 5$, respectively).

To make the necessary choice between U_1 and W_2 and avoid confusion later in the solution, we replace either of the zero constraint constants by the symbol i, denoting an extremely small but nonetheless positive number — for example, 0.00001. The other zero is replaced by i^2. (If more than two zeros are present we can go on to i^3, i^4 ... and so on.) This simple trick breaks the tie because $i > i^2$ ($> i^3 > i^4$ ...). Apart from this device to ensure the workability of the simplex method, no other change in procedure is called for. The initial simplex tableau is shown in Table 4.3, with i and i^2 as the initial solution values of W_2 and U_1, respectively.

In completing the solution the reader should treat all terms involving i *exactly* as he would straightforward numerical solution values, until it becomes possible to ignore them. This can be done when all variables in the solution are present in more than token amounts (which should occur after two iterations in this case). It is also important to bear in mind that in the gain-loss comparison at the foot of each column, as well as in the body of the tableau, a negative loss is equivalent to a positive gain.

Finally in this section on computational problems, we can note briefly that minimising an objective function can be performed in the same way as maximising. Two possibilities exist. One is to multiply the stated objective function by -1 and *maximise* the resulting expression in exactly the way we have been doing throughout this chapter. The other method is to leave the stated objective function unchanged and, instead of selecting the entering variable because it *adds* to the value of the objective function, select as the entering variable the one which most *reduces* the objective function value. Either method will lead to the identification of the lowest objective function value consistent with the constraints of the problem.

4.4 The Dual Formulation and the Valuation of Scarce Resources

4.4 (i) Formulating and Interpreting the Dual

Our original coffee blending problem involved two scarce resources and two different products. That problem was presented in familiar profit-maximising terms, but now we re-examine the same situation from an apparently different standpoint — that of the pursuit of optimal resource allocation. Although we can anticipate that the optimal allocation of scarce resources in the firm is the one which maximises profit, there is a lot to be learned from adopting a different standpoint for this purpose.

From its layout it is obvious that a linear programming problem such as the coffee blending problem can be read vertically as well as horizontally, with each column in the initial tableau (Table 4.1a) being seen as an 'activity' consuming scarce inputs and yielding a profit in direct proportion to the amounts of the latter consumed. Thus the activity of preparing one pound of C consumes 0.2 and 0.8 pounds, respectively, of scarce inputs of alpha and beta beans, and results in a contribution to profit of £0.50. This suggests the possibility of imputing values — 'shadow values' — to the scarce resources alpha and beta, reflecting their contributions to profit made through the defined activities. We can state, for example, that 0.2 pounds of alpha beans combined with 0.8 pounds of beta beans must be worth *at least* £0.50

to the firm (after meeting all expenses), since that is the contribution to profit made by that combination. Similarly, 0.6 pounds of alpha beans plus 0.4 pounds of beta beans make a contribution to profit of at least £1.00, which establishes a minimum shadow valuation for this resource combination. These statements suggest the following:

$$0.2v_a + 0.8v_b \geqslant £0.50 \tag{viii}$$

$$0.6v_a + 0.4v_b \geqslant £1.00 \tag{ix}$$

in which v_a and v_b are the as yet unknown shadow values per unit of the alpha and beta inputs respectively.

Symmetry suggests that having formed two new constraints, of opposite inequality type to the originals, using the *columns* of the original layout, with the objective function coefficients of the original as the new constraint constants, we can now expect that the original constraint constants will appear as the objective function coefficients in a *minimising* problem. But how are we to interpret this transformation of the *primal* (original, maximising) formulation into the *dual* (minimising) formulation? As shown in 4.3 (i), the shadow value of a scarce resource is its marginal contribution to profit — in this case after the additional expenses associated with its employment and the resulting changes in production have been met. But if management had failed to realise the significance of the information on implicit resource values contained in the solution to the primal problem, how could it try to elicit the same information directly? The importance of the loss of a unit of a scarce resource is measured by the consequential reduction in profit, so it would make sense for management to seek to allocate resources between activities in such a way that the total of these potential losses is minimised. This suggests an objective function of the form

$$minimise: \quad £(180v_a + 320v_b) \tag{x}$$

in which 180 and 320 are of course the physical amounts available, in pounds, of the resources alpha and beta, whose shadow values v_a and v_b management seeks to identify. The dual formulation of the coffee blending problem is now complete, and it is worthwhile to set it out alongside the primal formulation to which it is so closely related.

PRIMAL	DUAL

maximise: $0.50C + 1.00M$ *minimise*: $180v_a + 320v_b$

subject to: $0.2C + 0.6M \leqslant 180$ *subject to*: $0.2v_a + 0.8v_b \geqslant 0.50$

$0.8C + 0.4M \leqslant 320$ $0.6v_a + 0.4v_b \geqslant 1.00$

$C, M \geqslant 0$ $v_a, v_b \geqslant 0$

The reader who takes the trouble to solve the dual formulation of the problem, gaining useful experience in handling artificial variables in the process, will of course find that he learns nothing that could not have been gleaned from the primal solution obtained earlier. The decision on which formulation to use ought to turn only on the practical question of which one seems to involve less computational work, because the solution to each formulation can be read in the solution to the other. The dual's solution will show that the shadow value of a unit of alpha beans is £1.50, and that of a unit of beta beans is £0.25; the minimised shadow cost of the limited availabilities of resources is £350, implying that if management were to discover some new use for the same scarce resources (instant coffee?) their opportunity cost in terms of lost profit in their present uses would be £350. The basic linearity of the model dictates that this total valuation of scarce resources available to the firm be exactly equal to the sum of the per unit resource valuations multiplied by their respective quantities. Thus £270 (= 180 × £1.50) and £80 (= 320 × £0.25) represent the 'contributions' of the available quantities of alpha and beta beans, respectively, to the total profit of £350.

4.4 (ii) The Significance of the Dual

Some preliminary assessment of the dual's practical significance is in order. The shadow valuations identified in the dual solution and derived as by-products in the primal solution share the well-known characteristics of the concept of marginal revenue product in traditional micro-economic theory: the latter's dependence on other things being constant, and its proneness to change as the input in question actually changes. Even if all other inputs are held constant the marginal revenue product of the variable factor in traditional theory changes as (a) its marginal physical product changes (the 'law' of variable proportions), and (b) the price at which output can be sold changes as more is produced for sale. In our present model the price of output is constant over all feasible sales levels, so factor (b) does not operate (as Chapter 5 will argue, this need not mean that we are assuming the firm to operate as a price taker in a perfectly competitive market). Factor (a) cannot be so easily ruled out, but we can show that it operates quite differently to the smoothly declining marginal physical productivity of traditional theory.

In Figure 4.1 (p. 73) resource scarcities are shown as linear constraints, and by shifting one constraint outwards in a series of small, equal, parallel moves we can show the effects of progressively relaxing the constraint in question. As the alpha limit line is moved outwards to represent an increase in the availability of alpha beans its point of intersection with the stationary beta limit line slides upwards along the latter from Z, reaching higher and higher isoprofit lines as it does so. A given outward shift of the alpha limit line always produces the same amount of shift along the beta limit line, i.e. the same change in the profit-maximising pattern of output, as long as the point of intersection remains on the beta limit line. The marginal physical productivity of alpha beans, in terms of their effect on the profit-maximising combination of outputs, is constant throughout the range ZQ on the beta limit line; beyond point Q the changes in outputs that can be brought about by increased availability of alpha beans are zero. This abrupt discontinuity in marginal physical products is of course reflected in the marginal revenue productivity of alpha beans, and in their marginal contribution to profit. Each equal change in the maximum profit combination of outputs along ZQ produces a given change in the firm's sales revenue and a given change in its costs; beyond point Q, where the alpha limit line ceases to act as a constraint on output, the marginal revenue product and marginal contribution to profit of alpha beans both drop to zero.

If a problem's feasible solution space contains a greater number of corner points than OXZY in Figure 4.1, the same conclusion holds about the marginal revenue productivity of a variable input, except that the abrupt drop to zero may well occur before production is concentrated entirely on one type of output.

In the chapter which follows the theory of the firm and its short-period decision making will continue to be developed through the gradual enlargement of mathematical programming concepts, culminating in the presentation of alternative models of how management might resolve its resource allocation problem under risky demand conditions.

5.2 (ii) The LP Model of The Single-Product Firm

A convenient way of building a bridge between traditional theory and the LP theory of the firm is to employ the latter's framework to portray the single-product firm that is so strongly associated with the former. In the short period the firm may have open to it a limited number of different production processes, all capable of producing the single type of product in question. Each process combines inputs, including those in limited supply, in fixed proportions; and the levels of output achieved are in direct proportion to the levels of inputs. So far we have an exact analogy with the equiproportionate expansion of inputs and outputs along a 'ray' from the origin of a traditional constant-returns-to-scale production function (Koutsoyiannis, 1979, pp. 95-7); the difference between the LP model and the traditional production function is that in the former the number of different ways of combining inputs (i.e. the number of possible rays from the origin) is strictly limited. There is no continuous spectrum of production techniques as in the traditional isoquant (Allen, 1960, pp. 621-4).

As an example, suppose that a single-product firm can choose from among four different processes, combining resources in different proportions, and that two of the resources in question are in limited supply in the period we are considering. In the short period the part of the firm's technology (input–output relationships) that is relevant in determining production possibilities is that relating to the two scarcities, and this extract from the complete (and much more complex) table of input requirements is expressed in constraint form thus:

$$a_{11}x_1 + a_{12}x_2 + a_{13}x_3 + a_{14}x_4 \leqslant R_1$$

$$a_{21}x_1 + a_{22}x_2 + a_{23}x_3 + a_{24}x_4 \leqslant R_2$$

(i)

where x_j is the level of output from the jth process, a_{ij} is the amount of the ith scarce resource required in the production of a unit of output in the jth process, and R_i is the amount of ith scarce resource available ($i = 1, 2$ and $j = 1 \ldots 4$). Using this statement of production possibilities we can formulate linear programming problems for profit maximisation and for minimising the cost of producing a specified level of output. Although our main purpose at present is to consider 'supply' aspects, it will be helpful to deal briefly with profit maximisation before turning to the cost minimising problem.

If maximum profit is sought, how much output should the firm

5 LINEAR PROGRAMMING AND THE THEORY OF THE FIRM

My worthy friend, all theories are grey,
And green alone Life's golden tree.

> Goethe

5.1 Introduction

In this chapter we consider the linear programming model of the firm
as a possible framework for understanding decision making in the firm
on the central questions of which products should be produced and in
what quantities. In developing this theme it will be instructive to refer
occasionally and briefly to the traditional framework for modelling
the firm, so that the full significance of the LP presentation — its
advantages and limitations — can be appreciated. We consider both
'supply' and 'demand', and sandwiched appropriately between these
aspects we shall recognise and explore the area of 'policy' constraints.

Throughout the chapter discussion proceeds on the basis of
Chapter 4's introduction to linear programming theory and the simplex
solution method. However, the reader may find it helpful at some
stages — particularly in 5.2 — to refer to diagrammatic expositions such
as those of Dorfman (1953) or Baumol (1977), Ch. 12.

5.2 Aspects of Supply

5.2 (i) Introduction

The LP model of the firm's technology and supply constraints is
intended to represent conditions applying in a short period of time in
which production methods and productivity remain constant and some
resources are in limited supply. Although the 'short period' generally
has a planning connotation, in that it is intended to represent the
elapse of time between management decisions on production levels,
it is obvious that the frequency of decisions may, in turn, be
dictated by the frequency with which scarcity constraints change.
In Chapter 4, for example, the firm of F & M was described as
making a production plan for the duration of certain supply limitat'

produce, and in which process or processes? Output from all processes is sold at a standard price (assumed constant regardless of output) but the avoidable unit costs of production are likely to differ between processes. The amounts of the scarce resources consumed in each process per unit of output differ, so that if the costs of these resources are attributable to outputs in the short period we can expect the avoidable unit cost of output — and therefore the profit margin — to vary between processes. Even if the costs of scarce resources are completely fixed in the short period, different processes are likely to use differing amounts of non-scarce inputs, and this too gives rise to differing variable costs and profit margins per unit of output. The LP model for maximum profit is completed by introducing as the objective function the firm's profit function. In our example with four processes and two scarcities we have the following:

maximise: $m_1 x_1 + m_2 x_2 + m_3 x_3 + m_4 x_4$

subject to: $a_{11} x_1 + a_{12} x_2 + a_{13} x_3 + a_{14} x_4 \leqslant R_1$ $\qquad$ (ii)

$\qquad\qquad a_{21} x_1 + a_{22} x_2 + a_{23} x_3 + a_{24} x_4 \leqslant R_2$

$\qquad\qquad x_1, x_2, x_3, x_4 \geqslant 0$

in which the constraints stated in (i) are repeated, and m_j is the gross profit (sales revenue minus avoidable costs) earned on each unit of output from process j. With just two scarcity constraints we expect a solution to contain not more than two processes.

The LP formulation for minimum cost uses the same pair of scarcity constraints together with a specification of the level of output that is to be produced at least cost. In place of the profit-maximising objective function in (ii) we introduce a linear cost-minimising objective function, giving the following complete problem:

minimise: $c_1 x_1 + c_2 x_2 + c_3 x_3 + c_4 x_4$

subject to: $a_{11} x_1 + a_{12} x_2 + a_{13} x_3 + a_{14} x_4 \leqslant R_1$

$\qquad\qquad a_{21} x_1 + a_{22} x_2 + a_{23} x_3 + a_{24} x_4 \leqslant R_2$ $\qquad$ (iii)

$\qquad\qquad x_1 + x_2 + x_3 + x_4 = X^*$

$\qquad\qquad x_1, x_2, x_3, x_4 \geqslant 0$

where c_j is the variable cost per unit of output in process j and X^* is the output level for which total cost is to be minimised.

The general feature of a solution to either the profit-maximising

(ii) or the cost-minimising problem (iii) is that the number of processes employed does not exceed the number of resource constraints. In the profit-maximising formulation this is clear enough, as the problem contains only resource constraints. The possibilities there are that two processes will be employed, with both constraints fully effective, or that only one process will be employed and one of the resources will have unutilised 'slack'.[1] At first glance the cost-minimising problem (iii), having three constraints, appears to suggest the possibility of three processes being operated to achieve minimum cost at some level(s) of output. But such an inference contradicts the above 'rule' for maximum profit, and must be rejected; depending on its resource constraints, the firm's profit may be maximised at *any* level of output, and as the profit-maximising output is, by definition, produced at least cost, *no* level of output will involve the operation of more than two processes.

At the operational level, apart from its efficient handling of the standard operations of profit maximisation and cost minimisation, the LP framework may have other attractions for the management of a single-product firm. First, the simple rule about the relationship between the numbers of scarcity constraints and processes employed appears to provide a useful check on the firm's efficiency. As we shall shortly discover, however, the presence of constraints other than straightforward scarcity constraints diminishes the practical value of this check. Second, the LP framework greatly facilitates the identification of the firm's short-period marginal cost curve. Solving the cost-minimising problem (iii) for progressively higher output levels produces a total cost series from which marginal cost is readily obtained. Not surprisingly, the marginal cost function turns out to be discontinuous. The cost of additional output is initially constant as the most economical process is expanded to its limit, set by one of the resource constraints; then constant again at a higher level as output is expanded further by the progressive phasing-out of the most economical process and its replacement by a more expensive process requiring less of the 'bottleneck' resource per unit of output; and so on. Marginal cost rises in steps in this way until all scarce resources are fully utilised (Baumol, 1972, pp. 312–15). Third, management may be able to obtain helpful guidance from the 'shadow' resource valuations that can be read from both profit-maximising and cost-minimising solutions. The important proviso here is that these shadow valuations are determined by the parameters of the immediate problem, and are therefore of limited usefulness in medium- and long-term planning

(Henderson and Schlaifer, 1965; and Dorfman, Samuelson and Solow, 1958, pp. 183-4).

5.2 (iii) An Example of Cost Minimisation and Marginal Cost Measurement

We conclude our discussion of the single-product firm by illustrating some of the above points in a numerical example of cost minimisation in a four process — two constraint firm of the kind represented by (iii). The problem is stated as follows:

$$\text{minimise:} \quad \pounds(6x_1 + 5x_2 + 7x_3 + 6x_4)$$

$$\text{subject to:} \quad 10x_1 + 8x_2 + 6x_3 + 4x_4 \leqslant 40 \qquad \text{(resource}$$
$$2x_1 + 4x_2 + 7x_3 + 12x_4 \leqslant 50 \qquad \text{constraints)}$$

$$x_1 + x_2 + x_3 + x_4 = 6 \qquad \text{(required output)}$$

$$x_1, x_2, x_3, x_4 \geqslant 0 \qquad \text{(non-negativity conditions)}$$

The first tableau of the simplex solution to this problem is given below.

			6	5	7	6	0	0	M	
			x_1	x_2	x_3	x_4	w_1	w_2	U_3	
w_1	0	40	10	8	6	4	1	0	0	
w_2	0	50	2	4	7	12	0	1	0	
U_3	M	6	1	1	1	1	0	0	1	
	£6M		M	M	M	M	0	0	M	loss per unit (£)
			6	5	7	6	0	0	M	gain per unit (£)

Following the introduction to the simplex solution method given in Chapter 4, the above presentation needs very little explanation. In addition to the variables $x_1 \ldots x_4$, the problem contains slack variables for resources 1 and 2 (w_1 and w_2, respectively) and an artificial variable in the equation for required output, U_3, whose sole function is to provide a basis for an initial solution. The two slack variables, whose presence in the solution merely indicates excess capacity, have zero objective function coefficients; while in a minimising problem the artificial variable must take an extremely high, positive, coefficient — sufficiently high to ensure the exclusion of that variable from the solution. Here we use the symbol £M, representing, say, a 'cost' of one million pounds. Following the procedure explained in 4.3 (ii), the initial trivial solution is composed of three variables, each of which appears with a coefficient of unity in a different equation of the problem.

The initial solution is 'worth' £6M; a prohibitively expensive solution, particularly as no output is being produced! The most attractive move indicated in the loss *versus* gain display at the foot of the tableau is the introduction of x_2, which offers a net *reduction* in the objective function value of $£(M-5)$ per unit. The maximum amount of x_2 that can be introduced is five units, when w_1 is entirely displaced; so the new solution value will be $£(5M-25)$ lower than the original. The reader should now verify this point by identifying the second tableau, following the procedure shown in Chapter 4, and then the third tableau, shown below. (In doing this, recall that a negative loss is equivalent to a positive gain, and the cost of having an artificial variable in the solution is prohibitive.)

			6	5	7	6	0	0	M	
			x_1	x_2	x_3	x_4	w_1	w_2	U_3	
x_2	5	4	3/2	1	1/2	0	1/4	0	−1	
w_2	0	10	2	0	−1	0	2	1	−20	
x_4	6	2	−1/2	0	1/2	1	−1/4	0	2	
	£32		9/2	5	11/2	6	−1/4	0	7	loss per unit (£)
			6	5	7	6	0	0	M	gain per unit (£)

This third tableau is optimal. No further worthwhile change (that is, no *lowering* of the objective function value) is possible. Resource 1 is fully utilised, and its marginal valuation can be seen from the tableau to be £¼ (i.e. total cost *increases* by £¼ if a unit of w_1 is reintroduced into the solution, implying that total cost would *fall* by £¼ if an extra unit of resource 1 became available). Resource 2 is in surplus and its marginal valuation is accordingly zero. Processes 1 and 3 would each increase costs by £1½ per unit of output produced ($£(6-9/2)$ and $£(7-11/2)$, respectively), though as their respective columns show, this identity of financial effect comes about in quite different ways.

Finally, the U_3 column also carries some interesting information, though of course there is no question of deliberately re-creating a nonsensical solution. Recall that U_3 has its origin in an equation for required output:

$$x_1 + x_2 + x_3 + x_4 + U_3 = 6 \tag{iv}$$

With the constraint value constant at six units of output, the effect of reintroducing a unit of U_3 into the solution is simply to reduce the required total of $x_1 \ldots x_4$ from six units to five; and the resulting change in the objective function value (ignoring the amount £M which is clearly irrelevant in this connection) is a measure of marginal cost when output increases from five to six units. The U_3 column shows the detail of the calculation; when the output target is reduced by one unit, x_2 *rises* by one unit and x_4 *falls* by two units. Accordingly, the net change in costs is $1 \times £5 - 2 \times £6 = -£7$. The amount of resource 2 slack increases by 20 units. The solution also shows the range of output, below six units, within which marginal cost is constant at the level of £7; the maximum amount of x_4 that can be displaced by U_3 is just two units, so the substitution of U_3 for x_4 reaches its limit when $U_3 = 1$, i.e. when output has fallen by one unit from six to five units.

5.2 (iv) The Multi-Product Firm

We need not dwell on the fairly obvious parallels and differences between the linear programming picture of technology, limitations on production and the decision making of the single-product firm and that offered by the traditional approach (see Allen, 1960, pp. 618-21; Baumol, 1977, pp. 315-17; and Boulding and Spivey, 1960, pp. 94-129). Instead, we employ the LP model of the single-product firm as a convenient introduction to the theory of the multi-product enterprise — so convenient in fact that all we need to do to effect the transformation is to recognise that physically interchangeable outputs produced in different processes, having differing input requirements, variable costs and profit margins, are to all intents and purposes different products. Accordingly, much of what can be said about the single-product/multi-process firm can be expected to apply also to the multi-product firm.

The general features of the LP model of the multi-product firm in the short period are *linearity* and *scarcity*. Linearity implies a constant proportionality between the inputs into an activity and the latter's output and net revenue — in effect, constant physical and financial returns to scale — and this apparently very sweeping generalisation requires some substantiation. Our discussion of the 'demand' implications of linearity comes later; here we focus on the constancy of unit costs at different levels of output.

Given the fact that in a LP statement of the firm's technology an activity's rate of operation can be constrained within the range in which the linearity of inputs and output obtains, a breakdown of linearity is more likely to occur in the area of unit costs; and this likelihood is related to the ways in which scarcity manifests itself. For example, when the regular working hours of a given skilled workforce are fully utilised, overtime working is the only way in the short period of increasing the outputs of the products depending on the skill in question. Assuming that overtime working is arranged and paid for as required, the unit costs attributable to overtime production must exceed those of normal-time production, and this is recognised in the LP model of the firm by defining new variants of the activities affected. These variants retain the physical input requirements of the originals, but have objective function coefficients that are lower than the original in each case by the amount that unit cost is higher. The original and the new variant of each affected activity then exist side by side in an expanded LP model of the firm, and the solution method can be relied on to include a less profitable (more costly) variant only if a higher level of profit is thereby attainable; or if, in a cost-minimising context, required output exceeds the capacity of the less costly variant. (If the additional resources obtained at a higher unit cost are in fact less productive than the 'basic' amounts – e.g. because workers are less efficient during overtime working – the input coefficients of the affected activities as well as their objective function values must be appropriately modified in defining the variant activities.)

An implication of the last paragraph is that 'scarcity' is by no means a simple phenomenon. A simple classification of scarcity types followed by an example to illustrate the importance of that classification should clarify this point. The simplest scarcity type is a strictly limited availability of a resource which, in the period of the limitation, is costing the firm an amount that does not depend on the level of use. Obvious examples are the fixed normal working hours of a given workforce and warehouse space owned or rented on a long-term basis. In all such cases costs do not vary with the level of output or resource use within the limits stated, and traditional theory's recognition of the irrelevance of fixed costs for short-period decision making is completely applicable: management's presumed objective in the short period is to maximise the excess of revenue over *avoidable* costs, thereby making the maximum possible contribution towards fixed costs, profit and the retention and expansion of resources in the long run.

But scarcity can take other forms. In the coffee-blending problem discussed in Chapter 4, each grade of coffee bean could be purchased in any quantity at a stated price up to a stated maximum amount; the cost of beans *was* avoidable in the short period, by ceasing production, so the objective function coefficient for each blend of coffee had to reflect the costs of bean inputs (see 4.2 (i) for the relevant calculations).

Another variation is a limitation on the availability of a resource between an upper end and a lower limit (the latter may of course be zero). The cost of the minimum quantity has to be treated as a fixed, inescapable cost; but any quantities used above the stated minimum have to be paid for as used, the costs entering into the objective function coefficients of the activities responsible for them. For example, under a long-term supply contract the buyer may undertake to order at least a stated minimum quantity each month and the seller may state the maximum amount he will be willing to supply at the agreed price per unit.

5.2 (v) An Example Involving Different Scarcity Types

An example will show how easily a simple problem increases in complexity as scarcities other than the elementary type are recognised. As the example will show, the additional complexity arises from the attempt to observe the theoretically correct separation of fixed and variable outlays in the costing of output. Suppose that a firm produces two products, X and Y, which sell at fixed prices. Three resources are subject to one or other of the scarcity types described above. Resource 1 is available in a strictly limited amount, the cost of which is unalterable in the short period. Resources 2 and 3 are available in 'basic' amounts at fixed costs, as with resource 1, and in 'extra' amounts up to a stated limit at a constant price per extra unit in each case. Production of a unit of X requires three units of resource 1, two units of resource 2 and twelve units of resource 3. Production of a unit of Y requires five units of resource 1, one unit of resource 2 and seven units of resource 3. The amount of resource 1 available is 60 units; and the basic availabilities of resources 2 and 3 are 50 units and 100 units, respectively. Up to 20 extra units of resource 2 and up to ten extra units of resource 3 are available, at costs of p_2 and p_3 per unit of each resource type, respectively.

If we at first disregard the complications of the extra availabilities of resources 2 and 3, the linear programming problem presented by the above information is very straightforward. All scarce resources are 'free' to the firm's activities in the short term (i.e. their costs are overheads) and so the problem has a familiar appearance:

maximise: $\pi_x X + \pi_y Y$

subject to: $3X + 5Y \leqslant 60$ (resource 1)

$\qquad\qquad 2X + Y \leqslant 50$ (resource 2)   (v)

$\qquad\qquad 12X + 7Y \leqslant 100$ (resource 3)

$\qquad\qquad X, Y \geqslant 0$

in which π_x and π_y are the margins of selling price over avoidable costs for products X and Y, respectively. However, in recognising the potential supply elasticities of resources 2 and 3 we have to extend our simple model (v) in two ways: first, by defining new 'activities' to allow for the different (i.e. lower) profit margins on both products when the basic limits on availabilities of resources 2 and/or 3 are exceeded; and second, by adding constraints to indicate the limits on the availabilities of the 'extra' resources. In the first of these operations we distinguish between physically interchangeable units of output according to the avoidable costs of resources employed. With two resources whose availabilities can be increased at a cost, this involves defining three new categories of the output of each product in addition to the original, as follows:

X, Y   production using basic supplies of resources 2 and 3;
X′, Y′   production using basic resource 2, extra resource 3;
X″, Y″   production using extra resource 2, basic resource 3;
X‴, Y‴   production using extra supplies of resources 2 and 3.

This classification distinguishes units of output according to their avoidable costs, and for each category the objective function coefficient is computed accordingly. The full statement of the maximising problem, incorporating all necessary extensions, is as follows:

maximise: $\pi_x X + \pi_y Y + (\pi_x - 12p_3)X' + (\pi_y - 7p_3)Y' + (\pi_x - 2p_2)X''$

$\qquad\qquad + (\pi_y - p_2)Y'' + (\pi_x - 12p_3 - 2p_2)X''' + (\pi_y - 7p_3 - p_2)Y'''$

subject to:

	X	Y	X'	Y'	X''	Y''	X'''	Y'''		
resource										
1 (basic)	3	5	3	5	3	5	3	5	$\leqslant$ 60	
2 (basic	2	1	2	1	–	–	–	–	$\leqslant$ 50	
3 (basic)	12	7	–	–	12	7	–	–	$\leqslant$ 100	(vi)
2 (extra)	–	–	–	–	2	1	2	1	$\leqslant$ 20	
3 (extra)	–	–	12	7	–	–	12	7	$\leqslant$ 10	

The model of the extended LP problem is easy to interpret. For example, the activity labelled X'' is shown as drawing on the basic supplies of resources 1 and 3 and on the extra supply of resource 2; accordingly its objective function coefficient is lower than that for activity X by the cost of the two units of extra resource 2 that have to be purchased to produce it. This greatly enlarged LP problem (compare (v) and (vi)) can be solved in the usual way, once the actual objective function coefficients are introduced. With five constraints the solution may contain as many as five of the eight activities shown in (vi), and the solution method will of course tend to favour the variables with the highest profit margins. In this way resources of whatever scarcity type will be allocated to the most profitable set of activities. The output of each product will increase at a constant marginal cost *within* each category (i.e. X, X', etc.) and between categories marginal cost will undergo an upward step equal to the increase in the cost of inputs. The actual levels of production in each category cannot be predicted in advance of the solution.

5.3 Policy Constraints and Their Interpretation

Between 'supply' constraints and 'demand' constraints (the latter still to be considered) we must recognise a wide area within which discretionary managerial policies find expression. One simple suggestion in 4.3 (ii) was that managerial policy on the firm's product mix might override the dictates of unfettered short-run profit maximisation. Also possible are constraints on the numbers of products to be produced – in effect overriding the limitation on the number of products to a number not exceeding the number of constraints. If management wishes product i to be included in its production mix, nothing would be simpler than to add a constraint of the form

$$X_i \geqslant X_i^* \tag{vii}$$

in which X_i is the output of product i and X_i^* is the minimum level of production specified by management. Mathematically, an extra constraint requires the presence in the solution of an extra variable, and the form of this particular extra constraint ensures that X_i will be that extra variable (assuming it would have been absent from the profit-maximising solution).

The elimination or avoidance of unused capacity may be another 'managerial' objective that could conflict with or dilute the profit motive. Given time, new products may be found to absorb persistent excess capacity in relation to one or more of the firm's resources, or excess resources can be shed; but in the short period the presence of surplus capacity can be wholly or partly disguised by producing an unprofitably large number of products from the present range of possibilities. To bring this about, without altogether losing sight of its profit objective, management can attach arbitrary positive cost coefficients to the slack variables in the objective function that would normally, and correctly, be given zero coefficients. More radically, the whole problem might be restated in terms of minimising some fairly arbitrary valuation of excess capacities, subject to a minimum profit constraint. Under this approach the objective would become:

$$\textit{minimise}: \sum_{i=1}^{n} v_i W_i \tag{viii}$$

in which n is the number of resources, W_i is the amount of slack of resource i and v_i is the valuation or weighting given by management to a unit of slack of resource i. The minimum profit constraint would take the form:

$$\sum_{j=1}^{m} \pi_j X_j \geqslant \Pi^* \tag{ix}$$

in which m is the number of products from which management selects its product mix, π_j is the profit margin (sales revenue minus variable cost) per unit of product j, X_j is the output of product j, and Π^* is the minimum acceptable level of profit.

The varied class of 'managerial' constraints we have considered can be viewed in two lights. The LP framework is obviously well suited to the representation of short-term profit maximisation constrained, diluted or even replaced, by one or more purely short-term considerations. But some constraints should perhaps be seen as attempts by management to direct short-term activities towards a long-term goal of maximum (or at least adequate) profit, in conditions of uncertainty about the course and pace of future developments. Such an interpretation might apply, for example, to a constraint on minimum product numbers which has the effect in the short run of reducing profits and proliferating products, but which management may feel offers greater security of demand for the longer term.

5.4 The Representation of Demand

5.4 (i) Decisions on Prices

The undoubted advantages of the LP framework in representing short-period supply conditions and various managerial policies are not by themselves sufficient to make that framework a suitable one for representing short-period decisions in the firm. There remains the central problem of how to represent price and output decisions, and here our first task is to dispel the impression that our approach applies only to firms acting as price-takers in perfectly competitive product markets. Such an impression arises, understandably, because of our model's lack of a price-setting dimension and because of its assumption that product prices and profit margins do not vary with production and sales. These two aspects will be considered in turn.

First, the absence of a visible price-setting dimension presents no serious problem if, in reality, decisions on prices and outputs are made separately (and usually at different times). Indeed, a model in which periodic output decisions are made against a background of predetermined prices is arguably more realistic than one in which, in traditional textbook fashion, managers regularly adjust prices, outputs and other policies together. Apart from the kind of scepticism first articulated by Hall and Hitch (1939) in relation to firms' *ability* to equate marginal cost to marginal revenue — a policy which, if pursued with determination, would surely imply frequent price adjustments — we recognise various interpretations of why managers might *prefer* to adjust prices infrequently. These include 'sticky' oligopoly prices and non-price forms of competition, the costs of frequent price changes, and policies such as full-cost pricing and entry-preventive pricing which are obviously directed towards the attainment of long-term objectives. (Theories and evidence relating to pricing decisions are reviewed in Bridge and Dodds, 1975, Ch. 7; and Koutsoyiannis, 1979, Chs. 9–14.)

If out-and-out profit-maximising behaviour (simultaneous, co-ordinated decisions on price and output) appears unrealistic, the likelihood that output decisions are taken against a fixed-price background makes it easy to accept the curtailed version of profit maximisation embodied in our short-period LP theory of the firm. By contrast with the traditional model, the fixed-price maximisation of profit is a perfectly operational objective; and given that it can be constrained or diluted by 'managerial' considerations (5.3 (i)), it must surely appeal to managers as an eminently logical and appropriate objective.

5.4 (ii) Output Decisions and Demand Risk

The second criticism of our model of short-period decision making, that product prices are held constant regardless of levels of sales, is best considered in the context of uncertainty about the levels of demand for the firm's products.

Our first need is for a more general and realistic view of management's understanding of demand; then we can consider alternative models of decision making in the face of risk.

An interpretation of a managerial view of demand is illustrated in Figure 5.1, for the case of one particular product, X, in a particular time period. P_0 is the sales price that has been predetermined for the period in question. For each level of production, management estimates the probability that demand for X will be at or above that level; beyond a certain level, the greater the level of output the lower must be management's confidence in this sense. Thus, given the level of price, there is complete confidence in being able to sell a modest output of 50 units; but when output is set at 150 units, management's confidence drops to 90 per cent, and with output as high as 200 units the estimated probability that demand will fall short of production rises to 0.60 (i.e. $1 - 0.40$). By making similar estimates for different price levels, management can in principle draw a 'constant confidence demand curve' covering a range of prices for a given level of confidence; for example, the schedule D(0.90) shows for each price the amount of X consistent with 90 per cent confidence in the sense defined. But because we assume fixed product prices in the context of the firm's output decision, we can confine management's immediate task to the relatively simple exercise (to be performed for each of the firm's products) of assigning confidence levels to different sales levels at one price only.

Figure 5.1: Representing Demand as a Risky Variable

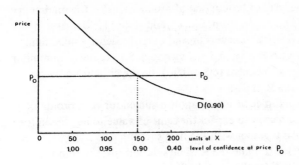

How should we picture the decision process when most levels of production, and mixtures of products, are believed to involve the risks of both excess production and unsatisfied demand? Various interpretations have been suggested, and we shall consider in turn two of the more interesting possibilities. Until 5.4 (vi) we shall assume that each production period is 'self-contained' in the sense that production in excess of demand has no value and underproduction represents permanently lost sales opportunities.

5.4 (iii) Chance-Constrained Programming

The general problem of introducing risk and uncertainty into the linear programming model of the firm is discussed in Naylor and Vernon (1969), pp. 319-22. Our first interpretation of the firm's behaviour in the face of a risky demand function is based on the LP technique known as *chance-constrained programming*, first suggested by Charnes and Cooper (1959). Our interpretation attempts to achieve a believable expression of management's attitude to risk while avoiding an over-ambitious picture of the implied probability calculations. In each 'self-contained' production period we assume that management formulates a maximum production constraint for each product. This is done in the light of the estimated demand probability distribution for the product, and its purpose is to place an upper limit on the probability of over-production. Other things being equal, the higher the cost of a lost unit of sales in relation to the cost of an unsold unit, the higher the upper limit on output (i.e. the maximum tolerable risk of overproduction) is likely to be.

The typical chance constraint of this type is

$$X_i \leqslant X_i(c_i^*) \qquad \qquad (x)$$

in which X_i is the level of production of product i, c_i^* is the minimum acceptable confidence level for product i, and $X_i(c_i^*)$ is the level of output at which the risk of having unsold output reaches a maximum acceptable level. Thus in Figure 5.1 if management's required minimum confidence level is 90 per cent ($c_i^* = 0.90$) the upper limit on production must be set at 150 units.

A chance constraint such as (x) can be assumed for each product, though there is no reason to expect the same c* value to be chosen for all products. Taken together with the firm's resource constraints, these chance constraints determine the feasible solution space within which a production mix will be chosen. The firm's objective function is unaffected by the introduction of risk into the problem; the objective function coefficient of each product is, as usual, its unit profit margin. It follows that the solution to the profit maximising problem is an indicated profit level and output/sales plan that will only be fully realised if all production is sold at the intended prices, that is, if all demands are equal to or in excess of their respective output levels.

While management, by definition, accepts the risk of unsold production for each product individually, there appears at first to be a lack of control over the risk that overall profit will fall short of its solution value. To illustrate this point we define a new variable, C_0. This is the probability of avoiding *any* overproduction, i.e. the probability of actually achieving the profit indicated in the solution to the chance-constrained programming problem:

$$C_0 = \prod_{i=1}^{x} c_i \qquad \qquad (xi)$$

in which x is the number of products or activities represented in the firm's production function, c_i is the confidence level actually achieved in the solution for product i and C_0 is the product of all c_i values. Equation (xi) assumes, for simplicity, that all demand probability distributions are independent. For each product, output is not permitted to exceed the level at which confidence would fall below management's c* value for that product; that is

$$c_i \geqslant c_i^* \quad (i = 1 \ldots x) \qquad \qquad (xii)$$

From this we obtain the following property of C_0:

$$C_0 = \prod_{i=1}^{x} c_i \geqslant \prod_{i=1}^{x} c_i^* \qquad \qquad (xiii)$$

Management's overall confidence in attaining the solution values of profit and sales is not identified until the solution production levels are identified and their respective c values calculated. But the product of the individual target confidence levels establishes a minimum value for the overall confidence measure. Taking this idea one step further, it would be a simple matter to choose a set of c* values for individual products with a view to their joint effect on the minimum value for C_0, rather than for their effects on confidence in relation to sales of individual products. However, if the relative costs of over- and underproduction vary considerably between products, the prospective value of C_0 may be of relatively little consequence; and management will probably then prefer to concentrate on setting c* values for individual products. Whichever approach is followed, it is clear that the framework of chance-constrained programming is one which facilitates experimentation in the search for an acceptable combination of risks and solution value of profit.

5.4 (iv) Stochastic Programming

Chance-constrained programming concentrates on identifying the profit outcome that will be achieved if all goes well, once acceptable risks have been determined and reflected in the problem's formulation. A very different approach can be expressed through the medium of *stochastic programming*. The principles of stochastic programming are described by Madansky (1963). Our particular interest lies in the solution of an LP problem containing a stochastic objective function, i.e. an objective function whose coefficients are subject to risk. Faced with the same kind of demand risks as those described earlier, we now assume that management maximises the expected value of profit. This approach contrasts with the chance-constrained approach in that it focuses on one central measure — the expected value — of the firm's uncertain profit outcome, rather than on the best that can be hoped for. Whether this different emphasis comes closer to picturing manage- ment's own attitude is arguable, but a comparison should focus on the practical aspects of the rival decision models as well as on their supposed psychological insights.

The probability calculations implied in the expected value maximis- ing approach are considerably more demanding than those required in chance-constrained profit maximising. At its simplest, the latter merely requires the decision maker to estimate for each product the level of output at which the risk of overproduction reaches the maximum level acceptable; complete estimation of each product's demand probability distribution is not required. By contrast, the expected value maximising approach – in principle at least – involves the decision maker in assigning an expected profit coefficient to each successive unit produced, of each product; so finely detailed estimates of demand probabilities *are* required. Inevitably, however, computational considerations and management's imprecision in formulating probability estimates result in probabilities being assigned to ranges or intervals of demand levels rather than to single values (see Mao, 1969, pp. 92-6; Garvin, 1960, pp. 172-9).

To illustrate both the structure of the expected value maximising approach and its sheer impracticability in the absence of fairly drastic simplification, we take as an example a firm producing just three products, X, Y and Z. The firm's objective function for maximising the expected value of profit is as follows:

$$maximise: \sum_{i=1}^{m} x_i \bar{\pi}_{xi} + \sum_{j=1}^{n} y_j \bar{\pi}_{yj} + \sum_{k=1}^{r} z_k \bar{\pi}_{zk} \qquad \text{(xiv)}$$

in which $x_i(y_j, z_k)$ is the ith (j^{th}, k^{th}) unit of production of product X(Y, Z); m(n, r) is the highest possible level of demand for that product; and $\bar{\pi}_{xi}(\bar{\pi}_{yj}, \bar{\pi}_{zk})$ is the expected value of the profit margin on the i^{th}(j^{th}, k^{th}) unit of sales of product X(Y, Z). As $x_i(y_j, z_k)$ is a variable representing a single unit of production, the value it takes in the LP solution to the problem must be either unity (if it is produced) or zero (if it is not produced). Each expected profit coefficient is determined according to the following procedure, taking $\bar{\pi}_{xi}$ as our example:

$$\bar{\pi}_{xi} = p_i \pi_x - (1 - p_i) v_x \qquad \text{(xv)}$$

in which p_i is the estimated probability that the ith unit of X produced will be sold, π_x is the profit achieved on each unit of X sold (the difference between constant sales revenue and constant variable cost), and v_x is the variable cost per unit of X. The all-important probability value p_i is simply the probability that demand for X will equal or exceed i units, but the calculation has to be performed in relation to each integer value of i between 1 and m; so a full estimation of the demand probability distribution for X is required. As the value of i increases, the value of p_i declines, and the expected value of $\bar{\pi}_{xi}$ declines too. This ensures that the solution to the expected value maximising problem will not yield an absurd result – for example rejecting the production of units 1 . . . 10 and recommending the production of units 11 . . . m.

The resource constraints of this problem are of course unaltered by management's objective or approach. But the output of each product must be expressed as the summation of all units produced. Thus, for example:

$$a_{1x}(x_1 + x_2 \ldots x_m) + a_{1y}(y_1 + y_2 \ldots y_n) + a_{1z}(z_1 + z_2 \ldots z_r)$$
$$\leqslant R_1 \qquad \text{(xvi)}$$

in which a_{1x} (a_{1y}, a_{1z}) is the amount of resource-type 1 required in the production of a unit of product $X(Y, Z)$ and R_1 is the maximum amount of resource-type 1 available in the period considered. Of course, resource constraints are present in all problems, the only difference here being the separate identification of each unit of each type of output. But we must recognise additional constraints for the present formulation, as well as the need for a modified solution method, to ensure that each variable $(x_1 \ldots x_m, y_1 \ldots y_n, z_1 \ldots z_r)$ takes only the integer values 0 or 1; that is, a particular unit of output is either produced $(x_i = 1)$ or it is not produced $(x_i = 0)$. Strictly speaking, integer solutions are required for *all* production planning problems unless the defined units of output are finely divisible. Thus far we have ignored this aspect of LP solution technique because it has not been central to our discussion; but in the present context, where each unit of production becomes in effect a distinct variable, the problem can no longer be ignored. Integer programming techniques will not be explained here, but they can best be envisaged as supplementing the basic simplex method, being brought into operation once the latter has yielded an optimal solution which contains fractional solution values to one or more variables that are not permitted to take fractional values. (Many texts describe integer solution methods: Baumol, 1972, Ch. 8; Naylor and Vernon, 1969, pp. 261–80; Mao, 1969, pp. 240–57; and Sasaki, 1970, pp. 192-201.)

5.4 (v) Comparison of Decision Models

Our outline of an approach to maximising the expected value of profit when product demands are subject to risk has no doubt served to demonstrate the method's computational impracticability in all but the simplest cases, as well as its great demands on the decision maker's capacity for making detailed probability judgements. In both respects the concept of expected value maximisation compares unfavourably with that of chance-constrained profit maximisation discussed in 5.4 (iii). Even when, as is usually the case, probabilities are estimated for ranges of demand levels instead of for each unit of sales separately, the problem inevitably remains a great deal larger than its chance-constrained alternative would be. However, in comparing the realism of the attitudes implied by the two approaches, a definite preference is less obvious. If management classifies its production-mix decision as one that recurs frequently, maximising the expected value of profit will perhaps seem appropriate, particularly if no risk of a loss serious enough to endanger the future of the business is thereby incurred. By contrast, the chance-constrained version emphasises the avoidance of 'excessive' risks, and this attitude, too, seems to deserve a place in any general theory of production planning. A compromise managerial objective might be expressed thus: 'maximise the expected value of profit subject to the attainment of minimum confidence levels in relation to individual products or the overall solution value.'

Our discussion has emphasised the suitability of the LP framework for experimentation and has suggested that management is likely in any case to wish to study the implications of various configurations of constraints. Given probability estimates for product demands, the probability distribution of profit for any production mix can be obtained, and this basic information can be employed in conjunction with a wide variety of decision criteria. Seen in this light, the LP framework is quite neutral on the question of managerial attitudes and motivations; it is quite capable of reflecting a considerable diversity of approaches to the central problem of risky demand conditions.

5.4 (vi) A Longer-Term Perspective on Demand Risk

Having shown how the presence of risk in relation to demands for the firm's products can be accommodated within a LP model of output decisions, we ought to note that the importance of this particular type of risk can easily be overstated. When output can be stored for future sale at little cost in relation to its profit margin, a relatively simple statement of the production mix problem may give an adequate representation of management's decision. Without embarking here on the vast literature relating to production and inventory planning, it will be obvious that plans are often prepared for several periods in advance (weeks, months, quarters, etc., as appropriate), based upon up-to-date demand forecasts and current inventory levels, etc. (For a comprehensive survey of techniques, including linear programming, relating to multi-period optimisation, see Niland, 1970.) Such plans will usually be up-dated and extended forward in time at the opening of a new period, in the light of recent

demand experience, changes in inventories and revised demand forecasts (Niland, 1970, pp. 125–32). In this kind of planning context
the financial costs of accumulating inventory are likely to appear
decidedly less alarming than in our one-period models; so much so
that management is likely to place equal or greater emphasis on having
enough inventory and current production to meet demands.

Recognising the extended horizon of planning and the double
function of inventory (as a means of absorbing excess production and
of meeting excess demands) does not necessarily invalidate our single-
period view of management's decision making, especially if the period
is lengthy enough to be seen as standing on its own financially.
After all, plans for future periods are understood to be provisional;
only the immediate period's plan is final. To illustrate this point we
can briefly sketch the kind of modifications to the chance-constrained
profit-maximising formulation and solution procedure that might
reflect management's altered consciousness of risks in the situation
now assumed. Constraints on the production of individual products
are now likely to be set with a view to limiting the risks of excessive
inventory accumulation, rather than with the intention of limiting the
risks of producing more than current demands. The higher the initial
inventory of a particular product, given its demand probability
distribution for the period in question, the lower will be its maximum
permitted output in that period. Management's objective function need
not change when inventory is recognised; so that apart from the altered
interpretation of production constraints, little of the problem's
basic nature and structure appears to have changed.

But the nature of the problem's *solution* has changed in a most
important way. Our earlier exposition of the chance-constrained
approach emphasised the inevitability of a compromise between, on
the one hand, the size of profit that could be achieved *if* all went well
and, on the other hand, the risk that all would *not* go well. The
seriousness of the latter risk is considerably lessened, even if the risk
is not entirely eliminated, in the context we are now considering.
Overproduction in one period now implies an accumulation of
inventory which is likely to be sold in the near future to yield a profit
probably not much less than that originally anticipated; so that the
overproduction risk in the chance-constrained maximum profit solution
is likely to be much less significant than in our original formulation.

It is also possible that management may wish to limit the risk of an
excessive accumulation of inventory for the firm as a whole. As indicated
above, the end-period inventory probability distribution for each

product is identified from its initial inventory, demand probability distribution and solution output level. Given estimates of the correlations between demands for different products, these individual inventory probability distributions can be combined into an overall probability distribution of the firm's total end-period inventory — measured in value terms, by weight, by cubic volume, or simply in units of production, as appropriate. (A technique for combining probability distributions will be described in Chapter 9.) All that remains is to calculate from this distribution the probability that total inventory arising from the profit-maximising solution will exceed the level defined as excessive; and if the risk so identified is unacceptably high, the profit-maximising production plan can be modified accordingly.

5.5 Conclusion

Our main concern in this chapter has been to demonstrate the suitability of linear programming as a mathematical framework for constructing the short-period theory of the firm, with particular emphasis on representing various managerial motivations and on the aspect of risky demand. Apart from showing the obvious versatility of the LP framework in theoretical matters, we have also been able to indicate its operational potential in quantifying such important concepts as marginal cost and shadow resource values. This theme of LP's operational usefulness is continued in Chapter 6, in terms both of applications and helpful variations in programming techniques.

Note

1. If by chance the most profitable process uses resources 1 and 2 in the same ratio as their availabilities, the solution will contain that process and a slack variable taking the value zero.

6 APPLICATIONS OF LINEAR PROGRAMMING

'The time has come,' the Walrus said,
'to talk of many things . . .'

Lewis Carroll

6.1 Introduction

This chapter rounds off our present interest in linear programming with
a brief and necessarily selective view of its application in various areas
of business decision making (Section 2), and a discussion of the related
subjects of *sensitivity analysis* and *parametric linear programming*
(Section 3). The latter section lays particular emphasis on the decision
maker's uncertainty, in many situations, about the values of objective
function coefficients, and this can be seen as complementing Chapter
5's discussion of decision making in conditions of risk. Optimisation
techniques such as stochastic or chance-constrained programming, both
considered in Chapter 5, appear to suggest a direct and unhesitating
choice of policy in the face of risk. On the other hand, sensitivity
analysis and parametric methods of programming may convey the
impression of a decision maker too uncertain about the values of
important constraints or coefficients to proceed directly, preferring
instead to evaluate the range of outcomes possible under each proposed
solution. Such a contrast between styles of decision making is certainly
overdrawn (e.g. in Chapter 5 the possibilities for experimentation with
different settings of chance constraints were discussed), but the point
that should be established is that programming techniques are quite
neutral on questions of decision criteria and approach. Linear programming in particular adapts readily, not only to the expression of many
different problem types, but also to the representation of widely
differing decision criteria and procedures.

6.2 Operational Applications of Linear Programming

6.2 (i) Introduction

This section describes a number of operational applications of linear
programming with the intention of demonstrating both the versatility
of LP techniques and the ways in which additional information can

usually be extracted from a problem's optimal solution. No account of LP's value in decision making would be complete without at least an introduction to the *transportation method* and its many possible applications, and 6.2 (iii) and 6.2 (iv) attempt to satisfy these minimum requirements.

6.2 (ii) Production Mix Problem with Order Size Constraint

The production of shirts involves four processes: cutting, assembly, button-holing/buttoning and inspection/packaging. One company produces three different shirt brands: 'Westminster', 'City' and 'Knightsbridge'. The number of minutes of labour time required for one dozen shirts of each brand in each process is as follows:

		brand		
		W	C	K
process	cutting	10	12	9
	assembly	18	15	17
	buttons	10	20	14
	inspection, etc.	6	6	6

In preparing a production plan for one week, management expects the numbers of man-hours available in the four processes to be 26, 50, 30 and 20 respectively. Labour is not transferable to other uses or dismissible in the planning period, so its cost is treated as fixed. The profit margins (selling price minus variable costs) per dozen shirts are £8, £10 and £7 for brands W, C and K, respectively. Firm orders for a total of 60 dozen shirts of brand C and/or K have been received, and these must be satisfied. Whatever else is produced can be sold or stockpiled for later sale at zero cost. How many shirts of each brand should the company produce in order to maximise its profit?

First, the reader should confirm that of the five constraints in the problem (four relating to resources and one to the level of orders), those relating to assembly and inspection are made redundant by those relating to cutting and button-holing, respectively. Omitting redundant constraints and using one minute of labour time as the common unit of measurement in the two remaining resource constraints, and one dozen shirts as the standard unit of output, the problem is expressed in equation form as follows:

maximise: $\quad 8W + 10C + 7K$

subject to: $\quad 10W + 12C + 9K + S_c = 1560$

$$10W + 20C + 14K + S_b = 1800$$

$$C + K - S_o + U_o = 60$$

in which the subscripts c, b and o attached to slack and artificial variables (S and U, respectively) represent 'cutting', 'buttons' and 'orders'.

The simplex solution to this problem proceeds straightforwardly, and in Table 6.1 only the first and final tableaux need be shown. The objective function coefficient for U_o is an unspecified amount, $-£M$, understood as being so overwhelmingly costly as to guarantee the exclusion of U_o from the final solution.

Table 6.1: Shirt Production Problem: Initial and Final Solutions

			8	10	7	0	0	0	−M	
			W	C	K	S_c	S_b	S_o	U_o	
S_c	0	1560	10	12	9	1	0	0	0	*initial solution*
S_b	0	1800	10	20	14	0	1	0	0	
U_o	−M	60	0	1	1	0	0	−1	1	
	−£60M		0	−M	−M	0	0	M	−M	loss per unit (£)
			8	10	7	0	0	0	−M	gain per unit (£)
S_c	0	60	0	−3	0	1	−1	−5	5	*final solution*
W	8	96	1	6/10	0	0	1/10	14/10	−14/10	
K	7	60	0	1	1	0	0	−1	1	
	£1188		8	118/10	7	0	8/10	42/10	−42/10	loss per unit (£)
			8	10	7	0	0	0	−M	gain per unit (£)

In addition to the inevitable 'slacks' in the assembly and inspection constraints, the optimal solution contains 60 minutes of slack in the cutting process. Thus only one of the firm's production constraints is fully effective, and the shadow value of one minute of this scarce resource, button-holing time, is shown to be £0.80. An extra minute of button-holing time would allow W to increase by 1/10, and as a result the level of S_c (slack in the cutting process) would fall by one minute. The limit on the expansion of W is set by the availability of surplus cutting time, 60 minutes; so the maximum increase in W that could be achieved by relaxing the button-holing constraint is six dozen shirts. This would allow profit to increase by £48, less the cost of achieving the necessary 60 minutes' increase in button-holing time.

The effect of the 'order' constraint on the solution can also be assessed from the final tableau shown in the lower half of Table 6.1. As in Chapter 5's discussion of marginal cost identification, the hypothetical introduction of a unit of the artificial variable U_o into the solution is equivalent to a reduction in the size of the firm order for brands C and/or K from 60 dozen to 59 dozen. On this understanding we ignore the cost coefficient of U_o and concentrate on its trade-offs – physical and financial – with the variables present in the optimal solution. Reducing the level of firm orders for brands C and/or K by one dozen allows W to increase by 1.4 dozen and K to fall by one dozen, increasing profit by the net amount £4.2 (1.4 × £8 – £7). At the same time, five minutes of surplus cutting time are brought into use. Given the solution's surplus of 60 minutes of cutting time, the improvement in profit through the reduction in firm orders could be carried as far as $U_o = 12$ (dozen), at which point the details of the solution would be:

$$S_c = 0, \quad W = 112.8, \quad K = 48, \quad \text{profit} = £1,238.4$$

Brand C fails to find a place in the optimal solution. In fact its profit margin would have to increase by £1.8 (£11.8 – £10.0) per dozen before it could begin to displace brands W and K. The C column of the solution shows how the optimum solution would change for every dozen C brand shirts introduced after a sufficient improvement in its profit margin.

The viability of new products can also be examined, at least in a preliminary way, using the original optimal solution as a reference point. For example, imagine a fourth brand of shirt, E, with the following estimated time requirements per dozen shirts in cutting, assembly, button-holing and inspection, respectively: 8, 14, 15 and 6 (minutes). How can we assess E's attractiveness? For small departures from the present optimal solution it is safe to disregard assembly and inspection as potential bottlenecks, and the decrease in profit implied by the diversion of resources to produce one dozen E shirts is therefore 8 × £0.0 for cutting resources (which are in surplus in the present optimal solution) plus 15 × £0.80 = £12.00 for button-holing. To complete the calculation, management needs to know the variable cost of E shirts and their selling price; only if the profit margin on E shirts exceeds £12.00 per dozen is it worth switching resources to their production. The next step would be to identify the limits on E production and the variable it would displace in the solution; calculations of this type have already been discussed in connection with other departures from the original optimal solution.

Full expositions and further discussion of the various techniques for analysing an optimal solution mentioned in this sub-section can be found in many texts, including Van de Panne (1971), Ch. 4, and Dantzig (1963), Ch. 12.4. The evident precision and simplicity of such techniques make it easy to overlook their limitations, and a note of warning should be sounded. An optimal solution to an LP problem reflects the current values of constraints, objective function coefficients, etc., and the profitabilities of adjustments to that solution calculated in the ways described here are similarly limited in relevance. It follows that some at least of the foregoing analysis should be seen as yielding only preliminary indications of profitable adjustments, for example in product lines and resource quantities. In such areas it is recognised that a full study of the long-run implications of a proposed change will normally be required.

6.2 (iii) The Transportation Method

Many LP problems can be formulated in such a way that less complex procedures will suffice to produce the optimal solution. Problems that can be solved by means of the *transportation method* vary widely in their content, as the example of the following sub-section will indicate, but are alike in the important aspects of their mathematical structure. The nature of that standard structure can best be conveyed by means of an example.

A chemical company produces a certain acid in three different locations, X, Y and Z; and supplies it to customers in towns A, B, C, D and E. Because of government regulations controlling the transport of dangerous chemicals over narrow and congested roads, towns C and D cannot be supplied from X and towns B and C cannot be supplied from Z. Transport costs per tanker-load of the acid between origins and destinations are as follows (in units of £100):

		destinations				
		A	B	C	D	E
	X	3	2	—	—	1
origins	Y	4	1	2	4	2
	Z	1	—	—	3	2

In one particular week the demands for the acid from towns A, B, C, D and E are for 20, 12, 8, 15 and 5 tanker-loads, respectively. The supply capacities of the plants in X, Y and Z are 23, 28 and 18 tanker-loads, respectively. Production cost is the same in each plant. How much acid should be produced in each plant, and to which towns should it be sent, in order to satisfy demands at least cost?

Formulated for solution by the simplex method, this problem would consist of eight constraints, three representing supply capacities and five representing delivery requirements. The number of possible origin-destination variables is eleven, and in addition the problem would involve three slack variables (one for each supply constraint) and five artificial variables (one for each requirements equation). The problem's objective function is as follows:

$$minimise: 3X_a + 2X_b + 1X_e + 4Y_a + 1Y_b + 2Y_c + 4Y_d + 2Y_e$$
$$+ 1Z_a + 3Z_d + 2Z_e$$

where X_a is the number of tanker-loads transported from X to A, and so on.

Although the simplex method could handle this problem, the computational prospects seem rather daunting. The alternative solution procedure known as the transportation method relies on the essential box-like structure of the problem and on the fact that every variable in every constraint possesses a coefficient of unity. Its standard layout adapted for the present problem is as shown in Table 6.2.

In Table 6.2 supplies from a particular plant to different towns are to be entered along the row denoting that plant, with the latter's

Table 6.2: Transportation Method: Chemical Deliveries Problem

	A	B	C	D	E	W	capacity
X	3	2	////	////	1	0	23
Y	4	1	2	4	2	0	28
Z	1	////	////	3	2	0	18
Requirements	20	12	8	15	5	9	69

maximum supply potential shown on the extreme right. Immediately to the left of this in each row is a space (W) in which the amount of unused capacity will be entered. Deliveries to each town will be entered in the appropriate column, the entries in each column summing to the requirement figure given at its foot. The entry at the foot of the W column is simply the difference, which must be non-negative if a full solution is to be attainable, between maximum supply capacity (69 tanker-loads) and total requirements (60 tanker-loads). Each box representing a permitted origin/destination variable has in its top left-hand corner the unit cost of the journey in question (in units of £100); boxes representing journeys not permitted are crossed out, and slack variables are given a zero cost.

The problem now is to allocate numbers into the permitted boxes of the table in such a way that each row (including slack) totals to the capacity figure given at its right-hand end and each column totals to the requirement figure given at its foot, *and* in such a way that the sum of costs implied by the chosen allocation is as low as possible. Without further insight into the nature of such problems a solution might seem to require a lengthy trial-and-error procedure because of the fact that the optimal allocation, if found, would not be recognised as such. However, three lessons from the simplex procedure are worth recalling. First, we are looking for a solution containing eight variables, that is, the number of variables should equal the combined sum of supply and requirements constraints. Second, the simplex method showed that when a new variable enters the solution is does not do so in a haphazard or unpredictable fashion; its effect on the value of every other variable is completely determinate, as is the identity of the variable that departs to make room for it. Finally, with the simplex procedure it is a very simple matter to check whether a solution is optimal, and if not to ascertain which changes would bring about improvements. We shall see that these convenient properties have their parallels in the transportation method, which is in fact very simple to operate in most cases.

Unlike simplex, the transportation method does not have to begin with a trivial solution. An initial solution can be obtained, more or less mechanically, by any one of a number of fairly simple allocation rules (Haley, 1967, Ch. 3; Horowitz, 1972, pp. 183-5, 193-4). The most mechanical of these is the 'north-west corner' rule, in which allocation begins with the largest possible entry in the top left-hand corner of the table, the limit being set by the smaller of the two constraints (horizontal and vertical) incorporating the variable in question. In the present problem X_a is initially set at 20 (tanker-loads) and is constrained at that level by the size of the total requirement at A. This completes the entry possibilities for the whole of the A column, but three units of X capacity remain to be allocated; so an entry of $X_b = 3$ is made, this being well within the limit set by demand at B (12 units). The X row is now complete, but a further allocation can be made lower down the B column. An entry of 9 units in Y_b completes the B column, leaving 19 units of Y capacity still to be allocated; and so on. The full initial allocation given by the north-west corner rule is given in Table 6.3, with the value of each entry shown below a diagonal line in its box.

The brevity of the present exposition precludes detailed discussion of the related problems of ensuring that the solution — initially and at each subsequent stage — is composed of the requisite number of variables and that these variables are located in such a way that any excluded variable can be introduced singly into the solution. These

Table 6.3: Chemical Deliveries Problem: Initial Solution

	A	B	C	D	E	W	capacity
X	3 / 20	2 / 3	▨	▨	1	0	23
Y	4	1 / 9	2 / 8	4 / 11	2	0	28
Z	1	▨	▨	3 / 4	2 / 5	0 / 9	18
Requirements	20	12	8	15	5	9	69

problems are the transportation method's equivalents of the problems of degeneracy already discussed in the context of the simplex method, and their resolution is usually comparatively straightforward (Sasieni *et al.*, 1959, pp. 211-18; Haley, 1967, pp. 32-3). Our initial solution shown in Table 6.4 does in fact contain the requisite number of variables, and we shall proceed to indicate how excluded variables might enter the solution singly to bring about a reduction in the total cost of meeting the stated requirements.

Total costs implied by the allocation in Table 6.3 are computed by summing the products of unit cost times quantity in each box of the solution. The initial solution is found to cost 157 ($\times$ £100). Only by accident could a mechanical rule have hit upon the most economical allocation, so it is necessary to consider the possibilities for cost saving. As with the simplex method, only one variable at a time can be introduced, and this has to be paired with the departure of one variable from the solution. Unlike the simplex method, the marginal contribution of an excluded variable to cost saving is not immediately visible; nor is its impact on the values of the variables presently in the solution.

As an example of the procedure for progressive improvement of the solution, consider an excluded variable that appears to be a strong candidate for inclusion: Z_a, with a unit cost of only £100. How can a unit of Z_a be introduced into the solution without infringing the supply constraints and requirements of the problem? Obviously one other entry in the A column and one other entry in the Z row must each fall by one unit, and these adjustments in turn will require at least one further balancing adjustment before all row and column totals are again correct. In the case of Z_a the chain of adjustments must be as follows: $Z_a(+1)$, $X_a(-1)$, $X_b(+1)$, $Y_b(-1)$, $Y_d(+1)$ and $Z_d(-1)$. (Recall that in the simplex method the entry of one variable at a particular stage is similarly uniquely linked to changes in the values of solution variables; the only difference in the present situation is that because of the structure of the problem all trade-offs are on a one-for-one basis.)

How does this identified series of changes in solution values affect overall cost? This question is answered by summing the relevant cost changes, with appropriate signs, for a one-unit introduction of Z_a:

Z_a	X_a	X_b	Y_b	Y_d	Z_d
+£100	−£300	+£200	−£100	+£400	−£300

The net value of this sequence is exactly zero; at this stage of the solution Z_a, in spite of its attractively low unit cost, cannot lower the cost of the solution. The repercussions of its introduction, not visible until this exercise is performed, have the effect of offsetting its obvious cost advantages over the existing entries in the A column and Z row.

Another superficially promising variable is X_e, again with a unit cost of only £100. To introduce a unit of X_e the following series of offsetting adjustments has to be made in relation to the variables already in the solution:

variable	X_e	Z_e	Z_d	Y_d	Y_b	X_b	Total
output change	+ 1	− 1	+ 1	− 1	+ 1	− 1	0
cost change	+£100	−£200	+£300	−£400	+£100	−£200	−£300

Here we find the opposite result to that obtained in respect of Z_a: the reduction in cost *exceeds* that indicated by a direct comparison with either of the entries in the immediately affected row and column.

It remains to establish the maximum possible amount of X_e that can be introduced into the solution. This limit is set by the contracting variable in the sequence of output changes with the smallest present allocation. The choice lies between Z_e, Y_d and X_b, and of these X_b has the lowest present allocation — three tanker-loads. So this amount is switched to the new variable X_e, variable X_b drops out of the solution, and the other intermediate variables in the chain of adjustment are all adjusted (up or down as appropriate) by three units. The total cost saving is thus $3 \times £300 = £900$.

The reader should continue with the solution independently, following the trial-and-error approach illustrated here. At each stage of the solution all excluded variables, including slack variables, are eligible for consideration, even if their entry has been rejected at an earlier stage. Indeed, although Z_a was rejected in our first attempt to improve the initial solution its entry will be found acceptable later on. With careful use of pencil and eraser one tableau can be progressively modified until no further cost-saving moves can be made.

Although the solution method outlined here seems lengthy and inefficient by comparison with simplex, mainly because at each stage the identity of the 'best' incoming variable is not at all obvious, the interested reader will find that a technique for the simultaneous evaluation of all empty boxes is available — in effect paralleling the simplex method's simultaneous evaluation of all excluded variables (see Krekó, 1968, pp. 21-4; Sasieni *et al.*, 1959, pp. 203-10). The present section concludes with an application of the method to a problem quite unconnected with the area of transport optimisation.

6.2 (iv) The 'Caterer' Problem

The timetable for completion of a four-month construction project requires the employment of given numbers of a certain type of machine in each month. These requirements are for 10, 15, 11 and 13 machines in months 1 . . . 4, respectively. After a month of use each machine requires an overhaul, which can be carried out in time to permit the machine's use in the following month, at a cost of £50 per machine; or the machine can be taken out of service for a month while a cheaper overhaul costing £20 is carried out. The cost of a new machine is £100. On completion of the project all machines will have a zero resale value.

Problems of this type are often referred to as 'caterer' problems, one of the earliest examples being the scheduling of table linen purchases and laundering arrangements in catering establishments. In its basic structure of 'origins' (new purchases and overhauled machines) and 'destinations' (requirements in different months) this problem is closely related to the standard transportation problem already considered, and it will be sufficient here to show how the standard transportation layout can be adapted to the special nature of a scheduling problem. (The formal structure of catering problems is explained in Smythe and Johnson, 1966, pp. 198-9.)

As in the standard layout described earlier, the rows of Table 6.4 represent the disposal of 'output' from 'origins'. Row X represents purchases of new machines for use in months 1 . . . 4, each at a cost of £100. An upper limit of 200 is placed on the total number of machines that can be purchased; this of course is much more than could possibly be required, but the shortfall of purchases below this limit will appear in the surplus box (column W) at zero cost. The row immediately below X, labelled D_1, shows the disposal of machines employed during month 1. Obviously these cannot be re-used during month 1, so box D_{11} is blocked off. If they are re-used during month 2, the relevant unit cost is £50 in box D_{12}; but if it is planned to re-use them in later months the slower overhaul is sufficient and the unit cost for D_{13} and D_{14} drops to £20. Any machines not re-used at all are entered in the

Table 6.4: 'Transportation' Layout for Scheduling Problem

	month				W	capacity
	1	2	3	4		
X	100	100	100	100	0	200
D_1		50	20	20	0	10
D_2			50	20	0	15
D_3				50	0	11
Requirements	10	15	11	13	187	236

surplus column at zero cost, and the total of row D_1 must therefore equal the number of machines employed during month 1. Analogous explanations apply for rows D_2 and D_3, representing the disposal of machines used during months 2 and 3, respectively, with the further blocking-off of boxes representing impossible flows. As an exercise the reader should now find an initial solution to this problem and improve upon it until the optimum purchase and overhaul schedule is obtained.

6.3 Uncertainty and Linear Programming

6.3 (i) Sensitivity Analysis and Parametric Linear Programming

When the objective function coefficients or constraint values of a linear programming problem are altered, the optimum solution to the problem must change in some respect. Two related kinds of question may arise. First, how wide is the variation that can occur in each coefficient or constraint value without the optimality of the present solution being affected? Second, how does the optimum solution change when coefficients or constraint values are varied over a certain range in a predetermined relationship? The first kind of question is answered by *sensitivity analysis*, the second by means of *parametric linear programming*. Quite a lot has already been said at various points on aspects of the sensitivity analysis of an optimal solution; examples are the identification and measurement of surplus resources and the identification of the changes in the objective function coefficients of excluded variables that would be necessary to bring about their inclusion in the solution. And of course we have studied the sensitivity of the solution to slight changes in the values of effective constraints, as well as the limits within which such adjustments can be made on unchanging terms. Techniques of sensitivity analysis are discussed systematically in Van de Panne (1971), pp. 70-8. This section concentrates on the second type of analysis, parametric linear programming (PLP), and in particular on the simultaneous and linked variation of objective function coefficients. The justification for ignoring the problem of variations in constraint values in the present context is that businessmen are likely to be more uncertain about the profit margins their goods will achieve when production and sale take place than about the values of most of the constraints they will confront. As far as resource constraints are concerned, no production plan can be implemented without the necessary resources, so a PLP exercise for resource constraint values has considerably less significance than one relating to objective function values which *can* change exogenously after decisions on output levels have been made. Besides, linked variations (not necessarily equal) in objective function coefficients are not at all unlikely — for example because of changes in the costs of inputs common to a number of products, or changes in market conditions affecting the prices at which the firm can sell its products. On the other hand, links between variations in the values of diverse and unrelated constraints seem rather implausible. PLP applied to both objective function coefficients and constraint values is described in Van de Panne (1971), Ch. 6. Krekó (1968), pp. 81-6, deals with parametric constraint values by applying the technique for a parametric objective function to the problem's dual formulation.

6.3 (ii) An Example of Parametric Objective Function Coefficients

A firm produces goods x and y, subject in a particular period to the following two resource constraints:

$$6x + 8y \leq 48$$

$$10x + 5y \leq 60$$

in which x and y are the output of goods x and y, respectively. In planning production for the period management makes the following assumptions about the profit margins it will achieve on goods x and y: (i) the 'central values' of unit profits on x and y are £3 and £6, respectively; (ii) actual profit margins may differ from these central values according to market conditions and costs, variations being in the same direction for each product and five times as strong for x as for y. These managerial assumptions suggest the following parametric profit function:

$$£[(3 + 5t)x + (6 + t)y]$$

in which t represents the amount of variation in profit per unit of good y. This approach is slightly unusual in that the underlying determinants of t — variations in costs, prices, taxes, etc. — are not shown directly in the profit function. If they were, only one variation at a time could be considered under the parametric programming procedure we are about to develop, and this would mean that management could learn very little from the procedure. It seems preferable, in a situation in which numerous factors interact in complex ways to determine profit margins, to represent management's thinking as impressionistic, along the lines suggested by our example.

The simplex solution to the firm's optimising problem proceeds normally, except that at each stage we have to identify the range of values of t within which the solution will actually be optimal. Without setting out the preliminary stage of converting constraints into equations we move directly to the initial simplex solution in Table 6.5.

Under what conditions will the solution of Table 6.5 actually be optimal? If $3 + 5t \leqslant 0$ *and* $6 + t \leqslant 0$, no production of x or y will be profitable and we need look no further than the 'do nothing' solution in the table, composed only of slack variables relating to the two resource constraints, w_1 and w_2. But if $t \geqslant -3/5$, production of x becomes profitable, and if $t \geqslant -6$, production of y becomes

Table 6.5: PLP Procedure: First Stage

			3+5t	6+t	0	0	
			x	y	w_1	w_2	
w_1	0	48	6	8	1	0	(optimal when $t \leqslant -6$)
w_2	0	60	10	5	0	1	
	£0		0	0	0	0	loss per unit (£)
			3+5t	6+t	0	0	gain per unit (£)

Table 6.6: PLP Procedure: Second Stage

			$3+5t$	$6+t$	0	0	
			x	y	w_1	w_2	
y	$6+t$	6	$6/8$	1	$1/8$	0	(optimal solution when $-6 \leqslant t$
w_2	0	30	$50/8$	0	$-5/8$	1	$\leqslant 6/17$)
	£$(36+6t)$		$(36+6t)/8$	$6+t$	$(6+t)/8$	0	loss per unit (£)
			$3+5t$	$6+t$	0	0	gain per unit (£)

profitable. As soon as the value of t rises above the *lower* of the two critical values (-6), production of the relevant variable (y) becomes profitable. As long as $t \leqslant -6$ no production will be undertaken and profit will equal zero (assuming for the moment that management is aware of the true value of t when its production decision is made).

Switching to a new solution proceeds normally, with y replacing w_1. The new tableau is given in Table 6.6. The value of the solution at this stage is £$(36 + 6t)$, which as expected equals £0 when t is at its lower critical value of -6. To find the upper limit of the range of t values within which this solution remains optimal we seek the value of t at which the entry of another variable first becomes profitable, and at this stage x is the only candidate. The introduction of x begins to be profitable when $(36 + 6t)/8 = 3 + 5t$, i.e. when $t = 6/17$. Thus the second stage of the solution is optimal when t lies in the range $-6 \leqslant t \leqslant 6/17$; and for higher values of t, x replaces w_2 in the solution. Table 6.7 shows the resulting third stage.

The third solution will evidently be optimal up to the value of t at which one of the slack variables can profitably be re-introduced. The two possibilities for the critical value of t are:

$$w_1: \quad 0 - \left[\frac{9-3t}{10}\right] = 0, \quad \text{i.e. } t = 3$$

$$w_2: \quad 0 - \left[\frac{-6+17t}{25}\right] = 0, \text{ i.e. } t = \frac{6}{17}$$

Obviously the latter result can be disregarded, as it describes the *lower* critical value of t for the present solution. For w_1 to be profitable

Table 6.7: PLP Procedure: Third Stage

			3+5t	6+t	0	0	
			x	y	w_1	w_2	
y	6+t	24/10	0	1	2/10	−3/25	(optimal solution when $6/17 \leqslant t \leqslant 3$)
x	3+5t	48/10	1	0	−1/10	4/25	
$£(\dfrac{288}{10}+\dfrac{264t}{10})$			3+5t	6+t	$\dfrac{9-3t}{10}$	$\dfrac{-6+17t}{25}$	loss per unit (£)
			3+5t	6+t	0	0	gain per unit (£)

Table 6.8: PLP Procedure: Fourth Stage

			3+5t	6+t	0	0	
			x	y	w_1	w_2	
w_1	0	12	0	5	1	−3/5	(optimal solution when $t \geqslant 3$)
x	3+5t	6	1	1/2	0	1/10	
£(18+30t)			3+5t	$\dfrac{3+5t}{2}$	0	$\dfrac{3+5t}{10}$	loss per unit (£)
			3+5t	6+t	0	0	gain per unit (£)

t must rise above the critical value of 3, at which point a fourth stage of the solution becomes relevant.

The fourth solution stage, shown in Table 6.8, remains optimal until one gain–loss calculation produces a positive result. In fact no value of t *above* 3 will produce a change in the solution, and the reader can confirm that all possible mixtures of variables have now been tried.

Having worked through the problem once, for a particular assumption about the determinants of the firm's profit, the main bodies of successive tableaux (each representing a different extreme point of the feasible solution space) can be re-used to study the implications of different linkages between objective function coefficients. The actual solutions remain unchanged in physical terms, but their cash values and the critical points at which they become optimal will be found to depend on the parametric structure of the objective function.

6.3 (iii) Decision Making with Uncertain Parameter Values

An exercise of the kind described in the previous sub-section should allow the production decision to be made with some confidence, or at least in the knowledge that opportunity losses associated with alternative decisions are evenly balanced. This point is made clear with the help of Figure 6.1.

Figure 6.1 shows the value of profit achieved under each solution to our two-product problem as a linear function of t. Within the range of t values for which a solution is optimal this relationship is shown as a solid line, and this is continued as a broken line for some distance beyond the ends of the range to show the levels of profit that would be earned with non-optimal policies in neighbouring ranges of t. The figure shows that opportunity losses, measured by the vertical distance between solid and broken lines for any value of t, are equal at any give distance to the left or right of each critical value of t.

Our original discussion of this problem made no direct mention of management's probabilistic judgements about the value of t, but the description of the £3 and £6 profit margins as 'central values' suggested that the value of t was seen as centred on zero, with positive and negative possibilities distributed fairly evenly in probability terms.

Figure 6.1: Objective Function Value under Optimal and Non-Optimal Policies

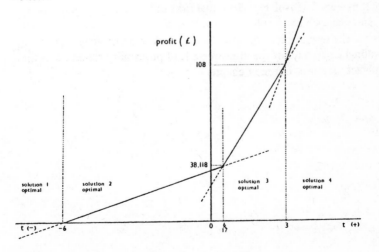

In Figure 6.1 this would place the centre of gravity of management's expectations towards the upper end of the range in which solution 2 is optimal, with probably some overlap onto the neighbouring range in which solution 3 is optimal. With a fairly even distribution of possible t values around t = 0, the preponderance of possibilities must lie in the range for which solution 2 is optimal, and the latter seems very likely to be chosen — whether by reference to a sophisticated criterion such as minimising the expected value of opportunity losses (see 7.3) or a more impressionistic approach lacking precise probability estimates for values of t.

In general, however, where t represents a specific variable whose value is difficult to predict, management's range of estimates need not centre on zero. When the range of estimates lies entirely or predominantly within one of the 'optimal solution ranges' shown in Figure 6.1, the solution in question is the one that will probably be preferred. But when the estimates of t centre on (or near) one of the critical values of t, it is clear from the figure that potential opportunity losses are the same (or nearly the same) whichever of the two solutions in question is chosen. In such a situation management must feel more in danger of making a seriously mistaken decision than when the range of possible t values it estimates lies entirely within one optimal solution range; but, paradoxically, the decision itself appears to be a matter of near-indifference — at least to a maximiser of expected money value or minimiser of expected opportunity loss (see 7.3). This odd implication would be weakened if management's utility function for profit were non-linear (3.3); but even with a linear utility function we may be sure that in a choice involving near-equal risks of substantial opportunity losses management would *not* treat the decision as a matter of indifference. The resolution of the paradox, in the shape of management's willingness to pay for the improvement of probability estimates, is the subject matter of our next chapter.

7 ACQUIRING AND VALUING INFORMATION

There is no knowledge which is not valuable.

Edmund Burke

7.1 Introduction

Business decisions typically have to be made in the absence of complete certainty about the behaviour of factors that will influence their financial outcomes. But in most situations a decision maker will not rely solely on his initial beliefs about the factors in question, presumably expressed in probability terms. He will often have the option of acquiring additional information, at a price known in advance, about at least some of the troublesome uncertainties.

This chapter is concerned with the techniques and motivations that may be involved in the acquisition of additional information. Beginning with the special case of paying for access to perfect information, we move to the more typical case in which new information, properly interpreted, is expected to produce revised probabilities for the various possible outcomes of the uncertain variable(s) under consideration — falling short of establishing complete certainty about any outcome. In the first case, where access to perfect information will enable the decision maker to reach a regret-free decision, the simple question that has to be answered is whether the price of that information is worth paying. But in the general case, where a decision based upon revised probabilities may still prove to be mistaken, two related questions have to be answered. First, a conditional (planned) response must be determined for every possible outcome of a particular expenditure on acquiring new information. Second, the optimum level of such expenditures has to be determined.

Fairly simple examples are employed throughout the chapter. In particular, variables subject to uncertainty are assumed to have a limited number of possible values rather than to vary on a continuous scale. This helps to minimise a problem's mathematical content without prejudice to its interest or relevance. In keeping with this desire for a comparatively non-technical approach, the introduction of highly specialised terminology from sampling theory has been kept to a minimum.

135

7.2 Valuing Perfect Information

7.2 (i) Introduction to Decision Tree Analysis

Suppose that a piece of equipment used by a firm has become unreliable
to the point of requiring major repair work within the next four
months — a relatively slack time of year during which repairs can be
carried out in any one month of the firm's own choosing. In month 1,
the present, the firm's own engineers can repair the equipment at a
cost of £3,500. In months 2 and 3 the repair cost will be £3,000 if the
firm's engineers have time to do the job, or £4,000 if it is done by
outside specialists. The probability that the firm's own engineers will
have time to do the job is 0.4 in month 2 and 0.3 in month 3. (These
probabilities are independent.) If the repair is delayed until month 4
it is anticipated that the worsened condition of the equipment will
necessitate the calling in of outside specialists and that the repair
will then cost £5,000, unless the specialists have by then managed to
perfect a new repair technique which they are known to be developing and which would reduce the repair cost to £2,000. The probability
that the new repair technique will be ready in month 4 (the earliest
possible month) is 0.4. In months 2 and 3 the repair cost will be known
at the beginning of the month, before a decision has to be taken.

Problems of this kind, in which the immediate decision evidently
depends on future prospects and conditional future decisions, can be
illustrated and resolved by means of decision tree analysis. (Many
expositions of this technique are available: see Moore, 1972, pp.
121–49; Moore and Thomas, 1976, pp. 53–73; and Magee, 1964.)

In Figure 7.1 points of decision are shown as square nodes
(I, A, B, G, D) and chance events as round nodes; C_i denotes the repair
cost in month $i (i = 1 \ldots 4)$; and decimal fractions on paths emanating
from chance event nodes are the probabilities of the events (cost levels)
in question.

It seems safe to assume that consciousness of future repair cost
possibilities will influence the firm's manager at point I (the present).
We can confirm this point and develop it into an analysis of optimal
decision making by assuming, at least for the time being, that the
manager intends to make each decision relating to the repair
according to the criterion of minimum expected value of repair cost.
On this understanding we begin with the more remote decision points
and work backwards in time, reversing the chronological sequence of
decision making, until we are in a position to consider the immediate
decision at I. This technique, known as the 'rollback' principle, means

Figure 7.1: Decision Tree for Repair Cost Problem

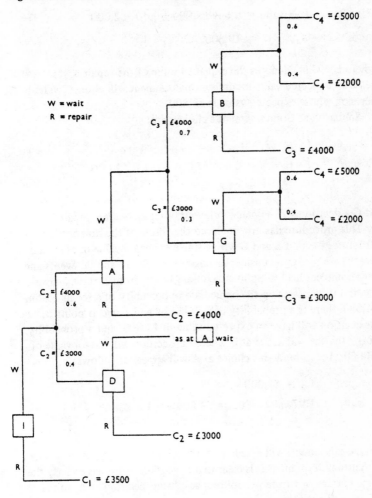

that each decision node will present a simple choice between a known immediate repair cost and an expected value representing optimal policy for the future assuming an immediate repair is not undertaken.

Point B will be reached as a result of the following sequence of repair costs and decisions: $C_1 = £3,500$, wait; $C_2 = £4,000$, wait; $C_3 = £4,000$. At B the manager's choice lies between the following:

repair: C_3 = £4,000

wait: EV(wait) = 0.6 × £5,000 + 0.4 × £2,000

= £3,800

where EV(wait) denotes the expected value of the repair cost in month 4. As an expected value minimiser, management will choose 'wait', a decision whose expected value is £3,800.

Similarly, at G management's choices are:

repair: C_3 = £3,000

wait: EV(wait) = 0.6 × £5,000 + 0.4 × £2,000

= £3,800

At G a decision will be made in favour of an immediate repair.

This procedure has now replaced the whole of the branched structures beyond B and G with a single expected value in each case, and we are ready to consider management's choice should events and earlier choices lead to point A. Looking ahead from A the manager can see that if he passes up the immediate opportunity of a repair costing £4,000, there is a probability of 0.7 that he will arrive at point B, where his decision will have an expected value of £3,800, and a probability of 0.3 that he will arrive at G where his decision will have a value of £3,000. Accordingly, his choice at A will appear as follows:

repair: C_2 = £4,000

wait: EV(wait) = 0.7 × £3,800 + 0.3 × £3,000

= £3,560

At A management will decide to 'wait'.

Turning to point D it is clear that a 'wait' decision has exactly the same pattern of future possibilities as a 'wait' decision at A, so the choice will appear as follows:

repair: C_2 = £3,000

wait: EV(wait) = £3,560

At D the immediately available repair cost of £3,000 will be preferred to the wide range of future possibilities (£2,000, £3,000, £4,000 and £5,000) implicit in a 'wait' decision.

We are now ready to consider the immediate decision that has to be

made at I, where the choice lies between an immediate outlay of
£3,500 and a probability-weighted average of the values of the optimal
decisions at A and D:

repair: $C_1 = £3,500$

wait: $EV(\text{wait}) = 0.60 \times £3,560 + 0.4 \times £3,000$

$\qquad\qquad\quad = £3,336$

The amount £3,336 represents the lowest expected value of repair cost
that is attainable, given the information available to the decision maker.
We define this expected value as EVC/U, the expected value of cost
given the decision maker's uncertainty about future costs. (In this
context the term 'uncertainty' obviously does not imply ignorance of
probabilities.) Evidently the immediate repair cost would have to fall
below £3,336 before the manager would change his decision at I, which
is in effect to await future developments and carry out the repair as
soon as the expected value of a 'wait' decision exceeds the immediately
available repair cost. The full probability distribution of repair cost
associated with the manager's decision rule is as follows:

Repair Cost	Probability		Sequence of Events
£5,000	0.252		$C_2 = £4,000, C_3 = £4,000, C_4 = £5,000$
£3,000	0.580	$\{$ 0.18	$C_2 = £4,000, C_3 = £3,000$
		0.40	$C_2 = £3,000$
£2,000	0.168		$C_2 = £4,000, C_3 = £4,000, C_4 = £2,000$

7.2 (ii) Valuing Information: an Introduction

Continuing with the same example we now raise the question of the
amounts the manager would be prepared to pay in order to eliminate
some or all of the aspects of risk of the repair cost problem. First,
suppose that it is possible to obtain a correct forecast of the sequence
of repair costs in months 2 . . . 4. How much would management be
prepared to pay *in advance* for this knowedge? For the moment we
continue to assume that all decisions, now and in the future, are made
with the objective of minimising the expected value of costs; this
implies that any forecast will be valued in terms of the reduction it
offers from the level set by EVC/U.

The value of EVC/U has already been calculated. Table 7.1 shows

Table 7.1: Probability Distribution of Repair Cost for Perfect Information

(1) Repair cost during month (£'000)				(2) Cost of repair (£'000)	(3) Probability of cost sequence	(4) Probability-weighted cost (£'000) (2) × (3)
1	2	3	4			
3.5	4	3	5	3	0.108	0.324
3.5	4	3	2	2	0.072	0.144
3.5	3	3	5	3	0.072	0.216
3.5	3	3	2	2	0.048	0.096
3.5	4	4	5	3.5	0.252	0.882
3.5	4	4	2	2	0.168	0.336
3.5	3	4	5	3	0.168	0.504
3.5	3	4	2	2	0.112	0.224

Expected value of costs given perfect information = £2.726 (× 1,000)

an analogous calculation based on the assumption that perfect information about C_2, C_3 and C_4 can be obtained during month 1. Given the assurance that the actual sequence of repair costs in months 2, 3 and 4 will be known during month 1, the expected value of repair cost is £2,726, a substantial improvement on the figure of £3,336 which obtains in the absence of perfect information. The full probability distribution of repair cost, assuming perfect information, is easily obtained from Table 7.1. We shall retain the term EVC/U to denote the expected value of repair cost without perfect information, and employ EVC/PI to denote the expected value of repair cost with perfect information.

The difference of £610 between EVC/U and EVC/PI sets an upper limit to the amount an expected value minimiser would be willing to pay during month 1 for a perfect forecast of C_2, C_3 and C_4. One thing that makes this difference as low as £610 is the fact that for some cost sequences perfect information would not lead to a different decision from that which would be made in its absence. For example, if the actual cost sequence in months 2 ... 4 is £3,000, £4,000 and £5,000, the manager will decide to pay C_2 = £3,000 whether or not he has perfect information about C_3 and C_4 (see point D in Figure 7.1).

The probability of this particular situation is shown in Table 7.1 to be 0.168. The greater the overall probability that perfect information will make no difference to the manager's decision, the smaller is likely to be its value in his estimation.

7.2 (iii) Valuing Partial Perfect Information

Obtaining a perfect forecast of repair cost in each month may seem a rather ambitious objective. Suppose instead that it is possible to obtain in month 1 perfect information about the availability of the new repair technique in month 4. What is the expected value of this information? To assess the expected value of such information, consider the effects in Figure 7.1 of management's knowledge of C_4. These are summarised as follows:

(i) If $C_4 = £5,000$ (prior probability = 0.6)

at B the decision becomes 'repair', $C_3 = £4,000$
at G the decision remains 'repair', $C_3 = £3,000$
at A EV(wait) becomes $0.7 \times £4,000 + 0.3 \times £3,000 = £3,700$, which remains preferable to $C_2 = £4,000$
at D EV(wait) becomes £3,700 (same as A), which remains inferior to $C_2 = £3,000$
at I EV(wait) becomes $0.6 \times £3,700 + 0.4 \times £3,000 = £3,420$, which remains preferable to $C_1 = £3,500$.

(ii) If $C_4 = £2,000$ (prior probability = 0.4)

the value of C will be £2,000 for certain.

Bringing these two conditional results together, the expected value of the repair cost assuming prior knowledge of C_4 is given by

$$0.6 \times £3,420 + 0.4 \times £2,000 = £2,852$$

The expected value of perfect information about C_4 is the difference between the original measure of EVC/U, £3,336, and £2,852, that is £484. Knowing that the expected value of perfect information about the whole sequence C_2, C_3 and C_4 is £610, we can deduce that the expected value of perfect information about C_2 and C_3 alone must be equal to the difference between £610 and £484, that is £126. This result, suggesting that information about C_2 and C_3 together is worth considerably less in expected value terms than information about C_4

alone, serves as a reminder that not all information is worth paying for. In fact, knowledge of C_2 and C_3 in addition to C_4 will lead to a different decision from that reached with knowledge of C_4 alone only in the case of one cost sequence: £3,500, £4,000, £4,000, £5,000. In this case if only C_4 is known, the manager will not carry out the repair in month 1, hoping to achieve a repair cost of £3,000 in month 2 or month 3. If C_2 and C_3 *are* both known in this case a saving of £500 will be achieved. The probability of this cost sequence is 0.252, giving an expected value of savings due to knowledge of C_2 and C_3 equal to $0.252 \times £500 = £126$.

7.2 (iv) The Expected Value of Perfect Information

We are ready to give the formal definition of a concept that has been close to the surface throughout this discussion. In the context of the repair cost problem the improvement (reduction) in the expected value of cost brought about by access to perfect information is denoted by EVPI, the expected value of perfect information, and is measured as follows:

$$\text{EVPI} = \text{EVC/U} - \text{EVC/PI} \qquad \text{(i)}$$

The value of EVPI obviously sets the upper limit to the amount management is willing to pay for perfect information when its objective is to minimise the expected money value of repair cost plus information cost. A forecast costing more than EVPI would cause the total of EVC/PI and the cost of the forecast to exceed EVC/U. The concept of EVPI is usually discussed in a profits context (Hamburg, 1970, pp. 626-9; Morgan, 1968, pp. 35-8), but our discussion has shown it to be completely applicable in situations where costs rather than returns are uncertain.

It follows from our earlier discussion that a relationship analogous to (i) holds for *any* piece of perfect information, including what we referred to as 'partial perfect information' in 7.2 (iii). Thus the expected value of perfect information about C_4 alone, EVPI (C_4), is measured as follows:

$$\text{EVPI}(C_4) = \text{EVC/U} - \text{EVC/PI}(C_4)$$

in which EVC/U has the same meaning as before and EVC/PI(C_4) denotes the expected value of cost given perfect information about C_4. Again, EVPI(C_4) sets an upper limit to the amount an expected value minimiser would be prepared to pay for perfect information about C_4.

All this may appear a rather pointless exercise in the sense that the option of paying for perfect information about some or all future developments is rarely likely to occur. But by indicating the *maximum* amounts that can sensibly be spent on the elimination of specific aspects of uncertainty, this approach at least directs the decision maker's attention in the most potentially 'profitable' directions. In any case, perfect information is not necessarily unattainable at any price. In a situation like our repair cost example it is probably unrealistic to imagine that C_2 and C_3 can be predicted uniquely, since they depend on the uncertain amounts of other work the firm's own engineers will have to handle in months 2 and 3; but in the case of C_4 it may well be possible to ascertain whether the new repair technique will be available in month 4. And, as shown earlier, this is potentially the most 'valuable' item of the missing information.

Notwithstanding this defence of the potential relevance of the EVPI concept, it remains true that what we have been considering is an extreme case of the general theory of the *ex ante* valuation of probability-revising information. In general we anticipate that additional information, correctly interpreted, will result in revisions of estimated probabilities of future events falling short of the establishment of complete certainties. In 7.3 we shall develop a more general approach to the identification of the expected value of additional information and the determination of the optimum amount of expenditure on additional information.

Throughout this section our implicit assumption has been that management's cash-utility transformation does not change its slope perceptibly over a range of £3,000 – the difference between the highest and lowest cost figures in the repair problem. This assumption, which is probably quite justified in our example, has allowed much of the discussion to be conducted in terms of money values rather than utility values. In general, the whole discussion of decision criteria and evaluation of information can be shifted very conveniently from a money to a utility dimension (Horowitz, 1972, pp. 62-5); and the examples given in Chapter 3 cover the techniques that are involved in moving from cash to utility values and from utility differences to their cash equivalents.

7.3 Principal Relationships in the Valuation of Information

In the general analysis of expenditures on information that will
concern us in Section 4, it will be useful to conduct much of the
discussion in terms of minimising the expected value of lost
opportunities rather than maximising the expected value of profit
or minimising the expected value of costs. In conditions of certainty
these two conceptual views are of course equivalent; maximum
profit (or minimum cost) implies a zero level of 'regret' or 'opportunity loss' (OL). Now we wish to establish an analogous equivalence
for conditions of risk, between maximising the expected money
value of profit (or minimising the expected money value of cost)
and minimising the expected money value of regrets or opportunity
losses.

When a decision maker faces a choice in conditions of risk there
usually exists a possibility that he will regret the choice he makes.
Events that are predictable only in probabilistic terms may cause the
outcome of his choice to be inferior to what could have been achieved
with a completely accurate forecast. The two terms 'regret' and
'opportunity loss' are both applicable to disappointments of this
kind, though in the present context the latter is generally employed;
each refers to the difference — in cash or utility units as appropriate —
between the result actually achieved and the best result that would have
been possible in the circumstances. The expected opportunity loss
(EOL) of a policy is the probability-weighted average of its various
possible regrets or opportunity losses, with each opportunity loss
weighted by the probability of the circumstances in which it will occur
(Moore, 1972, pp. 107-11). In general terms the expected opportunity
loss associated with policy j, EOL(j), is given by

$$\text{EOL(j)} = \sum_{i=1}^{m} p_i (R_i^* - R_{ij}) \tag{ii}$$

in which R_{ij} denotes the payoff or profit of policy j when event i
occurs ($i = 1 \ldots m$); R_i^* denotes the payoff, when event i occurs,
of the policy best suited to that event; and p_i denotes the probability
of event i. In a cost-minimising context the OL of policy k under event
f would be defined as $(C_{fk} - C_f^*)$, where C denotes cost and notation
is analogous to that in (ii). More generally, the utility equivalents of
cash values may be assumed, so that utility losses rather than cash
regrets are involved.

The equivalence between maximising the expected value of profit,

EVR, and minimising EOL can be shown by a simple manipulation of equation (ii):

$$EOL(j) = \sum_{i=1}^{m} p_i R_i^* - \sum_{i=1}^{m} p_i R_{ij} \qquad \text{(iii)}$$

In (iii), $\sum p_i R_i^*$ is constant irrespective of the policy under consideration; it represents the expected value of profit on the assumption that the decision maker will be able to choose the best policy for the prevailing circumstances, i.e. the expected value of profit given perfect information, denoted by EVR/PI. The term $\sum p_i R_{ij}$ is simply the expected value of profit under policy j in conditions of uncertainty, denoted by EVR(j)/U.

An expression analogous to (iii) applies to every policy open to the decision maker, and it is clear that in order to *minimise* EOL the policy with the *highest* EVR/U should be chosen. Having identified the policy with the lowest EOL, the relationship shown in equation (iii) indicates that this minimum value of EOL is equivalent to the expected value of perfect information, EVPI, which was earlier defined as the smallest attainable difference between the expected values of profit (or costs) under uncertainty and with perfect information (Hamburg, 1970, pp. 628-9).

7.4 Valuing Less-Than-Perfect Information on a Once-Only Basis

7.4 (i) Introduction

As admitted earlier, the valuation of perfect information may represent an exercise in the hypothetical, rather than the evaluation of a realistic option. Now we recognise that decision makers require a means of appraising prospective revisions of prior probabilities that fall short of establishing full confidence in any one future outcome. Throughout this section we shall assume that any new information obtained by management will be generated in a single exercise, e.g. a sample of potential customers or items of production. The reason for this limitation is mainly economic; in many situations the fixed costs of an information gathering exercise are high in relation to the marginal cost of information (e.g. sampling one extra potential customer once the exercise is under way), and this encourages decision makers to plan for a single operation of an 'optimal' size. In 7.6 we shall consider a more open-ended search for new information, in which the decision maker is assumed to continue to acquire new information in separate 'blocks' for as long as he finds it worthwhile to do so.

Chapter 2 included a number of examples of probability revision, and our first task is to graft onto such techniques a method for the evaluation of their financial attractiveness. We continue to assume that decisions are made according to the criterion of expected money value (or expected utility value). In building up an analysis of 'the economics of expenditures on information' the first step is a brief reminder of how the prospective results of a search for new information can bring about revisions in prior probabilities that are predictable in a probabilistic sense. To do this we introduce a new example.

An engineering consultancy firm is considering the introduction of a new energy economy advisory service. The size of the potential market for the service is known, and the consultancy manager believes that if it is launched the new service will attract 30 per cent, 20 per cent or 10 per cent of the firms making up that market. The manager's prior probabilities for these different market penetration levels are 0.25, 0.50 and 0.25, respectively. Because of the high costs of setting up and staffing the new service, the level of market penetration it achieves is crucial to its viability, as shown in the following table relating its prospective net present value (NPV)[1] to its market penetration level (M):

M (per cent)	30	20	10
NPV (£)	35,000	5,000	−40,000

The manager first makes a provisional decision on the basis of his prior probabilities of the various levels of M, and although this decision may not be implemented, its EOL value will serve as a reference standard by which to judge alternative policies involving the acquisition of new information. The most obvious alternative to the positive policy of launching the new service is to 'do nothing'. This simple alternative makes it easy to calculate meaningful opportunity losses, as Table 7.2 shows.

Applying the manager's prior probabilities for the various levels of M to the opportunity loss matrix in Table 7.2 (b) yields the following comparison of EOL values for 'launch' (L) and 'not launch' (NL) decisions.

EOL(L) : $0.25 \times £40,000 + 0.5 \times £0 + 0.25 \times £0$ $= £10,000$

EOL(NL): $0.25 \times £0 + 0.5 \times £5,000 + 0.25 \times £35,000 = £11,250$

Evidently, launching the new service on the basis of prior probabilities

Table 7.2: Derivation of Opportunity Loss Matrix for Advisory Service

		M (per cent)		
		10	20	30
policies	launch	−40,000	5,000	35,000
	do not launch	0	0	0

(a) Payoffs (£)

		M (per cent)		
		10	20	30
	launch	40,000	5,000	0
	do not launch	0	0	35,000

(b) Opportunity losses (£)

is preferable to abandoning the idea. The size of the lower EOL value, £10,000, sets a standard by which any alternative policy can be judged.

We can be fairly sure that some alternative(s) *will* be considered. After all, the value of EOL(L) is not far below that of EOL (NL), and the decision maker may hope that research into demand for the new service will, by causing him to revise his prior probabilities, produce a more emphatic verdict in favour of one policy or the other. As a preliminary to this research the decision maker may apply a kind of sensitivity analysis to the comparison of EOL(L) and EOL(NL), with the object of identifying all combinations of probabilities of M levels that would result in EOL(L) > EOL(NL). In general we do not expect to find that one policy is superior to its alternative for all combinations of probabilities, or even for all 'believable' combinations of probabilities (begging the question of the meaning of 'believable' in this context), so we anticipate that the decision maker will at least consider the option of acquiring additional information. (The sensitivity analysis approach is discussed by Moore, 1972, pp. 99–101, for the simple context of only two probabilities.)

Accordingly we begin with an analysis of a particular proposal for gathering information in this case. Later we shall consider whether this proposal is optimal in expected value terms. The consultancy manager decides to commission in-depth interviews with executives of ten potential users of the new service, chosen at random; each interview will give a definite and correct indication of whether or not the firm in question will make use of the new service.

There are two very different ways in which the consultancy manager can plan to make use of the information the survey will yield. First, he can adopt a 'wait and see' attitude to the as yet unknown result with no clear idea of the way in which any particular survey result will influence his final decision. Alternatively, he can commit himself in advance to a course of action conditional on the survey result. In the following discussion we shall be trying to give a precise meaning to the concept of an optimum level of expenditure on information, and commenting on the implications of the two broad approaches to the use of new information.

7.4 (ii) Use of Additional Information – No Predetermined Policy

If, in a situation such as we are considering, a decision maker receives new information without having any clear advance idea of how he will respond, his first problem is to decide how to employ the new data. Perhaps optimistically, we shall assume that the consultancy manager in our example wishes to employ the result of the sample survey 'scientifically', not in an impulsive or ill-considered manner. This entirely praiseworthy attitude presumably leads him first to revise his original (prior) probabilities for the various possible levels of market penetration (M) given earlier; then to recalculate EOL(L) and EOL(NL) using the revised probabilities.

To illustrate this process we assume that the survey actually yields two favourable and eight unfavourable responses. Given that the ten potential customers interviewed constitute a small sample of the total population of potential customers, it is appropriate to employ the Binomial theorem in conjunction with Bayes' theorem to generate revised (posterior) probabilities for the various levels of M. One such calculation will serve as a reminder of how this procedure is carried out (see 2.5).

The prior probability of a market penetration level of 30 per cent was stated to be 0.25, i.e. $p(M = 30) = 0.25$. Given the additional information that two customers of the ten interviewed gave favourable responses, this probability is revised as follows

$$p(M=30/\tfrac{2}{10}) = \frac{p(\tfrac{2}{10}/M=30)\,p(M=30)}{\left[\begin{array}{l} p(\tfrac{2}{10}/M=30)\,p(M=30) + p(\tfrac{2}{10}/M=20)\,p(M=20) + \\ p(\tfrac{2}{10}/M=10)\,p(M=10) \end{array}\right]}$$

in which the term '$\tfrac{2}{10}$' refers to the survey result. The values of the three conditional probabilities in this formula can be found most conveniently in tables of binomial probabilities on the assumption that M = 30 (20, 10) implies a probability of 0.3 (0.2, 0.1) of obtaining a favourable response from a randomly-chosen potential customer. (Binomial probabilities are given in many statistics texts and in compilations of mathematical and statistical tables; see Moore, 1972, and Kmietowicz and Yannoulis, 1976.) Substituting the appropriate conditional probability values and prior probabilities into the expression for $p(M = 30/\tfrac{2}{10})$ we obtain

$$p(M=30/\tfrac{2}{10}) = \frac{0.2335 \times 0.25}{0.2335 \times 0.25 + 0.302 \times 0.5 + 0.1937 \times 0.25}$$

$$= 0.2265$$

By substituting in turn the appropriate products from the denominator of the expression for $p(M = 30/\tfrac{2}{10})$ for the single product in the

numerator we obtain the remaining two revised probabilities:
$p(M = 20/\frac{2}{10}) = 0.5857$, and $p(M = 10/\frac{2}{10}) = 0.1878$.

Having revised his prior probability estimates in this way, the consultancy manager presumably uses the revised values to recalculate the values of EOL(L) and EOL(NL). The results of this are as follows: EOL(L) = £7,512; EOL(NL) = £10,856 (see Table 7.2).

As a result of the survey and the revision of prior probabilities, the launching of the new service is more emphatically recommended than before, at least on the basis of the EOL criterion.

7.4 (iii) The Need for Prior Evaluation of Expenditure on Information

A major disadvantage of even a sophisticated 'wait and see' approach to the use of sample information should now be obvious. Understandably, a decision maker will be reluctant to embark on a (possibly expensive) scheme to gather new information without any clear idea of the likelihood that the whole process will actually result in a different decision from that which he would otherwise make ('launch' in this case). In our example the new information merely results in the confirmation of the policy previously recommended in its absence, and in that sense the survey may appear to represent a waste of money. It is true that the decision to launch the new service can now be taken in greater confidence, but even if this extra confidence is worthwhile it is similarly not predicted in advance under the 'wait and see' approach. Besides, only by coincidence will an arbitrarily determined expenditure be optimal, in the sense that the difference between the *ex ante* valuation of its prospective results and its cost is maximised. For these reasons we should anticipate that a decision maker — especially one sophisticated enough to revise prior probabilities in the correct fashion — will wish to be better informed about the prospective results of the exercise before authorising large expenditures on gathering information. In other words, we assume that funds are committed to the acquisition of information on much the same basis as to any other outlay involving a risky return.

To illustrate the principles involved in the prior evaluation of information we shall continue with our example involving the sampling of customers' intentions. Instead of a 'wait and see' approach, the decision maker now determines the critical number of favourable responses (from a given size of sample) which will automatically 'trigger' the launching of the new service. Provided that this critical response is set at the lowest level which would, on the 'wait and see' principle, result in a deliberate decision to launch the service, the *decision rule* approach will not result in a different decision being taken; and we shall show that the prospective value of any amount of information obtained in this way can be evaluated in advance.

7.4 (iv) Evaluating a Decision Rule for the Use of New Information

We already know that two favourable responses out of ten will cause prior probabilities to be revised in ways which result in EOL(L) being significantly lower than EOL(NL). It is not yet possible to say whether this survey result ($\frac{2}{10}$) is the lowest number of favourable responses that would produce a 'launch' recommendation, but in view of the fact that a 20 per cent market penetration level is the lowest at which the new service will show a profit it seems a promising first guess. So, without yet committing ourselves definitely to a particular decision rule we examine the prospective working of 'two or more favourable responses' as an automatic trigger for launching the new service.

First, what is the probability at each level of M that the proposed decision rule $\frac{2+}{10}$ (two or more favourable responses from ten randomly-selected potential customers) will result in the choice of the wrong policy? If M = 10 a mistake will be made if the new service *is* launched, i.e. if two or more favourable responses are obtained. The probability of this result, given a probability of 0.1 that each response will be favourable (recall that M = 10 by assumption), is obtained from tables of binomial probabilities:

$$p(\frac{2+}{10}/M = 10) = 0.2639$$

Conversely, if M = 20 or M = 30, a mistake is made when *fewer* than two favourable responses are obtained. The probabilities of these errors are, respectively,

$$p(\frac{1-}{10}/M = 20) = 1 - p(\frac{2+}{10}/M = 20) = 0.3758$$

and

$$p(\frac{1-}{10}/M = 10) = 1 - p(\frac{2+}{10}/M = 10) = 0.1493$$

where $\frac{1-}{10}$ denotes 'one or less favourable responses out of ten'.

In the assessment of the $\frac{2+}{10}$ decision rule each possible opportunity loss (OL) is weighted by its probability and the resulting products summed to give the overall expected opportunity loss for following the decision rule. The probability of each OL is given by the product of the prior probability for the level of M in question and the probability of error given that level of M. Thus, for example, using 'e' to denote the occurrence of an error, we have

$$p(OL = £40,000) = p(M = 10)\, p(e/M = 10)$$

$$= 0.25 \times 0.2639$$

$$= 0.066$$

This probability, and the corresponding ones for the other two possible OL values, can be found at work in the formal evaluation of the $\frac{2+}{10}$ decision rule shown in Table 7.3, though the calculation is performed in two stages.

Table 7.3: Calculation of EOL for Decision Rule $\frac{2+}{10}$

(1) M (per cent)	(2) Prior probability	(3) OL for wrong decision (£)	(4) Probability of wrong decision, given M	(5) EOL, given M (3) × (4) (£)	(6) Overall EOL (2) × (5) (£)
10	0.25	40,000 (L)	0.2639	10,556.0	2,639.0
20	0.50	5,000 (NL)	0.3758	1,879.0	939.5
30	0.25	35,000 (NL)	0.1493	5,225.5	1,306.4
EOL condition on following $\frac{2+}{10}$ decision rule =					£4,884.9

The final result in Table 7.3 shows that the value of EOL for the $\frac{2+}{10}$ decision rule is £4,884.9, well below the lower of the two EOL values in the absence of additional information (EOL(L) = £10,000). Ignoring other possible decision rules for the moment, the consultancy manager would choose to follow the $\frac{2+}{10}$ decision rule unless he anticipated that the costs of interviewing ten potential customers would exceed £5,115.1 (£10,000 − £4,884.9). Ignoring the question of its cost, the survey's superiority is so marked that it is worth reminding ourselves that appreciable error probabilities renain, whatever the level of M (see column (4) of Table 7.3).

The next step is to examine alternative decision rules for the same size (and expense) of survey, to see whether there is one that offers an EOL value lower than £4,884.9. With such a small sample there is little chance of 'fine-tuning' the decision rule; the nearest alternative rules, $\frac{1+}{10}$ and $\frac{3+}{10}$, are in fact equivalent proportionately to the lowest and highest M levels envisaged by the consultancy manager. Table

Table 7.4(a): Calculation of EOL Values for Decision Rule $\frac{1+}{10}$

(1) M (per cent)	(2) Prior probability	(3) OL for wrong decision (£)	(4) Probability of wrong decision, given M	(5) EOL, given M (3) × (4) (£)	(6) Overall EOL (2) × (5) (£)
10	0.25	40,000 (L)	0.6513	26,052	6,513.0
20	0.50	5,000 (NL)	0.1074	537	268.5
30	0.25	35,000 (NL)	0.0282	987	246.7

EOL conditional on following $\frac{1+}{10}$ decision rule =   £7,028.2

Table 7.4(b): Calculation of EOL Values for Decision Rule $\frac{3+}{10}$

(1) M (per cent)	(2) Prior probability	(3) OL for wrong decision (£)	(4) Probability of wrong decision, given M	(5) EOL given M (3) × (4) (£)	(6) Overall EOL (2) × (5) (£)
10	0.25	40,000 (L)	0.0702	2,808	702.0
20	0.50	5,000 (NL)	0.6778	3,389	1,694.5
30	0.25	35,000 (NL)	0.3828	13,398	3,349.5

EOL conditional on following $\frac{3+}{10}$ decision rule =   £5,746.0

7.4(a) gives results analogous to those of Table 7.3 for the decision rule $\frac{1+}{10}$, and Table 7.4(b) does the same for decision rule $\frac{3+}{10}$.

As was to be expected, the first decision rule considered, $\frac{2+}{10}$, is the best attainable when only ten potential customers are to be interviewed. It is intuitively obvious that further departures from a trigger point of two favourable responses would produce even higher values of EOL than those obtained in Table 4(a) and 4(b).

Our final task at this stage is to confirm that the decision rule offering the lowest EOL value (given the size of the survey) does indeed have as its trigger point the lowest number of favourable responses at which the revision of probabilities would cause EOL(L) to be lower than EOL(NL). Table 7.5 shows the results of probability revisions conditional on survey results $\frac{1}{10}$, $\frac{2}{10}$ and $\frac{3}{10}$; the entries for $\frac{1}{10}$ and $\frac{3}{10}$ are calculated in the same way as those for $\frac{2}{10}$ shown earlier.

Table 7.5: Revised Probabilities for M Levels, Given Survey Results

	revised probabilities of M			EOL	
survey result	M = 10 (OL = £40,000)	M = 20 (OL = £5,000)	M = 30 (OL = £35,000)	EOL(L) (£)	EOL(NL) (£)
$\frac{1}{10}$	0.3707	0.5134	0.1159	14,828	6,623.5
$\frac{2}{10}$	0.1878	0.5857	0.2265	7,512	10,856
$\frac{3}{10}$	0.0792	0.5539	0.3669	3,168	15,611

Table 7.5 also shows, in the two columns furthest to the right, the EOL values for 'launch' and 'no launch' that will emerge from the probability revision process for each assumed survey result. These confirm that the result $\frac{2}{10}$ is the lowest number of favourable responses that will lead to a 'launch' decision on the basis of revised probabilities.

The advantage of the decision rule procedure is not that it is bound to produce better decisions than the 'wait and see' approach discussed earlier. Indeed, if both approaches are applied correctly they should arrive at the same decision for any given survey result. The real advantage of the decision rule procedure is that the value of the survey itself can be properly appraised beforehand. And if, as is usually the case, a choice exists on the amount to be spent on new information, a decision rule approach is essential in determining the optimum level of expenditure. The following sub-section discusses this aspect of optimisation.

7.4 (v) Determining the Optimum Level of Expenditure

We have shown how the optimal decision rule can be identified in advance of the acquisition of a given amount of new information. The remaining task in this section is to determine the optimal level of such expenditures, and it will be helpful to maintain continuity with the earlier discussion by retaining the example of the new consultancy service. (A full theoretical treatment of this topic is provided in Moore, 1972, Ch. 10).

Suppose that the survey of ten potential customers is expected to cost £1,300, made up of £300 of fixed costs and £100 per interview. Our result showed that the decision rule $\frac{2+}{10}$ would reduce the firm's EOL by £5,115.1 (£10,000 − £4,884.9), a figure which compares very favourably with the cost of the survey. But the prospective 'surplus' of £3,815.1 yielded by the acquisition and optimal use of additional information in this case (£5,115.1 − £1,300) raises the question of whether an even larger margin might be attainable at some other level of survey size and cost.

To illustrate one step in the process of reaching the optimum level planned expenditure on new information we examine briefly the implications of surveying 20 potential customers instead of the sample of ten originally considered. The first step is to find the optimal decision rule for a sample of 20, and the calculations involved are shown in parts (a), (b) and (c) of Table 7.6.

The optimal decision rule for a sample of 20 is to launch the new service if four or more favourable responses are obtained. In general of course there is no reason to expect the trigger point for the optimal decision rule to be constant in relation to sample size; indeed for obvious reasons this will usually be impossible. To increase the survey size from ten to twenty potential customers will cost an extra £1,000 (assuming marginal cost is constant at £100 per interview), and the reduction in EOL offered by the additional information is £1,589.3 − the difference between the EOL values for the optimal decision rules in samples of ten and twenty potential customers (£4,884.9 − £3,295.6). Accordingly, the additional outlay is judged worthwhile. Note, however, that the reduction in EOL achieved by the increase in sample size from ten to twenty (£1,589.3) is considerably smaller than that achieved by the increase in sample size from zero to ten potential customers (£5,115.1).

Generalising this last point, equal increments to the size of a survey yield diminishing reductions in EOL. The lower limit of EOL is zero, but this is attainable only through access to perfect information. When, as with sampling, information is necessarily less than conclusive, it becomes progressively more difficult (expensive) to achieve further reductions in conditional error probabilities through increases in sample size. The application of marginalist logic suggests that the size of sample should be increased up to the point at which the marginal

Table 7.6(a): Calculation of EOL Values for Decision Rule $\frac{3+}{20}$

(1)	(2)	(3)	(4)	(5)	(6)
M (per cent)	Prior probability	OL for wrong decision (£)	Probability of wrong decision, given M	EOL, given M (3) × (4) (£)	Overall EOL (2) × (5) (£)
10	0.25	40,000 (L)	0.3231	12,924	3,231.0
20	0.50	5,000 (NL)	0.2061	1,031	515.3
30	0.25	35,000 (NL)	0.0355	1,243	310.6

EOL conditional on following $\frac{3+}{20}$ decision rule =   £4,056.9

Table 7.6(b): Calculation of EOL Values for Decision Rule $\frac{4+}{20}$

(1)	(2)	(3)	(4)	(5)	(6)
10	0.25	40,000 (L)	0.1330	5,320	1,330.0
20	0.50	5,000 (NL)	0.4114	2,057	1,028.5
30	0.25	35,000 (NL)	0.1071	3,749	937.1

EOL conditional on following $\frac{4+}{20}$ decision rule =   £3,295.6

Table 7.6(c): Calculation of EOL Values for Decision Rule $\frac{5+}{20}$

(1)	(2)	(3)	(4)	(5)	(6)
10	0.25	40,000 (L)	0.0432	1,728	432.0
20	0.50	5,000 (NL)	0.6296	3,148	1,574.0
30	0.25	35,000 (NL)	0.2375	8,313	2,078.1

EOL conditional on following $\frac{5+}{20}$ decision rule =   £4,084.1

reduction in EOL resulting from a £1 increase in expenditure falls to £1 — subject of course to the condition that the *total* reduction in EOL due to sampling is at least as great as the *total* cost of sampling (see Moore, 1972, Ch. 10).

7.5 The Cost of Reducing Error Probabilities

Results in 7.4 were obtained on the assumption that the decision maker attempts to minimise the total of expected opportunity loss plus survey cost. Now we recognise that other considerations may influence his approach. In particular, he may be more concerned with the risks of making a wrong decision than with the actual monetary values of the payoffs. This would be true of a decision maker committed to risk avoidance or risk minimisation, but it might also occur when conditional payoffs are not as clearly or confidently identified as has been assumed so far. For example, market penetration may be only one of the factors determining the profitability of the proposed new consultancy service discussed in 7.4, and the manager may not have the kind of confidence in conditional NPV predictions that would allow him to proceed along the lines described.

Preference or necessity may therefore focus his attention on probabilities of error, rather than on the costs of errors. Table 7.7 illustrates the nature of decision making in this context by bringing together the error probabilities associated with the various combinations of decision rule and survey size considered earlier.

In Table 7.7, e_1 denotes the launching of the new service when it should not be launched, and e_2 denotes failure to launch the new service when it should be launched; $p(e_1)$ and $p(e_2)$ are the respective probabilities of these two errors. The overall probability of error in following any decision rule is denoted by $p(E)$, the sum of the probabilities of the mutually exclusive errors, e_1 and e_2:

$$p(E) = p(e_1) + p(e_2)$$

The exact definitions of $p(e_1)$ and $p(e_2)$ are as follows:

$$p(e_1) = p(L/M = 10)\, p(M = 10)$$

$$p(e_2) = p(NL/M = 20)\, p(M = 20) + p(NL/M = 30)\, p(M = 30)$$

in which the notation remains unchanged from 7.4 so that, for example $p(L/M = 10)$ denotes the probability that the new service will

Table 7.7: Error Probabilities for Stated Decision Rules and Survey Sizes

	Survey of 10			Survey of 20		
	Decision rule			Decision rule		
	$\dfrac{3+}{10}$	$\dfrac{2+}{10}$	$\dfrac{1+}{10}$	$\dfrac{5+}{20}$	$\dfrac{4+}{20}$	$\dfrac{3+}{20}$
$p(e_1)$	0.0176	0.0660	0.1628	0.0108	0.0333	0.0808
$p(e_2)$	0.4346	0.2252	0.0608	0.3742	0.2325	0.1119
$p(E)$	0.4522	0.2912	0.2236	0.3850	0.2658	0.1927

be launched when the level of market penetration is only ten per cent. The reader can confirm that all values of $p(e_1)$ and $p(e_2)$ in Table 7.7 are obtained from the appropriate conditional and prior probabilities given earlier in Tables 7.3, 7.4 and 7.6.

It is evident that for any size of survey a reduction in one type of risk can only be achieved at the price of an increase in the other. Only by increasing the size (and expense) of the survey is it possible to reduce both error risks simultaneously. In moving away from the EOL framework a decision maker faces an embarrassingly wide choice of criteria for responding to the results of a given survey and for determining the size of the survey to be undertaken, and no safe predictions can be made as to his thinking and behaviour. Two possible interpretations of decision making in the context of a given size of survey are that the decision maker seeks to minimise $p(E)$, the overall probability of error, or that he trades off $p(e_1)$ against $p(e_2)$ in a search for the least unattractive mixture of risks from those open to him. (There is in general no reason to expect the optimal decision in the EOL framework to have the lowest level of $p(E)$.) Given the marked difference between the natures of the 'regrets' or opportunity losses represented by the errors whose probabilities we are discussing, a straightforward minimisation of $p(E)$ seems an unlikely objective. In the case of e_1, the opportunity loss, if it occurs, will be highly 'visible', and apart from the financial setback suffered by the firm the decision maker's own standing and career prospects may be damaged. By comparison, e_2 represents an 'invisible' and relatively painless opportunity loss; indeed in some situations the decision maker will

never know whether a decision not to proceed with a new venture
was mistaken or not.

7.6 Evaluating the Option of Acquiring Information Sequentially

Throughout 7.4 and 7.5 we assumed that additional information would
be obtained on a once-only basis, and that the decision maker's task
was to determine the optimum size (expense) of such an operation.
Now we recognise that the circumstances and cost structure of
sampling may allow a quite different and potentially more
economical optimising process. The essence of this is that information
can be purchased in stages instead of in a predetermined amount.
At each stage the information obtained is used to revise prior
probabilities and then the EOL for each final decision is recalculated
using the revised probabilities. (A 'final decision' in this context is a
decision to proceed with the proposal in question or to finally reject
it.) The lower of the two resulting EOL values, denoted by EOL*, is
then compared with the cost of acquiring additional information plus
the EOL of continuing with the information gathering exercise; and if
the latter total is lower, the purchase of information will continue.
But if the value of EOL* is lower, the final decision in question will
be implemented. (The theory of sequential acquisition of information
is covered by Hamburg, 1970, Ch. 16; and Morgan, 1978, Ch. 6. Moore,
1972, pp. 196–202, offers an example which contrasts usefully with
our own, in *not* employing binomial probabilities.)

The major new concept at the heart of this process is the 'EOL
for continuing to acquire information'. To demonstrate its precise
meaning and method of computation we take as an example a
company which wishes to purchase new equipment for a certain batch
production process. All units produced in a batch are either uniformly
satisfactory (s) or defective (d), and the manager of the prospective
purchasing company believes that either ten per cent or fifty per cent
of batches produced with the new equipment will be defective. His
prior probabilities for these two rates are 0.6 and 0.4, respectively.
Thus $p(D = 0.1) = 0.6$ and $p(D = 0.5) = 0.4$, where D denotes the
proportion of batches that are defective. If the new equipment works
well ($D = 0.1$) the savings it will yield over the company's present
equipment will be such as to make its net present value (NPV) equal to
£60,000; while if the new equipment works badly ($D = 0.5$) its NPV
will be − £30,000.

This information yields the following opportunity loss matrix:

	D = 0.1	D = 0.5
Invest (I)	0	£30,000
Not Invest (NI)	£60,000	0

Using the manager's prior probabilities for D = 0.1 and D = 0.5, the EOLs for the final decisions 'invest' (I) and 'not invest' (NI) are as follows:

EOL (I)   =   0.6 × £0 + 0.4 × £30,000 = £12,000

EOL (NI)   =   0.6 × £60,000 + 0.4 × £0 = £36,000

In the absence of an opportunity to acquire more information about the new equipment, an EOL-minimising manager will decide to invest.

Suppose now that the company supplying the new equipment offers to allow prospective customers to use its own demonstration equipment to produce up to three test batches of output at a cost of £1,000 per batch. How should the potential customer respond to this offer?

Figure 7.2 illustrates the principles of sequential decision making as they apply to the potential customer in this example. Beginning at decision point A the decision maker's choice lies between the immediate final decision I, with EOL* = £12,000, and the EOL associated with producing one test batch and acting 'optimally' in the light of the result. Evidently the nature of this optimal follow-up is by no means obvious at A, but we shall show that the concept is capable of a very precise and meaningful interpretation.

First, the notation employed in Figure 7.2 must be explained. At each decision point A . . . G the company can either pay £1,000 to produce one test batch (T), or reach a final decision (FD) on the basis of the probabilities of D = 0.10 and D = 0.50 *as they will then be estimated*. The letters d and s denote a single test batch which is defective or satisfactory, respectively. A sequence of these letters, such as dss, denotes a particular sequence of results when testing is extended to more than one batch. At each decision point the EOL of the optimal final decision depends on the results of all earlier testing; thus at F, EOL*/ds denotes the EOL of the final decision having the lower EOL value in the light of the probability revisions that

Figure 7.2: Decision Tree for Sequential Testing Option

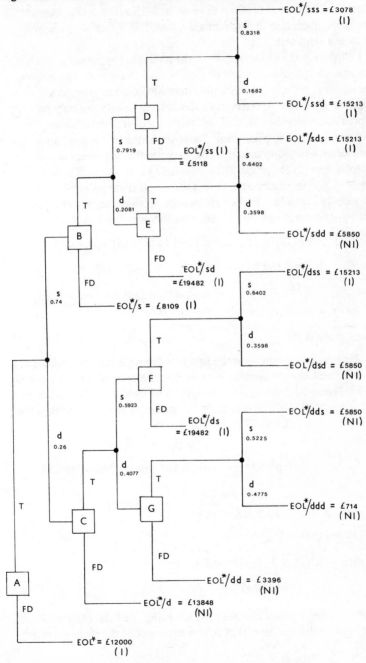

will follow the sequence of test results ds. In each case the actual final decision is shown in brackets beneath its EOL value. As explained earlier, a maximum of three tests is allowed, so a final decision must follow a third test.

Obviously the attractiveness of the sequential approach to the prospective purchaser is that he may be able to reach a final decision more economically than by a predetermined commitment to a particular amount of testing; but this type of option can only be appraised in advance, at A, if two related sets of probability calculations can be performed. These are (i) the revisions of prior probabilities conditional on the various possible sequences of test results, and (ii) the probabilities of results s and d at each stage of testing. A brief demonstration will show that these probabilities can indeed by identified. In the first test the probabilities of s and d, $p(s)$ and $p(d)$, respectively, are obtained as follows:

$$p(s) = p(s/D = 0.1)\, p(D = 0.1) + p(s/D = 0.5)\, p(D = 0.5)$$

$$= 0.9 \times 0.6 + 0.5 \times 0.4$$

$$= 0.74$$

$$p(d) = 1 - p(s)$$

$$= 0.26$$

Following the result s in the first test, how are the probabilities of $D = 0.1$ and $D = 0.5$ revised, in order that the optimal final decision at point B may be determined? The revised probability of $D = 0.1$ in this situation, $p(D = 0.1/s)$, is obtained by means of the standard Bayesian techniques as follows:

$$p(D=0.1/s) = \frac{p(s/D=0.1)\, p(D=0.1)}{p(s/D=0.1)\, p(D=0.1) + p(s/D=0.5)\, p(D=0.5)}$$

$$= \frac{0.9 \times 0.6}{0.9 \times 0.6 + 0.5 \times 0.4} = 0.7297$$

It follows that

$$p(D = 0.5/s) = 1 - p(D = 0.1/s)$$

$$= 0.2703$$

These revised probabilities are used to recalculated the EOL values for the final decisions I and NI at B, and the lower of the two resulting values is shown as EOL*/s in Figure 7.2.

This procedure is carried forward to the next stage of possible test results and probability revisions. If at B the decision maker decides to carry out another test, what probabilities will he assign to the outcomes s and d? Obviously at B the relevant probabilities for D = 0.10 and D = 0.50 will be those calculated after the result s in the first test. Thus, for a result s in a test conducted at B the decision maker's estimated probability, $p(s/s)$, will be determined as follows:

$$p(s/s) = p(s/D = 0.1) \, p'(D = 0.1) + p(s/D = 0.5) \, p'(D = 0.5)$$

in which $p'(D = 0.1)$ and $p'(D = 0.5)$ are the revised probabilities of D = 0.1 and D = 0.5, respectively. These have already been identified as 0.7297 and 0.2703, respectively; thus:

$$p(s/s) = 0.9 \times 0.7297 + 0.5 \times 0.2703$$

$$= 0.7919$$

and

$$p(d/s) = 1 - p(s/s)$$

$$=. 0.2081$$

At each stage of testing in Figure 7.2 the probabilities of s and d revised in the light of *all* previous test results are shown. The figure does not show the revisions that occur in the probabilities of D = 0.1 and D = 0.5 in the light of the test results, but these are summarised in Table 7.8. (The reader should confirm that the entries in the table are obtained by combining Bayes' theorem and the Binomial theorem in the way described in 2.5.)

It is important to note that although there are two distinct approaches to probability revision in a sequential testing procedure such as we are discussing, they will produce exactly the same set of revised probabilities in any given situation. Our assumption has been that the decision maker revises his original prior probabilities afresh after each test in the light of the whole sequence of test results he has experienced. But if instead he merely uses the latest test result to revise the probabilities he calculated after the last test, his conclusions will be exactly the same (Hamburg, 1970, pp. 731-2). This point is important in establishing the unambiguous nature of the conclusions the decision maker can draw from sequences of test results.

We are now ready to evaluate from the potential customer's stand-

Table 7.8: Conditional Revised Probabilities of D = 0.10 and D = 0.50

Sequence of test results	D = 0.10	D = 0.50
(no test)	(0.60)	(0.40)
s	0.7297	0.2703
d	0.2308	0.7692
ss	0.8294	0.1706
sd, ds	0.3506	0.6494
dd	0.0566	0.9434
sss	0.8974	0.1026
sds, ssd, dss	0.4929	0.5071
dds, dsd, sdd	0.0975	0.9025
ddd	0.0119	0.9881

point the testing option offered by the supplier. As usual with decision tree problems we operate the 'rollback' principle, under which conditional decisions and their EOLs at more remote decision points influence more immediate decisions. The choices at each stage of the decision process illustrated in Figure 7.2 can now be summarised without comment. At each decision point, EOL(T) denotes the EOL of producing a test batch and acting optimally thereafter. C(T) denotes the cost of making one test batch and EOL*(FD) denotes the EOL of the optimal final decision given the probabilities of D = 0.1 and 0.5 as they will be estimated at that point.

At D: C(T) + EOL(T)
    =   £1,000 + 0.8318 × £3,078 + 0.1682 × £15,213
    =   £6,119.1
or   EOL*(FD) = £5,118   (Invest)

At E: C(T) + EOL(T)
    =   £1,000 + 0.6402 × £15,213 + 0.3598 × £5,850
    =   £12,844.2
or   EOL*(FD) = £19,482   (Invest)

At F: same choice as at E

At G: C(T) + EOL(T)
    =   £1,000 + 0.5225 × £5,850 + 0.4775 × £714

$$= £4,397.6$$
or $\quad$ EOL*(FD) = £3,396 $\qquad$ (Not Invest)

At B: $\quad$ C(T) + EOL(T)
$$= £1,000 + 0.7919 \times £5,118 + 0.2081 \times £12,844.2$$
$$= £7,725.8$$
or $\quad$ EOL*(FD) = £8,109 $\qquad$ (Invest)

At C: $\quad$ C(T) + EOL(T)
$$= £1,000 + 0.5923 \times £12,844.2 + 0.4077 \times £3,396$$
$$= £9,992.2$$
or $\quad$ EOL*(FD) = £13,848 $\qquad$ (Not Invest)

At A: $\quad$ C(T) + EOL(T)
$$= £1,000 + 0.74 \times £7,725.8 + 0.26 \times £9,992.2$$
$$= £9,315.1$$
or $\quad$ EOL*(FD) = £12,000 $\qquad$ (Invest)

Having made conditional choices between T and FD for all future occasions, the decision maker is able to choose whether to embark on the testing option or reach an immediate decision. At A the value of C(T) + EOL(T) is appreciable lower than EOL*(FD), and at least one test batch should be produced before a final decision is taken.

Our example has introduced the main features of the prior analysis of a sequential information-gathering process, but a few general observations should be added. In the problem we have considered, testing (sampling) is conducted on a one-at-a-time basis; but in sequential sampling problems in general there need be no such restriction. Nor should we expect in general to find an arbitrary upper limit on the number of samples to be taken. The removal of such restrictions raises two sorts of problems. First, what size of sample should be taken on each occasion? Should the sample size be the same on each occasion? Obviously a sample ought to be smaller than the optimum size of sample would be if only one sampling operation were contemplated, and small enough to keep to a reasonable level the amount of computation involved in conditionally revising prior probabilities at each stage of the evaluation. Bearing these considerations in mind, it should be possible for a decision maker to do some preliminary experimentation with the rules for a sequential sampling exercise, just as we have done for a particular set of rules in Figure 7.2. His preferred set of rules from among those considered will be that offering the lowest initial value of C(T) + EOL(T), but it has to be accepted that complete optimisation in this area of choice is probably unattainable.

Second, if sampling is completely open-ended, how do we know that it will *ever* terminate in a final decision? We can be reasonably confident that in practice the build-up of information through sampling will eventually lead to probability revisions that yield a decisive superiority for one or other policy; and in the evaluation of an open-ended sampling option it is permissible if necessary to bring the chain of calculations to an arbitrary but sensible close (Morgan, 1968, p. 104).

7.7 Conclusion

This chapter's most complete and intellectually satisfying models are those which depict the decision maker as either optimising the level of planned expenditure on information (7.4) or evaluating a sequential information gathering exercise (7.6) — the approach being largely determined by the cost structure of acquiring information. But how wide are the gaps between business practice and pure theory likely to be?

Scepticism about the relevance of pure theory arises not only because conditional payoffs may be uncertain (7.5), but because the optimising processes outlined in 7.4 and 7.6 are conceptually complex. However, the equivalence between maximising expected money value and minimising EOL (7.3) means that we need not attribute to our decision maker a familiarity with obscure theoretical concepts. We should perhaps concede that decision makers allocate amounts to expenditure on information which they believe will produce decisive verdicts in favour of one or other course of action. However information is acquired, this probably means a larger than optimal outlay; but the decision then taken will be the correct one for that level of information and sample outcome.

Note

1. Net present value is one measure of an investment's profitability over its lifetime. The concept is explained and discussed in the Appendix to Chapter 9.

8 CAPITAL STRUCTURE AND COST OF CAPITAL

'tis not so deep as a well, nor so wide
as a church door; but 'tis enough, 'twill serve.

Shakespeare

8.1 Introduction

In Chapter 1 we discussed in general terms the objectives and coverage
of financial decision making in a business whose capital is widely owned
and traded on the stock exchange. The most widely accepted view of
management's overall financial objective, the maximisation of the value
of the enterprise to its owners, was shown to involve the formulation of
policies for the three main areas of investment choice, capital structure
and dividend policy. Our preliminary impressions of this tripartite
choice were: (i) that a three-way simultaneous maximisation exercise
seems both unlikely and impracticable; (ii) that in any case investment
decision making is by far the most important aspect of optimisation
within the broad area of financial decision making; and (iii) that
managements understandably wish to follow settled dividend policies
that are readily understood by the capital market and that allow them
to raise the great bulk of their regular equity requirements as retained
equity earnings.

Although this chapter concentrates on the capital structure decision,
we shall argue that this decision impinges on both investment decision
making, through its effect on the firm's cost of capital, and on dividend
policy through its effect on the size and risk of dividend prospects.
Our main interest is in the first of these connections — that between
capital structure and cost of capital — and we approach this question
by adopting the widely used but nonetheless artificial device of
assuming a static or comparative-static context (zero growth or a once-
only new investment by the firm) in which, because reinvestment of
earnings is not a regular occurrence, the firm's dividend policy is simply
a pale reflection of its capital structure decision. (For an attempt to
establish greater parity between the firm's dividend and capital
structure policies in a more dynamic context, see Baker, 1979, pp.
40-5.)

The significance of our discussion of cost of capital will be obvious.
Most readers will already be aware of the theoretical debate over the

relative merits of the *net present value* (NPV) and *internal rate of return* (IRR) methods of investment appraisal, a debate in which NPV has attracted wide support. (Readers unfamiliar with this debate should refer to the Appendix to Chapter 9 before studying 8.4.) A necessary input into the NPV approach, however, is an estimate of the relevant cost of capital; and this chapter tries to indicate the way in which this gap can be filled, as well as the limitations inherent in the chosen method.

8.2 Introduction to 'Traditional' Valuation Theory

This section sets itself an extremely modest target in relation to a subject of great breadth and fundamental importance, namely the determination of the market values of financial assets. Our presumed managerial objective of maximising the market value of investors' wealth can only be translated into specific policies through the medium of a predictive valuation model, and here we introduce the basic concepts in 'traditional' valuation theory on which much of this chapter's discussion will be based. It may be helpful at this early stage to identify the distinctive features of the traditional approach in order to prepare for critical discussion in this and in later chapters.

Although the traditional approach has often been accused of lacking a rigorous theoretical foundation, its influence on the literature and practice of financial decision making has been great, and remains considerable. And given the elusiveness of final and incontrovertible truth in the area of valuation theory, there is much to be said for a framework that recognises and incorporates major factors in valuation and seems to reflect the intuitive thinking of both investors and managers. (One of the most sympathetic and instructive expositions of traditional thought, on the narrow issue of valuation and on wider issues of managerial policy, is contained in Solomon, 1963.)

The traditional approach interprets the valuation of a financial asset in terms of the discounting of all expected future receipts accruing to its holder (or his successor(s)). The discount rate applying to a future expectation is assumed to reflect both pure time preference and the risk associated with the expectation, but it is common to assume a discount rate that does not vary with the remoteness of the expectation. (Discussion on this last point has been prolonged and remains inconclusive. The major alternatives to the interpretation of discounting discussed here can be found in Robichek and Myers, 1965, pp. 79–86, and 1966;

and Gordon, 1962.) Traditional analysis concentrates on the asset values that would prevail under equilibrium conditions, with all investors holding the same expectations of the future pattern of income, and no short-term disturbances in the capital market. Needless to say, market conditions rarely if ever approach this ideal, but on behalf of the traditional approach it can be argued that it is appropriate for management to employ a criterion relating to equilibrium valuation in this sense when it is considering long-term investment decisions.

In the traditional approach the term 'risk' generally refers to the variability of a future receipt. A suitable absolute measure of this risk is the estimated standard deviation of receipts, and a more useful relative measure is the coefficient of variation of receipts, i.e. the ratio of standard deviation to expected value. (For simplicity we assume that estimated probability distributions of future receipts are more or less symmetrical in appearance.) To preview the portfolio theory approach to the concept of risk, we should note that investors and business managers may differ on the relevance and importance of this type of risk measure as applied to a single company's earnings or dividend prospect. And, as we shall see in Chapter 10, the contrast between the traditional and portfolio theory interpretations of valuation is heightened by the latter's view of equilibrium in essentially short-run terms, rather than as a generally agreed appraisal of long-run expectations.

The equilibrium valuation of a company's equity capital is traditionally expressed in the following way:

$$S = \sum_{t=1}^{\infty} \frac{\bar{D}_t}{(1 + k)^t} \tag{i}$$

in which S is the present-day ex dividend equilibrium market value of the company's equity capital, $\bar{D}_t$ is the value of the company's dividend expectation for period t, and k is the market discount rate appropriate to the risk associated with the typical periodic dividend expectation. Given that it presumably represents investors' required rate of expected return on *any* investment of comparable risk, we should interpret k as the cost of equity capital to the business in question. In static conditions where the firm's dividend expectation is the same for all future periods, the general expression (i) reduces to

$$S = \frac{\bar{D}}{k} \tag{ii}$$

in which $\bar{D}$ is the unchanging dividend expectation. By contrast, when steady growth of expected dividend over time is anticipated, the valuation expression becomes

$$S = \sum_{t=1}^{\infty} \frac{\bar{D}_1(1+g)^{t-1}}{(1+k)^t} = \frac{\bar{D}_1}{k-g} \tag{iii}$$

in which $\bar{D}_1$ is the dividend expectation for period 1, i.e. one period hence, and g is the 'permanent' growth rate of $\bar{D}_t$ anticipated by the market. There is no need to fear that (iii) can be rendered meaningless by an anticipated permanent growth rate that is actually higher than the discount rate; see Modigliani and Miller (1959), footnote 17; and (1961), footnote 14.

Evidently the estimation of k from (ii) or (iii) or any other appropriate version of (i) involves inferring market expectations and the estimation of the equilibrium value of equity (as distinct from its actual value which may of course be subject to many short-term influences). This task is of considerable importance in any calculation of a firm's overall cost of capital, but discussion in this chapter is confined to the theoretical level. The practical identification of k is discussed in Baker (1978), pp. 168–79; various models of expected growth, of which (iii) is an example, are considered in Mao (1969), pp. 393–406.

The valuation of long-term debt capital is less controversial, and our present interest in it is a narrow one. We shall simply assume that a firm issues debt at a price at which, in the absence of interest rate changes, it will continue to be traded throughout its lifetime and at which it will be redeemed on reaching maturity. This assumption helps to simplify discussion of the firm's capital structure decision, and to this end we further assume that at any time a company's long-term debt is homogeneous in all respects; a change in the amount of debt is brought about by redeeming the outstanding block of debt, if any, at its nominal/issue/market value, then issuing the new amount of debt with uniform interest rate and other characteristics.

8.3 'Traditional' Capital Structure and Cost of Capital Theory

8.3 (i) Introduction

The theoretical debate on the importance of capital structure can easily take on an appearance of abstract unreality, given that it is often conducted in the context of static or comparative-static analysis of the firm and in terms of a drastically simplified choice between financing methods. In essence, capital structure theory is concerned with the question of the existence of an optimum capital structure (OCS) in the sense of a mixture of types of long-term finance that maximises the wealth of a firm's shareholders. To facilitate discussion we shall follow the standard practice of assuming that the risky earnings prospect of the firm is unchanging over time and is not influenced by management's capital structure decision. Specifically, we envisage an unchanging probability distribution of periodic earnings available for paying taxes and making payments to long-term investors (debt and equity). This earnings concept is usually referred to as 'earnings before interest and taxes' (EBIT); see Bierman and Hass (1975), pp. 27–30, 94–8. The probability distribution of EBIT is evidently a very useful catch-all concept, embracing (i) the firm's choice of capital equipment, location and other aspects of its physical make-up, (ii) its choice of products, markets and competitive behaviour patterns, and (iii) management's control over output and costs at all levels of demand for the firm's products (see Figure 8.1, p. 173). Cyclical influences on earnings prospects ought to mean that a 'period' in this context is defined by the anticipated length of the business cycle in the industry in question, so ensuring that each period's probabilistic earnings prospect is the same; in practice it is usual to equate the period with the standard accounting year. Throughout this section we shall assume that the 'static risk' firm we are considering is expected to survive in perpetuity; or, at least, that management's capital structure choice makes no difference to its chance of survival. We follow this approach in order to emphasise that the traditional belief in the existence of OCS does not depend in essence on differential survival prospects between alternative capital structures.

One convenient implication of our concentration on a 'static risk' business is that dividend policy is necessarily standardised regardless of capital structure. With no new investments occurring or anticipated, the firm regularly pays out as dividend 100 per cent of earnings after taxes and interest. The market valuations we shall discuss are those that would prevail under equilibrium capital market conditions, i.e. in the absence of speculative and cyclical distortions and with all investors holding the same view of the unchanging prospects of the firm in question. When corporate taxation features in our discussion the tax model assumed will be one in which interest payments on a firm's long-term debt are tax deductible.

Finally, some of the common terminology of the capital structure debate should be introduced. The terms 'leverage' and 'gearing' both refer to the relative importance of debt in a company's capital structure. Various methods of precise measurement of leverage have been suggested (Bierman, 1970, pp. 87-97), but at present the general concept is all that concerns us. The aptness of the two terms can be judged from a simple algebraic example in which the investment of an amount I will generate an unchanging periodic earnings expectation of $\bar{r}I$. Let the amount of debt capital raised by the entrepreneur in this case be bI ($0 < b < 1$), so that the amount of equity capital required is $(1 - b)I$; and let the interest rate on debt be i. The expected rate of return on equity capital, $\bar{r}_e$, is given by

$$\bar{r}_e = \frac{\bar{r}I - ibI}{I - bI} = \frac{\bar{r} - ib}{1 - b} \tag{iv}$$

from which it can be shown that if $\bar{r}$ exceeds i, $\bar{r}_e$ is an increasing function of b; the entrepreneur can employ debt to 'lever up' the expected rate of return on his own investment, provided the interest rate on debt is lower than the investment's expected rate of return.

The other side of the 'leverage' coin is of course the risk to which the equity investor is exposed because of the fact that interest payments constitute a prior charge on the project's (or firm's) risky earnings. Given the risk embodied in the firm's EBIT distribution, usually referred to as *business risk*, the variability of residual equity income in relation to its expected value is obviously an increasing function of the firm's fixed interest obligations (see Figure 8.1 below). The term *financial risk* is often used to refer to the additional risk facing the firm, on top of the basic and inescapable business risk, due to the existence of prior claims such as debt interest on its earnings.

8.3 (ii) The Importance of Capital Structure in the Traditional View

In the traditional view, management can maximise the value of shareholders' wealth by achieving the highest possible market value for the business as a whole through its choice of capital structure. After elaborating on the concepts of business and financial risk we shall be considering this important proposition about management's role.

Within limits, a company's periodic earnings distribution can be divided into a secure component, part or all of which can be assigned to meet fixed interest commitments, and a risky residual which provides the dividend paid to shareholders. Figure 8.1 shows how choice in this area is limited by the existence of an upper limit on the level of the firm's risk-free commitment.

In Figure 8.1, and henceforth in this chapter, we use the symbol Q

Figure 8.1: Business Risk and Financial Risk

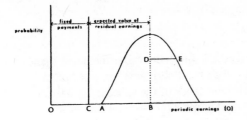

to denote the level of earnings (EBIT). The probability distribution of earnings will be referred to as the Q distribution and $\bar{Q}$ will represent the expected value of earnings. The positive minimum level of Q (that is, OA) in Figure 8.1 sets an upper limit on the level of fixed interest commitments management can undertake without some risk of having occasionally to default on at least part of its commitment (or run down cash reserves or increase short-term indebtedness). While a more general approach would recognise that firms may be willing to issue long-term debt (and investors to purchase it) on terms of less than perfect security for interest payments, the discussion of OCS can proceed quite satisfactorily on the assumption that firms limit their commitment in the way described. The fact that interest payments are kept within this limit, i.e. the amount OA in Figure 8.1, does *not* imply that the interest rate paid by the company will be constant irrespective of the amount borrowed (for example, see Lerner and Carleton, 1966, pp. 164–8).

Figure 8.1 clearly illustrates the distinction between business risk and financial risk mentioned earlier. The standard deviation and expected value of Q are shown as DE and OB, respectively; and the ratio of these two amounts, neither of which is affected by management's capital structure decision, is a satisfactory measure of the firm's business risk. If we now assume that OC is the level of fixed interest payments to which the firm is committed, the expected value of equity earnings is measured by CB and its standard deviation by DE. In general, as borrowing increases and interest payments rise from zero towards OA, the relative risk of the residual (equity) income prospect, as measured by its coefficient of variation, is increasing. This means that the risk associated with £1 of expected dividend increases with the level of the firm's debt, and we would expect the market value of that expectation to fall, i.e. the discount rate should increase.

The valuation implications of this discussion are best considered algebraically. Let the expected dividend of a 'static risk' firm be denoted by $\bar{D}$, defined as follows:

$$\bar{D} = (\bar{Q} - iB)(1 - t) \qquad \text{(v)}$$

in which i is the interest rate on the firm's debt, B is the nominal and market value of debt and t is the rate of corporate tax on earnings net of interest payments. The constancy of the expectation over time means that the present-day market value of the stream of future dividend expectations, S, is given by the capitalisation formula of equation (ii):

$$S = \frac{\bar{D}}{k} = \frac{(\bar{Q} - iB)(1 - t)}{k} \qquad \text{(vi)}$$

Accordingly, the expression for the market value of the firm's long-term capital as a whole, V, becomes

$$V = \frac{(\bar{Q} - iB)(1 - t)}{k} + B \qquad \text{(vii)}$$

As B is increased in (vii) the firm's overall market value is subjected to two opposing effects: the positive one-for-one effect of B on V, and the negative effect on S due to (a) the fall in the value of $(\bar{Q} - iB) \times (1 - t)$ and (b) the increase in k as the relative risk of residual earning rises. Central to the traditional approach is the presumption that as debt is increased from a zero or low initial level the first effect will outweight the second, but that beyond a critical point the second effect outweighs the first and V declines as B is increased. As we shall see, in the traditional view management's task is to fix B at the level yielding the maximum value of V, that is at the point at which an additional £1 of debt reduces the value of S by exactly £1.

The problem most frequently considered in theoretical discussions of capital structure is the capital structure decision of the established quoted company; and here it will be helpful to use a numerical example to illustrate the possibilities and techniques of adjustment. Table 8.1 shows the implications for a certain firm of a number of different assumptions about capital structure and the interest rate on debt. (Corporate taxation makes little difference to the general argument at this stage and is excluded from the example.)

In Table 8.1 the firm's Q distribution is given irrespective of its capital structure decision. The standard deviation of Q is not stated, but we assume the risk-free component of earnings to be at least £250

Table 8.1: Valuation Implications of Alternative Capital Structures

		1	2	3	4	5	3a	4a
$\bar{Q}$	(£)	1,000	1,000	1,000	1,000	1,000	1,000	1,000
i		0.05	0.05	0.05	0.05	0.05	0.055	0.06
B	(£)	0	2,000	3,000	4,000	5,000	3,000	4,000
$(\bar{Q} - iB)$	(£)	1,000	900	850	800	750	835	760
k		0.10	0.11	0.114	0.12	0.14	0.115	0.139
S	(£)	10,000	8,182	7,456	6,667	5,357	7,261	5,468
V	(£)	10,000	10,182	10,456	10,667	10,357	10,261	9,468

(the highest level of iB shown in the table). Assume the firm is initially an all-equity company (col. 1), with V = S = £10,000. Now (col. 2) the firm sells bonds with a market value of £2,000 carrying an interest rate of 5 per cent per annum. Its debt interest rises to £100 and the expected value of dividend, $\bar{D} = (\bar{Q} - iB)$, falls from £1,000 to £900. And because each £1 of expected dividend is now associated with greater variability, the equity discount rate rises from 10 per cent to 11 per cent. As a result of these two factors affecting the numerator and denominator of S in equation (vii), the value of S falls by £1,818, from £10,000 to £8,182. But assuming the proceeds of the bond sale to be distributed on a pro-rata basis among shareholders, each shareholder receives his fair share of the overall net gain in market value of £182 (£2,000 − £1,818).

Exactly analogous reasoning applies to further increases in B from the new level of £2,000 to any of the other levels shown in Table 8.1 Columns 3a and 4a are given in the table as alternatives to columns 3 and 4, respectively, on the assumption that the rate of interest on the firm's debt rises when B increases beyond £2,000. Not surprisingly they show that for a given increase in B, e.g. from £2,000 to £3,000, the drop in $(\bar{Q} - iB)$ is greater, the increase in k is greater, the fall in S is steeper and so the overall increase in V is smaller, than when i remains constant as B is increased.

The reader can confirm that for each possible change in capital structure the change in the overall market value of the firm is equal to the change in the market value of shareholders' wealth (cash holdings plus equity market value). Given that bondholders, by definition, cannot make either a capital gain or a capital loss as a result of capital structure change, this equivalence is inevitable. Its implication is obvious: the firm's management can maximise the wealth of share-holders — the sum of their holdings in the firm plus cash — by maximising the value of the firm itself.

An abrupt change in the capital structure of a static business of the kind shown in Table 8.1 may seem an unlikely policy move; but changes towards optimum capital structure (OCS) might be accomplished unspectacularly, through changes in debt matched by changes in dividend payments over a number of years. A more realistic perspective is to envisage capital structure change taking place as part of the process of financing new investments in a growing firm. Even in this context, however, a number of frictions are likely to prevent full and instantaneous optimisation in the area of capital structure policy. First, managers may be uncertain of the effect on the firm's equilibrium valuation of a given change in its capital structure. Each firm's Q distribution is unique, so the policies of other firms offer only limited guidance. The possibility that capital structure change may produce an adverse effect on valuation, and the suspicion that any gain achieved is likely to be slight, may diminish the importance managers attach to OCS. (In Table 8.1 the firm's value moves within a range of only £310 while debt moves within a range of £2,000, i.e. columns 3-5.)

A second reason to expect capital structure to be 'sticky' will be given in 8.3 (iv); briefly, we shall argue that the task of appraising investments will be eased if capital structure can be held more or less constant as the firm expands. Finally, changes in capital structure may create uncertainty about the firm's intentions and cause short-term disturbances in the market valuation of the firm's equity capital. These could complicate management's task of comprehending the valuation process in the pursuit of optimal investment policies.

8.3 (iii) Capital Structure and Cost of Capital

A different perspective on the problem of OCS provides an introduction to the concept of cost of capital, though our analysis remains for the moment anchored to the 'static risk' firm with no investment opportunities. Let the after-tax expected earnings of the firm in relation to its market value be denoted by c:

$$c = \frac{\bar{Q}(1-t)}{V} \qquad \qquad \text{(viii)}$$

Given $\bar{Q}$ and the corporate tax rate, t, maximising V is equivalent to minimising c, a concept whose meaning we shall now explore.

The right-hand side of (viii) expands as follows:

$$c = \frac{\frac{(\bar{Q} - iB)(1 - t)k}{k} + iB(1 - t)}{V} = \frac{S}{V}k + \frac{B}{V}i(1 - t) \qquad \text{(ix)}$$

Equation (ix) suggests that the problem of OCS can be seen in terms of minimising a weighted average of two net-of-tax cost components, k and $i(1 - t)$, with the weights given by the respective shares of equity and debt market values in the firm's overall market valuation. We shall shortly confirm that c, as defined in (ix) can be interpreted as the firm's cost of capital, that is as the minimum acceptable rate of expected return on new investment in the firm. First, however, the problem of OCS in the static firm can be visualised from the point of view of minimising c, rather than maximising V as in 8.3 (ii).

Figure 8.2: Weighted Average Cost of Capital: Traditional View

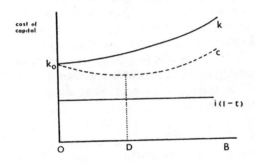

In Figure 8.2 the dashed schedule c represents the weighted average of the cost components k and $i(1 - t)$ as defined in (ix), for all values of B. (For the static firm the level of B is an unambiguous measure of leverage.) As in columns 1-5 of Table 8.1, the rate of interest on long-term debt is assumed constant because the total of debt interest is assumed to remain comfortably within the firm's risk-free earnings level. (Should the interest rate be an increasing function of B, as is the case in many expositions of capital structure theory, the conclusions of the traditional approach are strengthened.) As stated earlier, the value of k must increase with B because of the increase in risk associated with a given dividend expectation. The rate of interest lies below k at all levels of B, and of course the after-tax interest cost, $i(1 - t)$, is lower still. So we expect a weighted average of k and i(1 − t) to yield a value lower than k itself. Thus the c schedule coincides with that of k for a zero debt level (k_0 in Figure 8.2) and lies below it for positive values of B. More significantly, in the traditional view the c schedule actually falls when debt increases initially, as the weighted average of k and i(1 − t) is pulled downwards from k_0; the cost of i(1 − t) is lower than k, and with an increasing weight B/V and falling S/V such a tendency seems inevitable in the initial phase of debt expansion. Eventually, however, the high value of k outweighs the benefit of the lower net-of-tax cost of debt, and the c schedule turns upwards beyond the optimal debt level, OD. A rise in the interest rate − not shown in Figure 8.2 − would of course reinforce the tendency for c to turn upwards at some point.

The precise shape of the c schedule is an aspect on which the traditional approach offers no standard view, but a gently saucer-shaped schedule seems to be more commonly suggested than a markedly U-shaped schedule. In any case, firms' Q distributions are recognised as differing considerably both in shape and in the level of risk-free earnings, so a standard shape of c schedule should perhaps not be anticipated. From our discussion it should be clear that in the traditional approach the tax deductibility of debt interest makes no essential difference to the main argument; OCS contains more debt than it otherwise would, but the forces making for the eventual upturn of the firm's c schedule remain operative.

8.3 (iv) The Firm's Cost of Capital for New Investment

Switching our attention now to a comparative-static setting, we can demonstrate the relevance of c as a measure of the cost of capital to a business, that is the minimum acceptable rate of return expected on an investment. We assume that the investment in question represents a once-only, unanticipated opportunity to shift the firm's Q distribution outwards to a new permanent position. To simplify the analysis we assume further that the new Q distribution is more or less as risky as the original, for example in terms of its coefficient of variation. (The likelihood of this result is discussed in Baker, 1978, pp. 70–7.) It follows that if the firm's debt is increased in the same proportion as its unexpected earnings, and the interest rate on debt is unchanged, the relative risk of the residual earnings prospect is unchanged and the market rate of discount, k, can also be taken as unchanged. Since the expected value of residual earnings ($\overline{Q}$ − iB) evidently increases at the same rate as $\overline{Q}$ and B, it follows that in the situation envisaged $\bar{Q}$, B, S and V must all increase in proportion with one another; and given the constancy of both i and k the value of c is also unaffected by the investment/financing exercise. In developing a cost of capital concept against this background we shall assume that new equity capital is obtained by retaining equity earnings that would otherwise be distributed to shareholders as dividends. Comparable cost of capital measures for alternative methods of equity financing are derived by Brigham (1979), pp. 558–60, and Baker (1978), pp. 98–108.

To the extent that our analysis relates to (changes in) equilibrium valuations and assumes that debt financing takes place on terms that would apply in long-term equilibrium, it is correct to describe our objective as the identification of the long-run average and marginal cost of capital. Whether short-run capital costs actually differ significantly from their long-run counterparts obviously depends on the scale of the immediate financing requirement; when financing demands are modest in scale and capital markets are not noticeably distorted, it can be argued that the firm's short-run cost of capital approximates to the long-run average cost. (For the distinction between short and long-run in this context see Quirin, 1967, pp. 131–40, and Hawkins and Pearce, 1971, pp. 45–6.)

In the absence of the proposed investment, the value of shareholders' wealth (in the firm in question), denoted by W_0, is defined as

$$W_0 = D_0 + S_0 = D_0 + \frac{(\bar{Q} - iB)(1 - t)}{k} \tag{x}$$

where D_0 is the amount of dividend due to be paid in the near future and S_0 is the ex dividend equilibrium market value of the firm's equity (see equation (vi), p. 174). Acceptance of a proposal to spend an amount I on a new investment, financed in proportions b and $(1 - b)$ by new debt and retained earnings, respectively, would alter shareholders' wealth to W_0', defined as

$$W_0' = D_0 - I(1 - b) + \frac{(\bar{Q} - iB + \Delta\bar{Q} - ibI)(1 - t)}{k} \tag{xi}$$

in which $\Delta\bar{Q}$ is the expected value of the new investment's prospective earnings (unchanging over time). In (xi) the damaging effect of an immediate dividend reduction of $I(1 - b)$ is countered by the increase in the equilibrium market value of future dividend prospects capitalised at an unchanging rate, i.e. $[(\Delta\bar{Q} - ibI)(1 - t)] \div k$.

The obvious requirement for the investment's acceptability is that

W_0' be at least as great as W_0, and in terms of equations (x) and (xi) this implies the following conditions:

$$\frac{(\Delta\bar{Q} - ibI)(1-t)}{k} \geqslant I(1-b) \tag{xii}$$

With so simple a model of the earnings prospect of the new investment, we can define its expected rate of return, $\bar{r}$, as follows:

$$\bar{r} = \frac{\Delta\bar{Q}}{I} \tag{xiii}$$

This allows (xii) to be simplified as follows:

$$\frac{(\bar{r} - ib)(1-t)}{k} \geqslant (1-b) \tag{xiv}$$

or

$$\bar{r}(1-t) \geqslant k(1-b) + i(1-t)b \tag{xv}$$

The right-hand side of (xv) is a weighted average of the net-of-tax cost elements k and $i(1-t)$, the weights being equal to the respective proportions of equity and debt used in financing the new investment. Evidently the strict equality form of (xv) defines the minimum acceptable after-tax expected rate of return on a new investment, i.e. the company's cost of capital. Using $\bar{r}^*$ to denote this marginally acceptable value of $\bar{r}$, and b^* to denote the appropriate but as yet undetermined value of b, the strict equality form of (xv) is expressed as

$$\bar{r}^*(1-t) = k(1-b^*) + i(1-t)b^* \tag{xvi}$$

A fuller understanding of $\bar{r}^*$ and the appropriate value of b^* will emerge together. As stated earlier, we assume that for *any* investment the value of b is chosen to cause the firm's debt and debt interest to rise in the same proportion as its expected earnings, so allowing expected equity earnings also to increase at the same rate and the risk associated with that expectation to remain constant. This in turn allows k to remain constant. For a marginally acceptable investment the financing proportionality rule implies

$$\frac{b^*I}{B} = \frac{\bar{r}^*I}{\bar{Q}} \quad \text{or} \quad b^* = \bar{r}^*\frac{B}{\bar{Q}} \tag{xvii}$$

substituting $\bar{r}^*B/\bar{Q}$ for b^* in (xvi) yields

$$\bar{r}^*(1-t) = k(1 - \bar{r}^*\frac{B}{\bar{Q}}) + i(1-t)\bar{r}^*\frac{B}{\bar{Q}} \tag{xviii}$$

Collecting terms in (xviii) and rearranging gives

$$\frac{\bar{r}^*[\bar{Q} - iB)(1 - t) + kB]}{k} = \bar{Q} \tag{xix}$$

which simplifies conveniently to

$$\bar{r}^*(S + B) = \bar{Q} \tag{xx}$$

Finally, multiplying both sides of (xx) by $(1 - t)$ and rearranging yields

$$\bar{r}^*(1 - t) = \frac{\bar{Q}(1 - t)}{S + B} = \frac{\bar{Q}(1 - t)}{V} \tag{xxi}$$

Earlier we introduced the concept c, defined in equations (vii) and (ix) as follows:

$$c = \frac{\bar{Q}(1 - t)}{V} = \frac{S}{V}k + \frac{B}{V}i(1 - t) \tag{viii), (ix}$$

We now see that $\bar{r}^*(1 - t)$ as defined in (xxi) is identical to c as defined in (viii); and it follows that $\bar{r}^*(1 - t)$ defined as a weighted average in (xvi) is identical to c defined as a weighted average in (ix). This resolves the question of the values of b^* and $(1 - b^*)$ in equation (xvi); b^* is equal to B/V, the prevailing ratio of debt to the market value of the firm; and $(1 - b^*)$ is equal to S/V, the 'market value weight' of equity. Our cost of capital concept evidently deserves to be described as the 'market value weighted average cost of capital' (MVWACC).

As was demonstrated at the opening of this sub-section, our financing proportionality rule ensures that c (now recognised as the firm's cost of capital) will remain constant when a new investment is undertaken. However, representing the cost of capital as a weighted average can be somewhat misleading as far as the financing of intramarginal investments is concerned. Given management's intention of maintaining a constant MVWACC, the general requirement that debt must increase in the same proportion as $\bar{Q}$ obviously implies a greater amount of new debt in the case of a project with a higher value of $\bar{r}$. Generalising the financing rule stated in (xvii) for any investment j yields

$$b_j = \bar{r}_j\frac{B}{\bar{Q}} \tag{xxii}$$

For a marginally acceptable investment $(\bar{r}_j = \bar{r}^*)$, b_j will be equal to B/V; but when $\bar{r}_j > \bar{r}^*$ it is essential that $b_j > B/V$ by an equal proportion if the firm's MVWACC is to be held at its original level. The advantages of ensuring that this occurs are most obvious when numerous projects are being considered; if the firm's cost of capital were to change with each project selected, the problems of choice would be needlessly complicated. Besides, investments undertaken in the past are effectively revalued if the firm's cost of capital changes; and firms will be anxious to avoid a situation in which the reasoning behind current accept-or-reject decisions may be undermined by avoidable changes in the cost of capital in the future. Thus the value of MVWACC represents a hurdle or target rate of return for an investment project, but for most projects we do *not* expect financing to be arranged in the proportions embodied in MVWACC. This point seems to be implicitly recognised in Merrett and Sykes' critique of the MVWACC approach (Merrett and Sykes, 1963, p. 121).

8.4 A 'Traditional' Critique of Traditional Theory

8.4 (i) The Assumption of Constant Business Risk

The cost of capital concept we have derived from our representation of the traditional approach to capital structure is open to a number of critcisms and caveats, some of which can be considered within the traditional framework while others will emerge as we consider alternative theories of valuation. In the first category are a number of reservations concerning the practical relevance of our result, and since MVWACC has been widely recommended for use in investment appraisal — either for comparison with project rates of return, or as the appropriate discount rate in net present value calculations — these deserve consideration.

First, in deriving MVWACC we assumed that the investment in question would make no significant difference to the firm's business risk. In essence, the firm moves to a new 'static risk' equilibrium in which its new Q distribution is simply a scaled-up reproduction of the original. This might appear to confine the applicability of MVWACC rather narrowly, but in the more realistic context of fairly continuous investment decision making management may be confident of achieving an averaging of investment risks which will maintain the firm's business risk at more or less its present level (Baker, 1978, pp. 77-9).

8.4 (ii) The Relevance of MVWACC as a Discount Rate

But what if investments cannot be fitted into the convenient mould we have been shaping, i.e. a uniquely predictable and unchanging probability distribution of earnings (ΔQ)? These aspects (uniqueness and constancy over time) give rise to different problems and must be considered separately. If the characteristics of an investment's ΔQ distribution are themselves subject to risk or uncertainty, the MVWACC measure loses much of its relevance as an investment criterion because the consequential change in the equilibrium value of the firm, and in shareholders' wealth, cannot be predicted with certainty — as was assumed in deriving the criterion. In particular, if there is a possibility that the investment's $\bar{r}$ value will lie below $\bar{r}^*$, so that shareholders' wealth might actually decline if the investment is accepted, the MVWACC criterion by itself cannot settle the question.

When an investment's probabilistic earnings prospect is not expected to remain constant over time — again a fairly typical condition — our earlier analysis is no longer completely reliable. We can begin to appreciate the nature of the difficulty by reminding ourselves that in the procedure by which an investment's net present value (NPV) is calculated, each period's expected earnings is discounted to the present by the appropriate discount factor embodying the firm's cost of capital (Solomon and Pringle, 1977, pp. 261–71; Brigham, 1979, pp. 361–8). As we are trying to establish that the ideal measure of cost of capital is the firm's MVWACC, we shall employ the latter as the discount rate in considering a very simple investment proposal, but the issues involved can be discovered even in the case of the 'static risk' enterprise. Imagine that such a firm has the following equilibrium characteristics:

$$
\begin{array}{ll}
\bar{Q} = £100 & k = 0.10 \\
B = £400 & S = £800 \\
i = 0.05 & V = S + B = £1{,}200 \\
(\bar{Q} - iB) = £80 & c = \bar{Q}/V = 0.0833
\end{array}
$$

(We ignore taxation in this discussion.) The firm's MVWACC is 0.0833, obtained in equation (xxiv) from the general formula given in equation (xxiii):

$$
V = \sum_{t=1}^{\infty} \frac{\bar{Q}}{(1+c)^t} = \frac{\bar{Q}}{c} \tag{xxiii}
$$

$$
£1{,}200 = \sum_{t=1}^{\infty} \frac{£100}{1.0833^t} = \frac{£100}{0.0833} \tag{xxiv}
$$

In this summation of separate present values, each year's earnings expectation is discounted at the same annual rate, 0.0833. However, it can be shown that the separate valuations by shareholders and bondholders of any one year's prospects, using the appropriate discount rates, do *not* sum to the value predicted by the valuation formula. For example, the separate valuations of income prospects for year 2 sum as follows:

$$\frac{£80}{1.10^2} + \frac{£20}{1.05^2} = £84.257$$

$(£66.116) (£18.141)$

This sum is less than the value predicted by the relevant component of equation (xxiv), i.e. $£100/1.0833^2 = £85.212$.

Clearly, the firm's MVWACC does *not* give an accurate present-day valuation of any particular future expectation, but by definition the total value of the firm *is* correctly expressed by the use of MVWACC in capitalising an unchanging periodic expectation as in (xxiii) and (xxiv). (The reader can confirm that for more remote expectations the valuation bias shown in our comparison for year 2 is reversed.) What this means is that an investment such as we assumed in deriving MVWACC, having an unchanging periodic earnings expectation to infinity, can be evaluated perfectly satisfactorily by the MVWACC criterion; but that an investment having a finite life and possibly uneven time pattern of earnings expectations may require more careful consideration.

8.4 (iii) Using MVWACC in Net Present Value Calculations

To illustrate the problem of appraising realistic investments with the aid of MVWACC we now assume that the firm we have been discussing has the opportunity to undertake an investment costing £22.013. The expected returns from the investment are £10 at the end of year 1 and £15 at the end of year 2. We shall employ the net present value approach to investment appraisal, with the discount rate given by the firm's MVWACC (for brevity this will be referred to as the NPV/MVWACC approach). In order to allow this approach the maximum opportunity to demonstrate its suitability we shall assume that the firm's business risk in years 1 and 2 is completely unchanged by the investment, i.e. the investment's incremental earnings probability distributions for years 1 and 2 are simply scaled-down versions of the firm's permanent Q distribution, with which they both correlate perfectly. In addition, financing for the project will be arranged in such a way that bondholders and shareholders face exactly the same risks as at present, so that their respective discount rates of 0.05 and 0.10 should remain relevant. This rather strong set of assumptions allows us to proceed confidently to evaluate the investment by calculating the present value (PV) of its future expected earnings using MVWACC as discount rate:

$$PV = \frac{£10}{1.0833} + \frac{£15}{1.0833^2} = £22.013$$
$$(£9.231) \quad (£12.782)$$

According to the NPV/MVWACC approach, therefore, the investment is marginally acceptable, in the sense that it will increase the firm's value by an amount exactly equal to its cost.

To confirm the investment's marginal acceptability, as well as the reliability of the NPV/MVWACC approach, we now try to establish that its expected equity earnings when discounted by the equity discount rate ($k = 0.10$) are exactly equal to the amount of equity investment involved in its financing. Given our simplifying assumptions about the risks of the incremental earnings distributions and their perfect correlation with the permanent Q distribution, it is easy to calculate the appropriate levels of incremental equity earnings for years 1 and 2; these are £8 and £12, respectively (in each case 80 per cent of the full incremental earnings expectation, just as $(\bar{Q} - iB)$ is equal to 80 per cent of $\bar{Q}$). Incremental equity expectations of these amounts will create total equity expectations for years 1 and 2 (£88 and £92, respectively) that are exactly as risky as the regular expectation of £80, so the appropriate discount rate must be that applying to the latter, i.e. $k = 0.10$. This means that the incremental income prospects of bondholders for years 1 and 2 must be £2 and £3, respectively, which allows us to calculate the amount of new debt actually raised, ΔB at an interest rate of 5 per cent per annum, as a contribution to the investment's financing:

$$\Delta B = \frac{£2}{1.05} + \frac{£3}{1.05^2} = £4.626$$

This means that the new equity investment required is £17.387 (£22.013 − £4.626), and if our reasoning is sound this amount ought to equal the present value of the incremental equity income expectations for years 1 and 2, discounted at the firm's standard equity cost of capital. In fact the latter present value is as follows:

$$\frac{£8}{1.10} + \frac{£12}{1.10^2} = £17.190$$

As might have been expected in the light of our earlier doubts on the accuracy of MVWACC in relation to the valuation of *individual* expectations, the investment turns out to be unacceptable as far as equity investors are concerned. In effect, the NPV/MVWACC approach is shown to place higher valuations on early expectations than the separate discounting of their properly calculated components justifies. This means that in general the NPV/MVWACC approach is inclined to approve proposals that should be rejected, but in our example at least the degree of bias is not serious.

Evidently the NPV/MVWACC approach loses at least some of its authority when the investment in question possesses a ΔQ distribution that shifts over time, a characteristic that must surely apply to the great majority of investments. This line of criticism can obviously be extended to take into account the probability that – unlike the investment in our example – an investment's earnings prospects over its lifetime will *not* leave the firm's overall business risk unaltered. Of course it is open to a practically-minded proponent of NPV/MVWACC to point out that the degree of bias we have observed (i.e. the tendency for NPV/MVWACC to accept proposals that should be rejected) is slight, and that this bias is predictable and therefore easy to allow for.

In the light of these remarks it appears that a sensible compromise is within reach. The NPV/MVWACC approach can be applied to the generality of investment proposals with little risk of serious error. The method does require to be supplemented in each case by a calculation to determine the amount of debt financing and the time pattern of incremental payments to bondholders. This calculation affords an opportunity to identify for each year the incremental equity income expectation, assess the risk of the overall equity prospect for that year and decide whether any significant deviation from the standard or normal level of risk is implied by the overall earnings prospect and financing plan. The important question must be whether the value of revised equity prospects, discounted at the firm's equity discount rate, is higher in relation to the original equilibrium equity valuation by an amount at least as great as the amount of new equity capital required.

Finally, the market value weights embodied in MVWACC are clearly those of a 'static risk' enterprise; but if a firm has growth prospects that are anticipated by the market the value of its equity will exceed the simple capitalisation of its next expected dividend. In these circumstances should the (unobserved) static weights or the actual weights be used in calculating MVWACC? It can be shown that the use of static weights is correct (Baker, 1978, pp. 118-25), but even without a formal proof it is intuitively obvious, at least in the traditional framework of analysis, that in the absence of capital rationing the acceptability of one investment should not depend on the expectations of the market with regard to the firm's other and quite unrelated investment prospects.

A rather different criticism of actual market value weights is that the volatility of market valuations implies considerable, and possibly perverse, fluctuations in MVWACC (Merrett and Sykes, 1963, pp. 120-1). One direction in which such criticism points is towards the use of book value rather than market value weights. Without embarking on detailed discussion of this approach the objections to which should be obvious in the light of our analysis of MVWACC, it can be suggested that the foregoing argument in favour of the 'static' weights that would be observed in equilibrium capital market conditions also seems applicable to the difficulty raised by the likelihood of fluctuations in actual market values.

8.5 The Modigliani and Miller Debate

8.5 (i) The 'Irrelevance' of Capital Structure

In their celebrated 1958 paper, Modigliani and Miller (M & M) inaugurated a debate on valuation that remains unresolved after more than twenty years of vigorous and sustained interchanges between various points of view (Modigliani and Miller, 1958). This debate has ranged widely but is concerned ultimately with the nature of the equilibrium we should expect to observe in the capital market, given the beliefs and motivations of decision makers and the informational, legal and institutional constraints under which they operate. Our main purpose in this section is to show the implications of the M & M view of market equilibrium for a firm's cost of capital. With or without corporate taxation (for a different reason in each case), M & M dispute the traditional concept of optimum capital structure. We shall also try to confront the undoubted logic of the M & M position with some of the real-world considerations that have given rise to doubts about its practical relevance.

We begin by assuming the absence of corporate taxation, because it is in this setting that M & M's view of the relevance of capital structure to the firm's cost of capital differs most strikingly from the traditional. In their 1958 paper M & M argued that if individual shareholders can borrow on the same terms and in the same proportionate amounts as companies, and if transactions in financial markets are costless, it will be impossible for companies which are identical in all respects other than capital structure to have different overall market values; that is, the sum of S plus B must be constant irrespective of capital structure. If, for example, a company (L) with debt in its capital structure. momentarily enjoys a higher overall market value than an otherwise identical unlevered company (U), some shareholders in L will sell their holdings, borrow in amounts equal to the borrowing company L had undertaken on their behalf (and at the same interest rate) and purchase the shares of company U. Because U is cheaper than L, shareholders in L who engage in this kind of arbitrage are able to purchase larger holdings in U and have a higher expected income after interest payments, with no change in the effective risk or leverage in their portfolios. As long as the value of company L exceeds that of company U, arbitrage of this kind will be profitable; and M & M concluded that market forces would drive the overall values of U and L together and maintain their equality.

8.5 (ii) Comments on Modigliani and Miller

We have now outlined M & M's case for the irrelevance of capital structure in the absence of corporate taxation. The consensus among sceptics is that while the M & M logic is difficult to fault at its own level of abstraction, there are a number of real-world aspects, apart from corporate taxation which we shall consider shortly, which cannot be ignored. Some of these at least are thought likely to confer valuation (and cost of capital) advantages on levered firms. Here we offer no more than a brief enumeration of some of the main areas of the debate on the workings of the capital market that has grown out of M & M's original attack on traditional thinking (Bromwich, 1976, pp. 153–67, provides a wide-ranging review of the debate).

First, one may doubt whether individuals and institutions can in fact borrow on the same terms, or wish to borrow in the same relative amounts as companies. Yet these assumptions are crucial to M & M's capital structure 'irrelevance' proposition. If companies can borrow more cheaply than individuals, or in greater proportionate amounts, levered companies will retain a valuation advantage in the market. Quite apart from the empirically verifiable facts concerning rates of interest paid by companies and shareholders, and legal and institutional

constraints affecting some investing institutions' and private shareholders' borrowing or investing behaviour, we may be sceptical about
the proposition that an investor will be completely indifferent between
equal amounts of 'home-made' and 'built-in' leverage.

This doubt is partially related to a second factor, the possibility of
business bankruptcy; and here the arguments appear to point in
different directions. On the one hand it is argued that a given amount
of personal leverage involves the individual in a greater risk than an
equal amount of leverage provided by a company, if business bankruptcy resulting in losses by equity investors is a possibility.

To return to our earlier example, an investor in L stands to lose only
the value of his shares if L goes bankrupt while he is a shareholder. But
if he invests in company U with the help of borrowed funds, his
potential loss is greater by the amount of his personal leverage.

On the other hand, the presence of leverage in a company's capital
structure, having the effect of increasing its fixed costs, may actually
increase the risk of bankruptcy; and this would *increase* the attractiveness of unlevered concerns if bankruptcy is believed by investors to be a
potentially costly possibility. But if we assume that leverage is
deliberately kept within conservative limits by internal policy or
external pressures (Merrett and Sykes, 1963, pp. 117, 397–8), neither
side of the business bankruptcy argument can have much bearing on a
realistic evaluation of the M & M position.

M & M have also been criticised over the 'extreme leverage' implications of their argument that the firm's market value and cost of capital
are invariant with respect to leverage. If the total value of the firm is to
remain constant as debt is increased in the absence of corporate
taxation, the equity cost component of the firm's (constant) MVWACC
must eventually begin to behave in an implausible fashion. The rate of
interest on debt is bound to increase at some stage in the expansion
of debt as the bond market adjusts its views of the risks involved in
lending to the firm in question in larger and larger amounts. Whereas
the cost of equity, k, is usually assumed to increase when debt increases
(see Figure 8.2), M & M's theory implies that if V and MVWACC are
to remain constant the rise in the interest rate must be offset by, at
first, a decelerating rise in k; and eventually by a fall in k! Nor is it
correct to dismiss this issue as one of only theoretical interest, given
the unattainability of excessively high levels of leverage in practice.
As the reader can readily confirm with the aid of a simple numerical
example, the rise in k begins to decelerate as soon as the rate of interest
begins to rise; and this may occur at a level of debt well short of the

dangerously excessive levels envisaged by M & M in their ingenious but unsatisfactory explanation of the paradox (Modigliani and Miller, 1958, pp. 275-6).

8.5 (iii) M & M and Corporate Taxation

Once corporate taxation is recognised, M & M accept that capital structure is no longer irrelevant to the firm's value, but their reasoning and policy recommendation again differ from the traditional. Under a tax system in which interest payments are tax deductible, the after-tax level of earnings can be increased by greater leverage. In traditional·analysis this factor reinforces the argument presented earlier (8.3 (iii)) as far as the downward-sloping part of the c schedule is concerned, but ultimately c must increase with leverage as k (and probably i) increases. In the M & M analysis this upturn does not occur, and the cost of capital goes on falling as long as the firm continues to add to its tax saving by increasing its debt (Modigliani and Miller, 1963). However, this view appears to ignore the likelihood that at high levels of leverage the value of the firm *will* decline due to the increasing risk of bankruptcy, implying the existence of an optimum capital structure of a quasi-traditional kind (Van Horne, 1977, pp. 251-3; Archer *et al.*, 1979, pp. 246-8).

8.6 Conclusion

Our principal aims in this chapter have been to develop the MVWACC concept, to consider the possible effects of capital structure on MVWACC and to draw some preliminary conclusions on the relevance and usefulness of MVWACC in investment decision making. The last of these themes will return in Chapter 10, when we consider objections to the traditional approach to valuation and cost of capital from the standpoint of the portfolio theory of capital market equilibrium. For the moment we note that although the limitations of the MVWACC concept in investment decision making are widely recognised, not all theorists view these as sufficiently serious to disqualify the concept completely.

Qualified support for suitably modified variants of MVWACC is fairly common (Solomon, 1963, pp. 87-8; Samuels and Wilkes, 1975, p. 147; and Quirin, 1967, pp. 137-40); and for the present at least we concur with these pragmatic judgements. Compared with less sophisticated techniques of investment appraisal (see Merrett and

Sykes, 1963, pp. 219-40), any technique involving MWVACC, either as discount rate or target value for internal rate of return, must be strongly preferred; and much work remains to be done before an investment criterion developed from a portfolio theory-based valuation model can completely replace a criterion based on the traditional approach.

9 ASPECTS OF CAPITAL BUDGETING

There is such a choice of difficulties that
I am myself at a loss how to determine.

James Wolfe

9.1 Introduction

Capital budgeting has become an enormously wide-ranging discipline, and within a single chapter its variety of subject areas, techniques and theoretical connections can hardly be given full coverage. But our progression in this chapter is intended to give some idea of how the subject extends from somewhat mechanical but nonetheless useful variations on the basic theme of the NPV/MVWACC criterion (e.g. the lifetime/retirement calculations of Section 2) through areas of dispute on the application of basic theory (e.g. the capital rationing debate in Section 3) to the fringes of modern 'managerial' theories of the firm (the various models of risk taking in Sections 4 and 5).

Two topics in particular receive less attention here than is customary in expositions of capital budgeting theory and practice. The theoretical debate between the net present value (NPV) and internal rate of return (IRR) concepts of investment profitability is one which may already be familiar to readers, and it seems appropriate to deal with the main issues raised in this debate in an Appendix to this chapter. Readers who are uncertain of these issues should read the Appendix before proceeding with the material in the chapter. (The NPV *versus* IRR debate also figures in our discussion of capital rationing in 9.3.) Our broad preference throughout the chapter for the NPV approach to profitability measurement stems both from doubts about the IRR concept expressed in the Appendix, and from the obvious appropriateness of a measure of investment profitability defined in broadly the same terms as management is assumed to adopt in framing the firm's overall financial objective, namely the market's valuation of shareholders' wealth.

The second omission from this chapter is the application of decision tree analysis to sequential investment decision making. However, this topic is generally well covered in standard texts and in articles (e.g. Levy and Sarnat, 1978, pp. 196–202; Magee, 1964 and 1964a; and Hespos and Strassman, 1965), and the relevant principles have been explained in Chapter 7.

The reader's familiarity with the basic concept of discounting cash flows, and with the use of discount tables, is taken for granted. Discount tables are widely available, either as appendices to texts on business finance and capital budgeting, or in compilations of mathematical, statistical and financial tables such as Kmietowicz and Yannoulis (1976). Our treatment of cash flow discounting conforms to standard practice in that we adopt the convenient assumption that cash flows occur at the *end* of the year in question. This has the obvious attraction of greatly simplifying the calculations involved in cash flow analysis, at the cost in most cases of a minimal amount of bias in the results.

9.2 Replacement, Retirement and Timing

9.2 (i) Optimum Lifetime for a Once-only Investment

Many textbooks give examples of NPV or IRR calculations in which the lifetime of the asset in question is stated without discussion. (Similarly, the timing of an asset's introduction is often not discussed.) We shall distinguish two different theoretical rules for the optimum lifetime of an asset, but as we shall see it is not always possible in practice to determine at the planning stage which rule is applicable.

First we consider a once-only investment, one that as far as can be seen at present will not be replaced on the eventual disposal of the assets involved. Strictly speaking, the investment must be self-contained in the sense that no other investment's timing (introduction or termination) is affected by the decision taken about its lifetime. In this case the obviously appropriate plan is to choose the investment lifetime having the highest NPV. A single investment's NPV depends on its planned lifetime, n years, as follows:

$$\text{NPV}(n) = -I + \sum_{t=1}^{n} \frac{R_t}{(1+c)^t} + \frac{D_n}{(1+c)^n} \qquad \text{(i)}$$

where $\text{NPV}(n)$ is the net present value for a planned lifetime of n years, I is the initial cost of the investment, R_t ($t = 1 \ldots n$) is the return generated by the investment in year t, D_n is the disposal value of the investment on its retirement after n years and c is the firm's cost of capital. At the planning stage the firm chooses n to maximise $\text{NPV}(n)$.

It is obviously important for the logic of this criterion that the planned retirement date will continue to appear optimal throughout the project's life, assuming cost and revenue develop as expected. Given that $NPV(j - 1) < NPV(j) > NPV(j + 1)$, so that j years is the optimum lifetime for the project as seen from the present, the reader can easily confirm that retirement after j years will continue to appear optimal by comparing the NPVs of (a) retention for one more year and (b) immediate retirement that will obtain at any date up to and including end-year j. (Recall that at any date all past expenditures and revenues are bygones, and should not influence decision making; see Mao, 1969, pp. 331-6.)

9.2 (ii) Optimum Retirement Age for Investments in a Series

Turning now to investments that will be replaced at the end of their physical lifetimes, it will be useful to begin by discussing a revenue-generating project, though this part of optimum lifetime theory is perhaps more applicable to cost-minimising investments. In the absence of definite information about the future, one convenient assumption is that of an 'infinite chain' of replacements, identical in all respects, exploiting a continuing and unchanging investment opportunity. Management's proper objective now is to maximise the NPV of an infinite series of identical assets, each replaced at the same age. Let this overall net present value measure for a standard asset life of k years be denoted by $NPV(k)$, and let the net present value of each separate k-year lifetime at its starting date be npv_k. Then

$$NPV(k) = npv_k + \frac{npv_k}{(1 + c)^k} + \frac{npv_k}{(1 + c)^{2k}} + \frac{npv_k}{(1 + c)^{3k}} \cdots \infty \qquad \text{(ii)}$$

$NPV(k)$ is to be maximised with respect to k. Our commonsense expectation is that an optimum replacement date does exist, balancing the considerations of frequent *versus* infrequent capital outlays, and high average earnings from a frequently replaced asset *versus* lower average earnings from an infrequently replaced asset.

The determination of the optimum value of k is made simple if we recognise that in essence the firm is seeking to maximise its annual average return from the opportunity in question. (An alternative solution approach is explained by Mao, 1969, pp. 336-41. Whichever method is used must give the same result, so a choice can be made on the grounds of convenience.) This implies that the lifetime of *each* investment in the chain should be such as to maximise the average annual return it yields; by choosing this lifetime, k*, for all identical investments in the chain, the value of $NPV(k)$ will by definition be maximised. The costs incurred and the gains generated by the investment during its lifetime can be averaged to yield an *equivalent annual* *benefit* (EAB), a concept that differs from a simple annual average only in its recognition of the importance of discounting. Thus for an assumed asset lifetime of k years, for which the net present value is known to be npv_k, we identify the hypothetical average annual return, EAB_k, to which the actual cash flows of the investment are, by definition, equivalent:

$$npv_k = \frac{EAB_k}{1+c} + \frac{EAB_k}{(1+c)^2} + \ldots \frac{EAB_k}{(1+c)^k} = EAB_k \sum_{t=1}^{k} \frac{1}{(1+c)^t} \qquad (iii)$$

Finding EAB_k for any value of k simply involves (1) finding npv_k from the project's actual cash flows over a k-year lifetime and (2) dividing npv_k by the sum of the discount factors for that lifetime:

$$EAB_k = \frac{npv_k}{\sum_{t=1}^{k} \frac{1}{(1+c)^t}} \qquad (iv)$$

By choosing k to maximise EAB_k, that is k^*, management attains its objective of maximising NPV(k). (Note that in (iv) if c = 0, EAB_k reverts to a simple annual average of the investment's cash flows over k years.) The reader may wish to confirm algebraically that maximising the EAB of an individual asset actually maximises the NPV of an infinite chain of identical assets; and that for any lifetime k, NPV(k) = EAB_k/c.

If the investment in question is 'well-behaved' in the sense that its annual return and disposal value both decline with the age of the asset in the range of lifetimes we consider, we expect EAB_k to behave in the way shown in Figure 9.1a (Figure 9.1b is discussed in 9.2 (iii) below).

Figure 9.1: Equivalent Annual Benefit (EAB) and Equivalent Annual Cost (EAC)

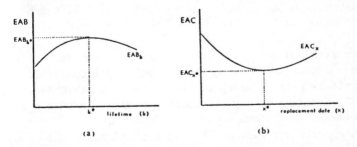

9.2 (iii) Minimising the Present Value of Costs

The relevance of the infinite chain assumption in replacement planning is perhaps greatest in cost-minimising situations. Items of equipment which perform a continuing function in the firm's production process, and whose contribution to profit is best expressed in terms of the lowering of costs rather than the direct generation of revenue, fall into this category. Again we assume an infinite chain of identical replacements, and apart from conducting a minimising rather than a maximising exercise the procedure is exactly as described in 9.2 (ii). Let the cost in year t of operating the equipment in question be C_t. (Other symbols retain their earlier meanings.) The net present value of costs for a lifetime of n years, $npvc_n$, is given by

$$npvc_n = I + \sum_{t=1}^{n} \frac{C_t}{(1+c)^t} - \frac{D_n}{(1+c)^n} \tag{v}$$

where the negative sign preceding the final term reflects the fact that D_n is a negative cost in this context. As before, it is convenient to convert $npvc_n$ into its hypothetical annual equivalent, in this case the *equivalent annual cost* (EAC). Following the same argument used in 9.2 (ii), we obtain a relationship between $npvc_x$ and EAC_x for any given lifetime, x:

$$EAC_x = \frac{npvc_x}{\sum_{t=1}^{x} \frac{1}{(1+c)^t}} \tag{vi}$$

The firm chooses x to minimise the value of EAC_x, thereby minimising the net present value of all future costs in an infinite chain of identical replacements. If the time patterns of C_t and D_t are 'well behaved', we expect the schedule of EAC_x to have the shape illustrated in Figure 9.1b, with x^* the optimum lifetime of each item in the series.

This framework has proved extremely versatile and helpful in such areas of decision as (1) the choice between alternative items of equipment, (2) the optimal date for 'switching' from a current model to a superior model, (3) whether a replacement due in the near future should be delayed until an anticipated improved model becomes available, and (4) whether an existing asset is worth overhauling rather than replacing. The analysis is very similar in all cases, and is illustrated by a composite example involving applications (2) and (4).

A newly developed machine will form part of a continuing and unchanging production process. Its initial cost is £100,000, and its end-year operating and maintenance costs and disposal values are as follows (£'000):

	end-year					
	1	2	3	4	5	6
operating and maintenance costs (C_t)	20	25	32	40	50	62
disposal value (D_t)	70	50	35	22	12	7

The company uses a discount rate of 8 per cent per annum.

The reader can confirm that a lifetime of three years is optimal, the relevant calculations being the following:

$$\text{npvc}_3 (\text{\pounds'000}) = 100 + \frac{20}{1.08} + \frac{25}{1.08^2} + \frac{32}{1.08^3} - \frac{35}{1.08^3}$$

$$= 137.5691$$

$$\text{EAC}_3 (\text{\pounds'000}) = \frac{\text{npvc}_3}{\sum_{t=1}^{3} \frac{1}{1.08^t}} = \frac{137.5691}{2.5771} = 53.3813$$

When should the new type of equipment, whose optimum lifetime we have now determined, replace the firm's existing equipment? The latter's time patterns of C_t and D_t in the future are estimated to be as follows (£'000):

	end-year			
	0	1	2	3
C_t		40	50	60
D_t	35	25	19	13

The question the decision maker must ask himself at the close of each year is 'should I retain my present equipment for one more year, or replace it with the new equipment whose minimum EAC I know to be £53,381.3?' The cost of continuing to use existing equipment for one more year is the sum of three components: (1) operating and maintenance cost for the coming year, (2) the decline in disposal value during the coming year, and (3) the opportunity cost of 'investing' funds in the existing equipment for one more year (in this case 8 per cent of its disposal value at the close of the present year). Applying this three-part cost concept to the data given above, the cost of continuing with the existing equipment for one more year will be £52,800 (£40,000 + £10,000 + £2,800) – a lower figure than the equivalent annual cost implied by an immediate switch to new equipment. An analogous calculation for a second year of delay yields a cost of £58,000 (£50,000 + £6,000 + £2,000), and it follows that the old equipment should be replaced after just one more year of use.

Suppose now that an immediate overhaul of the present equipment is possible, so that instead of the cost and disposal values given in the last paragraph, the following values would apply (£'000):

	end-year			
	1	2	3	4
C_t	35	40	49	58
D_t	30	20	13	10

Given the firm's cost of capital of 8 per cent per annum, how much should the firm be prepared to pay for the overhaul? Before answering this question we must first determine the optimum lifetime of over-hauled equipment, bearing in mind that once undertaken the cost of the overhaul becomes a bygone expense and should not influence subsequent decisions. This preliminary question is answered in terms of the comparison described above, and inspection of the data shows that replacement should occur after *two* more years:

cost for year 2 (£'000) = 40 + 10 + 2.4 = 52.4 (£'000)

cost for year 3 (£'000) = 49 + 7 + 1.6 = 57.6 (£'000)

We are now in a position to calculate the present value of the savings that will be generated by the overhaul during the two years in which present equipment will continue to operate. The proper comparisons are shown in Table 9.1. For each option a dotted vertical line marks the date at which the present equipment will be replaced. The actual cash flows for each option up to replacement are shown, with X representing the as yet unknown overhaul cost; thereafter the minimum EAC on new equipment is shown. This procedure, which limits the comparison between options (1) and (2) to just two periods in this case, is perfectly

Table 9.1: Cost Comparison for Overhaul Decision (£'000)

		end-year			
		0	1	2	3
(1)	No overhaul		$\begin{bmatrix} 40 \\ -25 \end{bmatrix}$:	53.3813	53.3813 ...
(2)	Overhaul	X	35	$\begin{bmatrix} 40 \\ -20 \end{bmatrix}$:	53.3813 ...
(3)	Savings due to over overhaul	−X	−20	+33.3813	0 ...

justifiable in the sense that investors are by definition indifferent between a hypothetical constant annual cash flow and the actual cash flows to which it is equivalent. The final line of the table shows the savings due to the overhaul, and it is easy to calculate the value of X at which the net present value of savings would equal zero. Denoting this critical value of X by X*, we have

$$X^* = \frac{-20}{1.08} + \frac{33.3813}{1.08^2} = 10.099 \ (\text{£'000})$$

An overhaul costing up to £10,099 is worthwhile; beyond that amount the overhaul would have a negative net present value.

This extended example illustrates both the versatility and simplicity of the equivalent annual cost (or benefit) concept and the importance of the timing aspect of investment decisions. In this context at least it can be seen that the admittedly unrealistic assumption of an infinite chain of identical replacements does not have a major influence on the decision, which is obviously dominated by the immediate and near-immediate cash flow prospects (or their equivalents); and these are known with a high degree of confidence. And whatever the true value of EAC for the remote future, it can hardly differ significantly between options (1) and (2) in Table 9.1. In this and other commonsense ways the lack of realism in the infinite chain assumption can usually be adequately bypassed.

9.3 Capital Rationing

9.3 (i) Capital Rationing Situations

Many writers use the term 'capital rationing' in a very broad sense, to include any situation in which a firm experiences a supply schedule of investment funds that is not horizontal at the level of the firm's long-run average cost of capital. Such situations are usually categorised as either 'external' or 'internal' in origin. External capital rationing refers to factors outside management's control which may in the short term limit the amount of finance available or alter the terms on which finance can be obtained. The need to resort to external equity financing (perhaps during a period of depressed stock market prices) and temporarily high costs of long-term debt financing are examples of factors which can cause a firm's short-run marginal cost of capital to exceed its long-run average cost. Given an investment demand schedule descending in steps and a marginal cost of capital schedule rising in steps, a solution is easy to envisage when the heights and lengths of all steps on each schedule are known (Brigham, 1979, p. 575). But when one or other or both schedules are not identified with certainty, e.g. when a period's investment opportunities are not all apparent at exactly the same date, an approximate step-by-step matching of anticipated demands and supplies of funds can produce a reasonable approximation to the neat but unattainable textbook solution (Porterfield, 1963, pp. 82–4).

Some writers are inclined to minimise the significance of external capital rationing, arguing that firms often deliberately limit their demands for funds to the horizontal sections of their short-run marginal cost curves, where short and long-run costs are equal (see following paragraph). An alternative interpretation is that a firm's investment planning proceeds broadly in step with its forecasts of internally generated capital supplies, so that on most occasions no question of external constraints arises. This interpretation is strengthened if the firm's planning period is of longer duration than the standard accounting year, giving management time to schedule its investment outlays and financing in such a way that no departure from long-run average cost need occur.

To argue in this way does not of course dispose of the issue of capital rationing, for we have conceded that rationing may be imposed internally, in the form of a strict upper limit on the amount of funds the firm permits itself to invest. Few writers approve in principle of an arbitrary limit on investment, a limit which implies an infinitely high marginal cost of capital. But numerous explanations of such a policy have been suggested, not all of them unsympathetic (contrast Van Horne, 1977, pp. 98-9, and Solomon and Pringle, 1977, p. 409). These include a simple reluctance on management's part to become involved in external equity financing; a scarcity of one or more key non-financial resources in the firm, making it impossible to absorb more than a limited amount of new investment (Weston and Brigham, 1979, pp. 227-8; and Penrose, 1959, Ch. 4); and a multi-divisional company structure in which each division or branch is assigned a strict spending limit (Archer, Choate and Racette, 1979, p. 480). These explanations are readily understandable even if their effects are condemned, and here we concentrate on the theoretical and practical problems to which internal capital rationing gives rise.

9.3 (ii) One-Period Rationing, One-Period Projects

Because of the great variety of possible assumptions relating to such aspects of capital rationing as the nature of the rationing, the post-ponability of projects and the relationships between proposals, it seems sensible to theorise on a case-by-case basis. Here we consider only the most tractable of rationing problems, that of a strict upper limit on the volume of investment that is expected to operate for one period only. We also assume that each proposal considered is independent, that is, its acceptance or rejection (a) neither precludes nor requires the acceptance of any other proposal, and (b) makes no difference to the prospects of any other proposal. Assuming management is generally successful in bringing forward investment plans broadly matching capital supplies at a constant cost of capital, the most probable reason for a one-period rationing situation is an unusual 'bunching' of investment demands within the period in question. There are two separate cases to consider: (1) where investments that cannot be undertaken for lack of finance are lost forever, and (2) where some investments at least can be postponed. In this and the following sub-section we consider case (1), and in 9.3 (iv) case (2) is discussed. We must also recognise that our recommendation may depend on whether or not investment projects are divisible.

The main theoretical issue posed by capital rationing is whether the firm's cost of capital, based as we have seen on the assumption that capital is available at a constant cost (the long-run average cost of capital), loses its relevance for calculating project NPVs in a rationing situation. The practical importance of this theoretical debate can be shown by developing the one-period rationing problem from its

Table 9.2: One-Period Rationing, Alternative Project Rankings

Project	Initial outlay (£)	Payoff after one year (£)	IRR	NPV (£)	NPV per £ (£)
A	100	120	0.20	9.091	0.0909
B	300	345	0.15	13.64	0.045
C	60	70	0.167	3.636	0.061

simplest form to more complex possibilities. Table 9.2 presents data for three one-year investment projects (A, B and C). For each project the initial outlay and terminal payoff (after one year in each case) are given, along with three different measures of investment acceptability: internal rate of return (IRR), net present value (NPV), and net present value per £ invested (NPV per £). The company's normal cost of capital, used in calculating NPVs, is assumed to be 10 per cent per annum.

When investment funds are scarce it is logical that the allocation criterion adopted should reflect that fact, and both IRR and NPV per £ can claim to meet this need. Accepting projects in descending order of IRR is one commonsense way of ensuring a maximum return from scarce funds, though this rule is complicated as we shall see when projects are not completely divisible. Similarly, accepting projects in descending order of NPV per £ seems sensible, though the appropriateness of the firm's 'normal' discount rate for this purpose may be questioned. In fact, for one-period investments the rankings given by IRR and NPV per £ for *any* given discount rate must be the same, as the reader can readily demonstrate algebraically, so the issue of which discount rate is theoretically correct can be shelved for the moment.

Divisibility of Projects. If the firm can invest in any fraction of any project to obtain the project's NPV per £ and IRR per £, the solution to the one-period rationing problem is straightforward. In Table 9.2, for any budget up to £100 management should invest in A; for a budget between £100 and £160, A and a fraction of C should be chosen; and beyond £160 projects A, C and part of B should be chosen. This procedure maximises the firm's NPV from its temporarily scarce supply of investment funds; or, in terms of a rate of return ranking, it ensures the maximum return from the available funds. Full divisibility of projects may be a physical impossibility, but the scale on which a project is undertaken may well be variable; whether the profitability of each £1 committed to a project is identical is, of course, doubtful.

Indivisibility of Projects. If projects are evaluated on an 'all-or-nothing' basis, it may happen that acceptance of a small project with a high IRR and NPV per £ results in the exclusion of a larger project that is less profitable per unit of funds invested but more profitable in total. In this situation it is perhaps more helpful to think in terms of maximising the net present value to investors of the investments chosen, and Table 9.3 shows the choices that would be made at different levels of spending constraint, F. We assume that money not invested in projects has a zero net present value, being used for example to pay dividends to the shareholders (who are not themselves subject to capital rationing).

Table 9.3: Investment Choice for Various Levels of Budget Constraint

	Project indivisibility		Choices assuming project divisibility
	Choices	NPV (£)	
F < £60	no investment	0 ⎱	part of A
£60 ≤ F < £100	C	3.636 ⎰	
£100 ≤ F < £160	A	9.091	A + part of C
£160 ≤ F < £300	A and C	12.727 ⎫	
£300 ≤ F < £360	B	13.640	
£360 ≤ F < £400	B and C	17.276 ⎬ A, C + part of B	
£400 ≤ F < £460	A and B	22.731	
£460 ≤ F	A, B and C	26.367 ⎭	A, B and C

The choice of projects assuming indivisibility should be compared with that under divisibility, also shown in Table 9.3. The latter is obviously a smooth progression, each project in its turn being admitted in larger amounts as the budget constraint is relaxed. When projects are indivisible a good deal of switching can occur, with projects entering the selection at one level of constraint, departing at a higher level and finally re-entering when the constraint ceases to apply. One particularly interesting switch occurs when F reaches the level of £300: project B is marginally preferred to A plus C, although *both* of the latter have higher IRR and NPV values per £ than B. This illustrates the possibility of a large but low yielding project being preferred to one or more high-yielding but smaller projects.

9.3 (iii) One-Period Rationing, Multi-Period Projects

When projects have a longer life span than the anticipated one-period duration of rationing, a more difficult problem in choice of criterion presents itself, because the equality of project rankings according to IRR and NPV per £ no longer holds. One suggestion is that the firm should select projects in descending order of IRR (subject of course to the need to allow for the 'crowding out' problem already described in the case of project indivisibility) until the investment budget is exhausted (Quirin, 1967, pp. 179-81). This procedure identifies the IRR of the best project *not* selected, which by definition exceeds the firm's normal cost of capital, and this rate can be employed as the appropriate discount rate for the calculation of the NPVs of the chosen projects. The reasoning behind this approach is that the firm's normal cost of capital has lost its relevance as a measure of opportunity cost for the time being; but in the case of a multi-divisional company structure in which each division has its own capital constraint the true opportunity cost for the business as a whole is unlikely to be apparent to any individual decision maker.

An alternative view is that the best interests of investors are served by maximising the net present value of investments chosen, using the normal cost of capital as discount rate, on the grounds that investors themselves are not subject to capital rationing in the way that the firm is (Lorie and Savage, 1955; Elton, 1970; and Myers, 1972). According to this view, investors will prefer management to select those investments which the market will value most highly, because this will place them in the best possible position — given the firm's constraint on investment — to maximise their own utility through consumption and saving or borrowing. This certainly begs the question whether, in the short period during which capital rationing is in force, the market valuation of the firm actually reflects the investment decisions it takes; but in terms of the valuation of benefits accruing to long-term investors it seems a stronger argument than its alternative. The implications of both approaches are clearly demonstrated in Bromwich (1976), pp. 204-21.

However, the choice between the IRR and NPV per £ measures of profitability in this context may be a false and unnecessary one. As stated, the two criteria give identical rankings when projects all mature in one period, and a reconciliation between the two for the general case of multi-period projects depends on transforming each project into an 'equivalent' one-period project. This can be done by using the method explained in the Appendix to this chapter (9A (v)), reducing each future cash flow to the present value it will have in one year's time, when rationing is over and the normal discount rate is once again relevant. For each project the cash flows due at end-year 2 and later are discounted at the normal rate to end-year 1 and added to the amount due at that date. This results in each project being represented by just two cash flows: an immediate outlay and an amount at end-year 1 equal to the market valuation at that date of its current and future returns. Once projects are converted into the equivalents of one-year projects in this way, the equivalence between IRR and NPV per £ rankings already referred to resolves any dilemma over choice of criterion.

However, an argument for ranking projects according to their *unadjusted* IRRs in a capital rationing situation is that cash flow in the near future is thereby likely to be maximised (Quirin, 1967, pp.179-81). This may help to relieve capital shortages in the near future, though of course no explicit expectation of future shortage has been incorporated in our calculations (nor is it obvious that the idea would appeal to managers who anticipated a possible recurrence of capital shortage in the more distant future). One other possible justification for this approach is that the prospect of substantial early cash returns on investment may actually help to relieve the immediate capital shortage, for example by making the firm's bankers more willing to finance current investment spending.

9.3 (iv) Postponability of Projects

Our discussion so far has focused on what is arguably the less likely case — that projects not accepted during a period of capital rationing are lost forever. Posing the problem in terms of 'which projects should be postponed?' is probably more realistic. Table 9.4 illustrates the nature of one-period capital rationing when some projects at least can be postponed — at a cost.

All of the proposals listed in Table 9.4 are acceptable, having positive NPVs (using the firm's normal discount rate), and with the exception of U all projects will be accepted in the future if not undertaken immediately. Each entry in column (iv) is the NPV *at the present*

Table 9.4: NPV Losses Through Postponement

(i) Project	(ii) Cost (£)	(iii) NPV (start now) (£)	(iv) NPV (start next year) (£)	(v) NPV loss per £
P	100	30	27	0.03
Q	200	50	36	0.07
R	50	10	7	0.06
S	50	9	8	0.02
T	100	15	14	0.01
U	50	5	0	0.10

day of the project in question, assuming its start to be delayed by one year. The sensible objective here is to minimise the overall loss of NPV due to capital rationing, and to do this it is helpful to know the NPV loss per £ of investment due to postponement; this is shown in column (v) of the table. If all projects are divisible, project selection can proceed in descending order of loss per £, so that for example if the sum available for investment is £350 the projects chosen will be U, Q, R and half of P. If projects are indivisible the 'crowding out' problem described in 9.3 (ii) may occur. Thus, if funds are limited to £200 it would be possible to select project U, which has the highest NPV loss per £, along with R and P – making a total NPV 'saving' of £11. But project Q, which would absorb the whole of the available £200, offers a saving of £14 although its NPV loss per £1 is lower than that of U.

9.3 (v) Relaxing the Capital Constraint

The striking feature of the capital rationing framework we have been considering is its rigidity, and this is obviously its least believable aspect. One indication of this is that in the selection procedures we have discussed the shadow value of scarce investment funds has usually been readily identifiable, and it is perhaps sensible to see those procedures as establishing a preliminary selection of projects as well as a measure of the cost imposed on the firm by the funds constraint. As an example, with an investment budget of £200 in Table 9.4 above, and no project divisibility, the NPV saving attributable to an additional £50 would be £5 (due to the inclusion of U in the investment plan).

Moves to improve the preliminary solution to the rationing problem can take a number of forms. First, the search for additional resources can proceed on the basis of an accurate measure of their contribution to the valuation of the firm. Second, the timetables of many projects embody possibilities for delaying outlays that are not immediately crucial. Third, even if projects are not fully divisible, it is often the case that an investment opportunity permits considerable discretion as to the size of the outlay. It is interesting that the preliminary solution, in addition to yielding a measure of the shadow value of resources on the basis of project indivisibility, indicates the size of gain that could be achieved through project divisibility or scaling. Returning again to Table 9.4 and an investment budget of £200, the NPV saving of £14 under indivisibility could be increased to one of £15.5 if project Q could be scaled down to three-quarters of its originally planned size (£5 for project U and 0.75 × £14 for project Q).

9.3 (vi) Mathematical Programming and Capital Rationing

When rationing is expected to extend over a number of years and project NPVs depend on their starting dates, the optimising process becomes much too complex for a simple ranking approach, and mathematical programming models come into their own. A preliminary problem for such models is the way in which the objective function should be expressed; but for computational convenience most writers seem to recommend the firm to maximise the net present value of all its present and future projects, using its normal cost of capital as discount rate. We have already referred to theoretical doubts about this procedure when funds are scarce (and in the context we are considering they are expected to remain scarce for some years), but at least the investment choice problem becomes soluble in principle through its use. Following Weingartner's pioneering work (1963), many texts describe the application of linear programming methods to the capital rationing problem, e.g. Bromwich (1976), Ch. 11; Levy and Sarnat (1978), Ch. 18; Samuels and Wilkes (1975), pp. 200–5; and Wilkes (1977), Ch. 5.

The attraction of programming methods lies not only in their ability to resolve complex problems of investment choice over time, but also in their identification of the prospective shadow values of scarce investment resources at different dates during the extended period of scarcity. And although programming techniques suffer from the obvious disadvantages that no perfect forecasting of investment opportunities and resources is possible, and that they cannot fully allow for the kinds of flexibility discussed in 9.3 (v), their ability to yield prior indications of future shadow valuations of funds allows management to concentrate on the problems that appear to have the most depressing effects on the market value of the firm.

9.4 'Managerial' Appraisal of Single, Risky Investments

9.4 (i) Introduction

In our treatment of investment appraisal so far we have been able to represent the selection process in comparatively simple terms, for two distinct reasons. First, it has been possible to evaluate projects in terms of a single measure — NPV or IRR — thanks to our assumptions that future cash flows are all subject to a standard level of risk and that serial correlation between cash flows at different dates is absent.[1] These assumptions relate to the nature of the risks inherent in a project. Second, we have disregarded the 'portfolio' aspect of project selection, each project being seen as acceptable or not on the basis of its own characteristics (apart from the problem of capital rationing). When investments are expected to leave the firm's overall business risk unchanged there is no need for a portfolio dimension to the task of investment appraisal. In the remainder of this chapter we shall consider the effects of removing these admittedly restrictive assumptions, beginning in this section with the evaluation of single investments and concluding in 9.5 with a managerial model of portfolio choice.

9.4 (ii) Realistic Cash Flow Prospects

Our assumptions about cash flow prospects in the context of Chapter 8's cost of capital discussion were both explicit and restrictive (8.3 (i) and 8.4 (i)). A more realistic representation is given in Figure 9.2, which shows the cash flow prospects of an investment in two successive periods and the conditional probability linkages between later and earlier prospects. Probabilities are shown in brackets.

In Figure 9.2 the cash flow probability distribution for period 2 is conditional on the result in period 1, and although each possible period 2 distribution is a scaled replica of that for period 1, the prospect for period 2 viewed from the present (period 0) is inevitably more risky than that for period 1. A more extended forward view assuming the same kind of 'propensity to diverge' in cash flow prospects of later periods would obviously imply steadily increasing risk as seen from the present. Our example is only illustrative, and of course quite different

Figure 9.2: Probability Linkages Between Cash Flows (£) in Two Periods

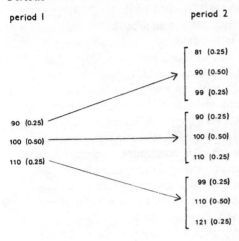

beliefs may be held; but the general idea of a degree of positive correlation between an investment's early and later performance is fairly widely accepted and does imply the kind of perception of increasing risk shown in Figure 9.2 (models of cash flow correlation are discussed in Van Horne, 1977, pp. 125-31; see also Hillier, 1963). This means that management will require a valuation model of considerably greater sophistication than that underlying the NPV/MVWACC criterion if it wishes to follow an exclusively investor-oriented policy. And if its inclination lies in the direction of a 'portfolio' interpretation of valuation, as suggested in 9.5 (i), the task of quantifying that interpretation will appear doubly difficult.

9.4 (iii) Appraising Risky Investments

For the moment we confine our interest to the comparatively uncontroversial area of appraising risky investments singly, leaving questions of acceptance or rejection for later. Arbitrary rules such as 'payback period' are at best a substitute for serious study of an investment's prospects and risks, and these we disregard. (Such rules are evaluated in Merrett and Sykes, 1963, Ch. 7.) Among methods suggested for handling risk within a conventional discounting framework, a major choice exists between: (1) a progressive downward scaling of future expectations (in the numerator of the discounting formula) to reflect the presumed increasing uncertainty of more remote cash flows (Robichek and Myers, 1966, and 1965, pp. 79-86); and (2) including an essentially arbitrary risk premium in the discount rate (i.e. in the denominator) to reflect the kind of risks the project is believed to involve (see Bierman and Hass, 1975, pp. 200-5). Either of these approaches, if applied by managers in an attempt to reflect investors' thinking, inevitably involves a good deal of arbitrariness — quite apart from the 'portfolio' dimension of the market valuation of the firm's prospects. Although each approach produces a simple verdict, a single estimate of the investment's NPV, it can be argued that this very simplicity, however it is achieved, constitutes a suppression rather than a clarification of the facts regarding the investment's risk. (In Chapter 10 we shall have much more to say on the subject of the risk premium approach, but from the quite different standpoint of the portfolio theory of capital market equilibrium.)

When an investment's prospects appear to be dominated by the behaviour of a comparatively small number of variables it may be possible to meet such criticism by means of sensitivity analysis. A 'central estimate' of the investment's NPV is calculated by combining the estimates of the most probable values of each of the key variables identified, e.g. investment cost, annual profit or cost saving, lifetime and disposal value. This central estimate of NPV is then subjected to sensitivity testing by varying each of the key estimates in turn within limits that seem appropriate. What emerges is a comprehensive but not necessarily helpful picture of the possible range of NPV for the investment, and the method is open to some fairly obvious criticisms. First, even if the key variables are statistically independent, their most likely values may coincide with only a very low probability, so the 'central estimate' of NPV may be a very misleading measure. Second, where the key variables are not statistically independent, their separate variation in the sensitivity test may disguise the important aspect of the simultaneous variation of a number of connected factors. Third, investment performance may be affected by more factors operating in more complex ways than this rather mechanical approach can accommodate. Finally, the approach leaves open the crucial question of what discount rate should be employed in NPV calculations (in I.C.E., 1969, pp. 92-4, the discount rate itself is treated as one of the key variables in the sensitivity analysis of a project).

The direction in which such criticisms point, at least for projects of importance and complexity, is towards a full simulation approach to identify the variability of NPV. In principle each possible future time-path of an investment's cash flow can be expressed as a net present value; and if the probability of each time-path is estimated an overall probability distribution of NPV for the project can be obtained. It is generally agreed that the discount rate employed in obtaining the NPV of each time-path of cash flows should be the risk-free interest rate. Each time-path, if it could be valued by itself as a certain prospect, would be discounted in the capital market by the ruling risk-free interest rate; on this view the project's risk lies in the multiplicity of possible time-paths, not the presence of risk on any given time-path.

A different way of making the same point, this time from the decision maker's point of view, is to note that the suggested procedure yields the most informative and objective picture of an investment's risk. Had we calculated the NPV probability distribution using any other discount rate, the resulting picture of the investment's risk would have been distorted, and a 'double counting' of risk would have occurred — once in the 'objective' phase of project appraisal and once in the decision process itself (Van Horne, 1977, p. 119).

Figure 9.3 shows the substance of this discussion in a highly simplified form. In Figure 9.3 (a) four possible cash flow time-paths are shown. The project in question may have a gestation period that is short and inexpensive (A) or prolonged and expensive (A_1). Similarly, once its profit-earning phase begins, the project can have a long and profitable life (B) or a short and less profitable life (B_1). To obtain the project's NPV probability distribution the probability of each sequence (AB, AB_1, etc.) must be estimated. In our simplified example this involves estimating the probabilities of A and A_1 and the probabilities of B and B_1. In reality, cash flow time-paths are likely to diverge on

Figure 9.3: Construction of NPV Probability Distribution

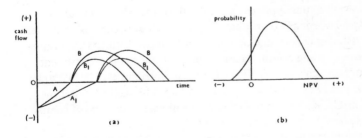

more than a single occasion, but Figure 9.3 (a) does show the essential nature of what is involved. Given a more detailed identification of possible time-paths and the necessary probability estimates, the discounting of each time-path by the risk-free interest rate should produce a reasonably smooth probability distribution of NPVs, as in Figure 9.3 (b).

Although the NPV probability distribution represents an objective view of a project's risk characteristics, its underlying calculations belie its tidy appearance. What is required, in principle, is a full-scale simulation exercise involving not only the separate probability distributions of such variables as investment cost and lifetime, but — much more demanding — all correlation coefficients *between* pairs of variables. The full simulation approach is clearly and interestingly described by Hertz (1964); simulation of the outcomes of business decisions is discussed in Jones (1972), pp. 206–12, and I.C.E. (1969), pp. 94–9.

9.4 (iv) Choosing Between Risky, Mutually Exclusive Investments

So far we have not discussed the general principles that govern management's decision when an investment's NPV is subject to risk in the way described above and a 'contrived' single-value NPV is believed inappropriate. Before considering this issue we can point to a technique that helps to supplement the objective picture available to a decision maker faced with the fairly common problem of choosing between risky, mutually exclusive, investments.

Management may wish to know the probability that one alternative will out-perform the other, an approach that echoes the 'most probable winner' calculation discussed in 3.3 (iii). Such an approach is particularly appropriate because the fact that one project has a higher expected value of NPV than another does *not* guarantee that it is more likely to produce a better result.

We explore this approach to choice through a highly simplified example involving two projects, K and L, each of which has a risky level of investment cost (I) and present value of future returns (PV). Table 9.5 gives cost and returns data for the two projects. The investment cost of K is either £10 or £15, with equal probabilities. The investment cost of L is either £8 or £13, again with equal probabilities. But the relationship between these two investment costs is not one of complete independence. The table shows that if I_K is at its lower level of £10 the probability that I_L will be at its lower level is 0.7; while if I_K is at its higher level the probability that I_L will be at its higher level is 0.7. We

Table 9.5: Investment Costs and Returns for Two Mutually Exclusive Projects

investment cost (£)

I_K probability			I_L probability		I_L probability	
			8	0.7		
			13	0.3		
10	0.5		-----		8	0.5
15	0.5		8	0.3	13	0.5
			13	0.7		

PV of future returns (£)

PV_K probability			PV_L probability		PV_L probability	
			12	0.8		
			21	0.2		
17	0.5		-----		12	0.45
20	0.5		12	0.1	21	0.55
			21	0.9		

can confirm that the two conditional probability distributions for I_L combine to give equal probabilities for I_L = £8 and I_L = £13; for example

$$p(I_L=8) = p(I_L=8/I_K=10) \times p(I_K=10) + p(I_L=8/I_K=15) \times p(I_K=15)$$

$$= 0.7 \times 0.5 + 0.3 \times 0.5 = 0.50$$

The derivation of the overall probability distribution of PV_L from the two conditional distributions shown is exactly analogous to this procedure.

If we assume that for both K and L the factors influencing investment cost are independent of the factors affecting future returns, we obtain the probability distributions of NPV (NPV = PV − I) shown in Table 9.6. Evidently L has a marginally higher $\overline{NPV}$ than K, but a considerably wider spread of possible outcomes. Faced with such an evenly balanced choice, management may wish to know the probability

Table 9.6: Probability Distributions of NPV for Projects K and L

NPV_K (£)	Probability	Cost and returns	NPV_L (£)	Probability
7	0.25	(cost low, returns low)	4	0.225
10	0.25	(cost low, returns high)	13	0.275
2	0.25	(cost high, returns low)	−1	0.225
5	0.25	(cost high, returns high)	8	0.275
$\overline{NPV}_K$ = £6.00		expected value of NPV	$\overline{NPV}_L$	= £6.45
σ_K = £2.915		standard deviation of NPV	σ_L	= £5.128

that NPV_K will exceed NPV_L. As a first step in answering this question, we identify the conditional probability that NPV_K exceeds NPV_L for each possible value of NPV_K.

If NPV_K = £7 (I_K = £10, PV_K = £17) the conditional NPV_L distribution is constructed as follows:

I_L (£)	PV_L (£)		NPV_L (£)	Probability	
8 (0.7)	12 (0.8)		4	0.56	√
13 (0.3)	21 (0.2)		13	0.14	
			−1	0.24	√
(probabilities in brackets)			8	0.06	

From the conditional NPV_L distribution we can immediately identify the required probability, denoted by $P(NPV_K > NPV_L / NPV_K = £7)$. NPV_K exceeds NPV_L with a probability of 0.80, i.e. when NPV_L equals £4 or −£1 (shown by ticks against the relevant probabilities). Exactly analogous calculations are possible for the other possible NPV_K outcomes, and the full set of results is as follows:

$$p(NPV_K > NPV_L / NPV_K = £7) = 0.80$$

$$p(NPV_K > NPV_L / NPV_K = £10) = 0.37$$

$$p(NPV_K > NPV_L / NPV_K = £2) = 0.56$$

$$p(NPV_K > NPV_L / NPV_K = £5) = 0.10$$

(It is interesting that when NPV_K is at its lowest level, £2, the probability of K producing a superior result is considerably *greater* than when NPV_K is at the more satisfactory levels of £10 or £5.)

Bringing all four conditional probabilities together by giving each the probability weight of the NPV_K to which it relates, we obtain the overall probability that NPV_K will exceed NPV_L:

$$p(NPV_K > NPV_L) = 0.80 \times 0.25 + 0.37 \times 0.25 + 0.56 \times 0.25 +$$
$$0.10 \times 0.25$$

$$= 0.4575$$

Since $NPV_K = NPV_L$ is not a possibility, our result implies

$$p(NPV_K < NPV_L) = 0.5425$$

This information may help to influence the decision between K and L. For example, it is possible that on observing that the two projects in this example are pretty evenly matched in terms of chance of 'winning', management may feel justified in following its natural inclination towards K, with its lower dispersion of NPV, or L with its higher $\overline{NPV}$. It is easy to imagine other situations, in which the result of a 'most probable winner' calculation would be more decisive; but the complexity of the calculation should not be ignored. The greater the number of areas of statistical dependence between the projects (and the greater the number of projects), the greater the number of conditional probability estimates required and the more involved the calculation becomes. But for a major choice between a small number of competing alternatives it is likely that management will wish to know which alternative offers the best chance of zero regret.

9.5 'Managerial' Evaluation of Combinations of Risky Investments

9.5 (i) Appraising Combinations of Investments

In many cases the capital budgeting problem can be likened to the financial portfolio decision confronting the ordinary investor-saver. That decision is generally described in terms of a trade-off between the level of expected return on the portfolio and the level of risk associated with that return, and we shall have more to say on this subject in Chapter 10. For a business this aspect of choice becomes particularly important when it appears that the 'portfolio' of investments chosen will significantly affect the risk of the firm's overall earnings prospects.

By appraising investments in groups rather than accepting or rejecting them singly, management may hope at the very least to be aware of the characteristics of the resulting probability distribution of the firm's overall NPV. Here we assume that management behaves 'managerially', seeking to select the grouping of investments offering what it sees as the most satisfactory combination of overall expected net present value (a 'good') and risk (a 'bad'). Our discussion in this section owes much to Van Horne's application of portfolio theory to an essentially 'managerial' objective (Van Horne, 1966, and 1977, pp. 149-55).

The mathematical formulae for combining probability distributions of NPV (or any other variable) are straightforward. When the separate NPV probability distributions of projects 1, 2 . . . x are to be combined into a single distribution (0), the latter's mean value, $\overline{\text{NPV}}$ (0), and standard deviation, $\sigma(0)$, are determined as follows:

$$\overline{\text{NPV}}(0) = \overline{\text{NPV}}_1 + \overline{\text{NPV}}_2 \ldots + \overline{\text{NPV}}_x = \sum_{i=1}^{x} \overline{\text{NPV}}_i \qquad \text{(vii)}$$

$$\sigma(0) = \sqrt{\begin{array}{l} \sigma_1^2 + \sigma_2^2 \ldots + \sigma_x^2 + 2r_{12}\sigma_1\sigma_2 + 2r_{13}\sigma_1\sigma_3 \ldots \\ + 2r_{(x-1)x}\sigma_{x-1}\sigma_x \end{array}}$$

$$= \sqrt{\sum_{i=1}^{x} \sigma_i^2 + 2\sum_{i=1}^{x-1}\sum_{j=i+1}^{x} r_{ij}\sigma_i\sigma_j} \qquad \text{(viii)}$$

In these formulae $\overline{\text{NPV}}_i$ and σ_i ($i = 1 \ldots x$) are, respectively, the expected value and standard deviation of NPV for project i; and r_{ij} is the correlation coefficient between NPV_i and NPV_j. The interpretation of this crucially important correlation coefficient is fairly obvious, though in practice estimation may be difficult and may have to be performed impressionistically. A high positive value of r_{ij} means that projects i and j tend to perform well or badly together; their NPVs are influenced in the same direction by factors common to both (e.g. double-glazing and wall insulation). A strong negative correlation means that under conditions which give one project a low NPV, the other project will tend to have a high NPV (e.g. umbrellas and sunshades). A zero correlation indicates that the performances of the two projects are completely unrelated, presumably because they are affected by completely different sets of unrelated factors (e.g. knitwear in Brazil and pocket calculators in Norway).

Before discussing a model of managerial 'portfolio' choice, a brief example of these formulae at work may be helpful. In Table 9.7 (a) the

Table 9.7: Financial Prospects (£) and Correlation Coefficients for Three Investments

(i)	(ii)	(iii)	(iv)	(v) [(iii) − (ii)]			Project		
Project	Cost	$\overline{PV}$	$\sigma(PV)$	$\overline{NPV}$			1	2	3
1	10	12	2	2		1	1.0	0.5	0.2
2	15	18	4	3	project	2		1.0	0.6
3	18	22	3	4		3			1.0

(a) data relating to each project   (b) values of r_{ij}

necessary data on each individual project (1, 2 and 3) are given. Column (v) shows the expected net present value, $\overline{NPV}$, of each project as the difference between the expected present value of its future returns, $\overline{PV}$, and its known immediate cost. Column (iv) gives the standard deviation of the present value of future returns. Given that in this example project costs are known for certain, the value of $\sigma(PV)$ is identical to the standard deviation of the project's NPV; that is $\sigma(PV) = \sigma(NPV)$. Table 9.7 (b) gives the correlation coefficients between NPVs for all possible pairings of projects. The overall characteristics of any 'portfolio' of projects are now readily ascertainable. As an example, if all three projects are adopted the resulting NPV(0) distribution has the following properties:

$$\overline{NPV}(0) = 2 + 3 + 4 = 9 \; (£)$$

$$\sigma(0) = \sqrt{\begin{array}{l} 2^2 + 3^2 + 4^2 + (2 \times 0.5 \times 2 \times 4) + (2 \times 0.2 \times 2 \times 3) + \\ (2 \times 0.6 \times 4 \times 3) \end{array}}$$

$$= \sqrt{53.8}$$

$$= 7.355 \; (£)$$

The reader is invited to substitute different values of r_{ij} ($i \neq j$) in Table 9.7 (b) and re-work the above calculation of $\sigma(0)$ to demonstrate the crucial importance of the intercorrelation aspect of the portfolio's overall risk.

A project's risk-reducing potential can be seen clearly by imagining a fourth project being added to a three-project grouping whose $\sigma(0)$ is obtained as in (viii). The change in $\sigma(0)$, denoted by $\Delta\sigma(0)$ is given by

$$\Delta\sigma(0) = \sqrt{\sigma_4^2 + 2\sigma_4(r_{14}\sigma_1 + r_{24}\sigma_2 + r_{34}\sigma_3)} \qquad \text{(viiia)}$$

Using C to denote $\Sigma r_{i4}\sigma_i$ (i = 1 ... 3), we can see that $\Delta\sigma(0)$ *may* be negative if one or more r_{i4} values is negative. Given $C < 0$, the value of $\Delta\sigma(0)$ will actually be negative if $\sigma_4 < -2C$. This favourable effect actually *increases* as the new project's individual risk *increases* in the range $0 < \sigma_4 < -C$, and is diminishing but still favourable in the range $-C < \sigma_4 < -2C$.

Figure 9.4: Properties of Portfolios of Investment Projects

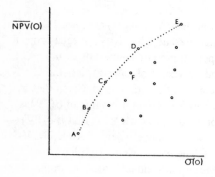

In Figure 9.4 each possible grouping or portfolio of investments is indicated by a point showing the mean and standard deviation of NPV(0) for that grouping. Each grouping making up the frontier ABCDE is efficient in the sense that no other possible selection from the same set of opportunities is superior in *both* characteristics, i.e. possessing a higher $\overline{\text{NPV}}(0)$ *and* lower $\sigma(0)$. It is important to note that because of the very limited divisibility of physical investments, a frontier such as ABCDE does not represent a continous range of attainable combinations of $\overline{\text{NPV}}(0)$ and $\sigma(0)$. Whatever project divisibility is possible is reflected in the limited number of groupings shown; and it is not possible to supplement this number by, for example, investing partly in group B and partly in group C to achieve a compromise between the characteristics of these two groups (although it is quite likely that groups B and C do have certain projects in common). By the same token, the 'efficiency frontier' may not possess the smooth curvature shown in Figure 9.4; in the absence of group C the frontier would become ABFDE because the investments in groups B and D could not be combined in variable proportions to create a continuous frontier between points B and D.

9.5 (ii) The 'Managerial' Optimum Investment Calculations

As indicated earlier, our model of 'managerial' motivation imputes to managers a desire to achieve the 'best' combination of overall expected performance and risk; and this general concept obviously adapts readily to the framework of investment appraisal we have outlined. At any time management's choice of investments extends to all new proposals and those of the firm's existing investments that can be disposed of. Of course many existing investments cannot readily be disposed of, and each of these *must* appear in every investment grouping considered. Because their original capital outlays lie in the past, these investments are represented by the mean and standard deviation of the present value of their future cash flows. Existing investments that are disposable can be treated, in effect, as new proposals, with the disposal value substituting for the purchase price as the immediate opportunity cost of the investment in question.

Managerial utility in this context is represented by a function in which, unlike the utility function derived in 3.3 (i), risk is an explicit and direct determinant:

$$U = U[\overline{NPV}(0), \sigma(0)] \tag{ix}$$

In (ix), U denotes present-day managerial utility, which is affected positively by $\overline{NPV}(0)$ and negatively by $\sigma(0)$. The diagrammatic representation of this relationship is shown by indifference curves U_1, U_2 and U_3 in Figure 9.5. Curves U_1, U_2 and U_3 represent progressively higher levels of managerial utility. The upward slope of the typical indifference curve is explained by the fact that at any given level of utility an increase in $\overline{NPV}(0)$ must be offset by an increase in risk, as measured by $\sigma(0)$. The increasing slope of the curve reflects an increasing reluctance to accept greater risk at any given level of utility.

Also shown in Figure 9.5 are the points originally shown in Figure 9.4, each representing one possible combination of investments open to the firm. (We now recognise that these points relate to the firm's existing assets as well as to new proposals, as described above.) Management's preferred investment combination is obviously C, the only one that enables it to reach indifference curve U_2. The optimum point is

Figure 9.5: Determining the 'Managerial' Optimum

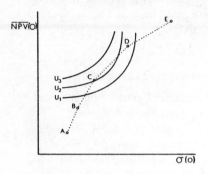

not one of tangency between an indifference curve and the firm's efficiency frontier because, as argued earlier, the latter is not a continuous range of attainable points; management cannot combine groupings C and D to reach an indifference curve beyond U_2. Evidently the shape of the typical indifference curve is crucial to the combination that will be chosen: a shallower indifference curve slope (greater risk tolerance) could have led to the choice of combination D, or even E; while a greater degree of risk aversion could have shifted management's choice to B, or even A. Only if management's indifference curves are completely horizontal or if the investment combination with the highest $\overline{NPV}(0)$ also possesses the lowest $\sigma(0)$, can we be certain that all investments with positive $\overline{NPV}$s will be selected.

Before we attempt to evaluate this interpretation of a managerial selection of projects, we should note its potential usefulness for identifying subjective shadow valuations of individual investments. If an investment's initial cost is unknown (e.g. because it will be the subject of negotiation) management can determine the maximum price it ought to be willing to pay, according to its own scheme of preferences, to add the investment's PV distribution to that of the firm's planned portfolio of assets.

9.5 (iii) Critique of the 'Managerial' Portfolio Choice Model

In evaluating the capital budgeting model outlined in 9.5 (ii) we must recognise the practical and conceptual difficulties it poses. Not only are the correlations between (present values of) pairings of multi-period returns likely to be difficult to estimate with any pretence of accuracy; but for unknown future investments, which enter into the firm's 'true' NPV(0) distribution and which probably depend in part on present choices, the necessary calculations cannot be performed at all. It would not be too surprising, therefore, if managers were to employ a portfolio approach as no more than a final check on the overall acceptability of a group of proposals chosen individually.

On the other hand, a major attraction of the portfolio approach must be the assurance it offers that a portfolio of projects chosen from among those forming the efficiency frontier (ABCDE in Figures 9.5 and 9.6) cannot be inferior to another group of projects in terms of *both* $\overline{NPV}(0)$ and $\sigma(0)$. For a management concerned about the market value implications of its choice, yet unable to predict exactly how the market would value each possible grouping, this assurance may represent an acceptable degree of fulfilment of its theoretical obligations to shareholders.

This comforting impression of near-harmony between managerialism and a value-maximising motivation rests on the interpretation of valuation to which we have committed our hypothetical managers, namely that the firm is valued, as a whole, for its own inherent risk and return properties. In Chapter 10 we shall question this interpretation and examine the radically different prescriptive conclusions for business investment choice that have developed from the portfolio theory of capital market equilibrium.

Appendix to Chapter 9: Basic Concepts of Investment Profitability

9A (i) Introduction

The aim of this appendix is to provide an introduction to (or reminder of) the theoretical debate between the net present value (NPV) and internal rate of return (IRR) measures of investment profitability. Although a recognition of risk might help to strengthen the case we shall make in favour of the NPV concept, we shall follow standard practice in such discussions and confine our attention to projects assumed to have uniquely predictable time patterns of cash flow. At an earlier stage in the popularisation of discounted cash flow (DCF) techniques it could be argued that the IRR concept enjoyed an important practical advantage in that it 'made more sense' to businessmen who were perhaps accustomed to making unsophisticated profitability calculations in terms of a periodic rate of return (see Merrett and Sykes, 1963, pp. 149-50). However, after nearly two decades of widening awareness of DCF principles and techniques, it seems safe to concentrate on the theoretical merits of the two main DCF profitability concepts rather than on their putative 'selling points' in the eyes of investment decision makers.

9A (ii) Internal Rate of Return

In operational terms, an investment's internal rate of return is defined as the periodic compound rate of discount which has the property of making the discounted sum of the investment's cash flows equal to zero. If we imagine a project with a 'normal' cash flow pattern involving an initial outlay (I_0) at the present day and positive returns (R_t) in years $t = 1 \ldots n$, the project's IRR is given by r in the following equation:

$$ -I_0 + \sum_{t=1}^{n} \frac{R_t}{(1 + r)^t} = 0 \qquad\qquad \text{A (i)} $$

The uniqueness of the solution value of IRR in this case is easily confirmed; any higher (lower) rate of discount would give the sum of discounted future cash flows a lower (higher) value, and the left-hand side of A (i) would become less (greater) than zero. It should be noted that a project's IRR is a 'self-contained' measure of its profitability, unaffected by the cost of capital of the investing firm.

It is easy to show that the value of r for such an investment constitutes a 'break-even borrowing rate' in the sense that the project could in principle borrow its initial capital requirement, I_0, at an annual interest rate of r, and just succeed in repaying principal and accumulated interest over the project's n-year lifetime. The following example of a three-year project illustrates this property of IRR, which in this case is 12 per cent per annum (identified by solving equation A (i)).

	end-year			
	0	1	2	3
project's accumulated debt (£)	100	112	114.24	54
minus project earnings (£)		−10	−66.0	−54
project's end-year debt (£)	100	102	48.24	0

The project borrows its initial capital of £100 at the present day (end-year 0) at an annual interest rate of 12 per cent. This debt accumulates to £112 at end-year 1 under our hypothetical financing scheme, but at that date the project earns £10; so at end-year 1 the outstanding debt is £102. The processes of debt accumulation and repayments out of earnings are repeated up to end-year 3, at which point the final earnings of £54 result in an exact 'balancing of the books' at the end of the project's life. The project remains 'in debt' throughout its lifetime, so we need not worry about how a temporary surplus might be invested. It is clear that a lower borrowing rate would leave a surplus at the end of the project's life, and a higher borrowing rate would leave a deficit.

The 'break-even borrowing rate' implication of IRR seems harmless enough and it suggests an obvious investment criterion, namely that if IRR exceeds the actual cost of capital of the investing firm the project should be accepted (on the grounds that the project would actually be financed by resources costing less than its implied break-even borrowing rate and would therefore produced a 'surplus' over its lifetime).

A different perspective on the IRR concept can be gained by multiplying equation A(i) throughout by $(1 + r)^n$ and presenting the result as follows:

$$\sum_{t=1}^{n} R_t (1 + r)^{n-t} = I_0 (1 + r)^n \qquad \text{A (ii)}$$

This shows that *if* the positive cash flows from the project could be reinvested as they occur, *outside* the project, to earn an annual rate of return equal to the project's IRR up to the end of year n, the terminal value of the reinvested cash flows would be $I_0 (1 + r)^n$ — exactly what the investing firm would have achieved over the same period had it been able instead to 'bank' the amount I_0 to yield a steady rate of return of r per annum. Not only does r represent the project's break-even borrowing rate, it also represents the implied rate of return on reinvested cash flows given that the project is equivalent in terminal value to a straightforward 'bank deposit' investment yielding a periodic return of r over the same lifetime. Once again, the investment criterion suggested by this way of looking at IRR is to accept a project if r exceeds the investing firm's cost of capital — interpreting the latter as the rate of return on alternative investments actually open to the firm or its shareholders.

9A (iii) Net Present Value

In contrast to the IRR approach, in which the discount rate satisfying a certain condition is identified separately for each project, the NPV concept assumes that the relevant discount rate is that given by the investing firm's cost of capital, and that the significant measure of a project's profitability is the sum of its discounted cash flows. Employing largely the same notation as before, the project's NPV is obtained as follows:

$$NPV = \sum_{t=1}^{n} \frac{R_t}{(1+c)^t} - I_0 \qquad\qquad A\ (iii)$$

in which c is the discount rate equal to the firm's opportunity cost of capital. The NPV concept too has its own implied reinvestment rate, as can be seen by multiplying equation A (iii) throughout by $(1+c)^n$ and rearranging thus:

$$\sum_{t=1}^{n} R_t (1+c)^{n-t} = (I_0 + NPV)(1+c)^n \qquad\qquad A\ (iv)$$

The left-hand side of A (iv) shows the project's cash flows being reinvested outside the project, as they occur, to earn a periodic return at the rate c up to the end of the project's life. The terminal value accumulated in this way is $(I_0 + NPV)(1+c)^n$. Given that the alternative use of funds would by definition have yielded a terminal value of $I_0(1+c)^n$, it can be seen that the project 'breaks even' if NPV is zero, shows a 'profit' if NPV is positive or a 'loss' if NPV is negative.

9A (iv) Common Ground between IRR and NPV

Notwithstanding their differing implications, the IRR and NPV measures of profitability must yield identical recommendations in relation to 'normal' investments evaluated individually in the absence of capital rationing. We shall elaborate on these conditions shortly, but a comparison of equations A (i) and A (iii) makes clear the sense in which the two measures can be seen as interchangeable.

Project profitability	Should project be accepted?
r > c implies NPV > 0	Yes
r = c implies NPV = 0	On the margin
r < c implies NPV < 0	No

Assuming that under the NPV criterion only investments with positive NPVs will be chosen, and that under the IRR criterion only investments with internal rates of return higher than the company's cost of capital will be chosen, the two criteria should *in practice* yield identical recommendations.

9A (v) Abnormal Cash Flow Patterns

However, there are three kinds of circumstance in which the choice of investment criterion is not a matter of indifference. One of these is capital rationing, and this is discussed in 9.3. The second, considered here, is the possibility that a project may have a 'troublesome' pattern of cash flows; and the third, to be discussed in 9A (vi), is the problem of mutual exclusiveness between two or more investments which are all acceptable individually.

When a project's cash flow pattern includes negative flows in some period(s) following periods of positive earnings, the possibility exists that more than one value of IRR will be found; that is, more than one discount rate may yield a zero NPV for the project in question (see Lorie and Savage, 1955). Before analysing this difficulty we should recognise that the circumstances in which negative cash flows follow positive ones are not so unusual as to relegate the problem to the status of a *curiosum* or footnote in discounting theory. Two quite different examples can be suggested to demonstrate the nature and prevalence of the problem. First, an investment may be intended to speed up an anticipated time pattern of cash flows, raising the investing firm's cash flow in early periods but inevitably reducing it in later periods; the incremental cash flows *attributable to the project* are initially positive but inevitably negative after its benefits cease. This possibility may be generally relevant in problems of investment timing. A second possibility is that a project may involve large inescapable outlays at the conclusion of its working life; for example, a mining operation may be approved on condition that costly landscape restoration will be undertaken once mineral extraction is discontinued.

When an investment is 'normal' in the sense that a series of outlays is followed by a series of positive returns and the undiscounted sum of all cash flows is positive (NPV > 0 when the discount rate equals zero), the investment's IRR must be unique. An increase in the discount rate lowers the present value of positive cash flows by more than it lowers the present (absolute) value of negative cash flows. (The positive flows, being more remote and larger in absolute value than the negative flows, are more sharply reduced in absolute present value by a given increase

in the discount rate.) Typical relationships between NPV and discount
rate for 'normal' projects are illustrated in 9A (vi) below.

An example of a 'troublesome' cash flow pattern is given in the
following table, and the implications for the project's NPV at different
discount rates are shown in the NPV 'profile' alongside. (The profile
shows the project's NPV for all values of discount rate.)

end-year	cash flow (£)
0	−26.4
1	10
2	35
3	30
4	−50

Not only does the profile show multiple solutions for IRR ($r = 0.07$ and
$r = 0.16$), but the project has positive NPVs at discount rates *above*
0.07 (up to 0.16) and negative NPVs at discount rates *below* 0.07.
In our earlier discussion of 'normal' investments we found that a
project's IRR carries the alternative implications of a break-even
borrowing rate or an earnings reinvestment rate; but in the case of a
multiple IRR project such as that in our example, we shall find both
implications *simultaneously* in effect. This point is illustrated by
working out the financing pattern implied by borrowing at the rate
of 16 per cent per annum to finance the project.

	end-year				
	0	1	2	3	4
project's accumulated debt (£)	26.24	30.44	23.71	−13.10	−50
minus project earnings (£)		−10.0	−35.0	−30	+50
project's end-year debt (£)	26.24	20.44	−11.29	−43.10	0

It is clear from this example that given the time pattern of its cash
flows, the project's hypothetical financing must actually be in surplus
during its lifetime. At end-year 2 the project has repaid its initial
borrowing and has emerged with a surplus of £11.29. By end-year 3

this surplus accumulates to £13.10, the rate of accumulation being the same as the interest rate paid earlier on the project's debt. By end-year 4 the surplus accumulates to £50, exactly what is required to cover the project's negative cash flow due at that date. (The reader can confirm that a similar general picture of financing emerges if a borrowing/reinvestment rate of 7 per cent per annum is assumed.)

Generalising our conclusions from this example, we can see that it is at least possible that a project having an 'abnormal' time pattern of cash flows will have multiple values of IRR, each of which will carry the implication that the project can both borrow *and* lend at that rate during its lifetime. But only by coincidence will one of the implied borrowing/reinvestment rates associated with such a project actually equal the investing firm's true opportunity cost of funds, i.e. its cost of capital.

Without actually resolving the problem posed by the borrowing/reinvestment rate implication of the IRR concept, it is at least possible to restore the property of a unique IRR to projects such as that in our example. The price of this restoration is that the modified rate of return we shall calculate necessarily depends on the investing firm's cost of capital, and is therefore no longer 'internal' to the project in the original sense. The table below shows what is involved in this calculation, again using our example and assuming the investing firm to have a cost of capital of 8 per cent per annum.

| | | | end-year | | |
	0	1	2	3	4
actual cash flow (£)	−26.24	10	35	30	−50
actual/equivalent cash flow (£)	−26.24	10	35 / 27.78 / −42.87		

In the row 'actual/equivalent cash flow' the first two entries are the actual cash flows at the dates shown, but the entry for end-year 2 £(35 + 27.28 − 42.87), which equals £19.91, is the amount which at that date will represent the project's present value to the firm's owners, who are assumed to employ the firm's cost of capital in valuing future expectations. Thus £19.91, the 'equivalent' cash flow at end-year 2, is made up of the actual cash flow due at that date (£35) *plus* the value at that date of the £30 due in one year's time (£30 × $(1.08)^{-1}$ =

£27.78), *minus* the value at that date of the £50 outlay due in two years' time ($-£50 \times (1.08)^{-2} = -£42.87$).

The reason for choosing end-year 2 as the date for identifying an equivalent cash flow is that, working backwards from end-year 4, end-year 2 is obviously the first occasion on which a positive equivalent value is obtained — and the first occasion therefore on which the troublesome aspect of the project's *actual* cash flow pattern is eliminated. The project's cash flows as modified in this way are now bound to possess a unique discount rate yielding a zero NPV; but because this discount rate is inevitably influenced by the value of the investing firm's cost of capital used in obtaining the end-year 2 equivalent cash flow, it is advisable to find an alternative definitional term to internal rate of return. Suggestions that have been made include 'return on invested capital' (Mao, 1969, pp. 201–2) and 'extended yield' (Merrett and Sykes, 1963, pp. 158–65).

The reader may confirm our example project's modified IRR is identified uniquely as 0.0822, so that the project is barely acceptable given a cost of capital of 0.08. But it should be emphasised that the paradoxical implications of an abnormal cash flow pattern are not completely removed by the suggested modification to the IRR concept. A cost of capital of only 5 per cent per annum, would give the project a modified rate of return of *less* than 5 per cent per annum, which would suggest rejection.

9A (vi) Mutual Exclusiveness among Investments

Earlier it was stated that for 'normal' investments viewed in isolation and in the absence of capital rationing the IRR and NPV measures of profitability are interchangeable, in the sense that they are bound to yield identical accept-or-reject recommendations. Here we elaborate on the second aspect of this complex condition by considering a situation in which two or more investments are mutually exclusive for reasons other than scarcity of capital. Examples are to be found in the existence of alternative uses for the same plot of land, and the availability of different models of capital equipment designed to perform a specific task in a production process. Mutual exclusiveness is also present in questions of investment timing — a particular project undertaken at the present day cannot also be undertaken at some future date.

The common sense of the problem raised by mutual exclusiveness is easy to grasp by imagining a choice between a relatively inexpensive investment with a high rate of return (IRR) and a larger project with a less attractive rate of return than the first, but, by virtue of its size, a higher NPV. The following table of alternative cash flow patterns and matching set of NPV profiles for two projects, A and B, will illustrate the issue in greater detail. (Ignore the 'project' shown as [A − B] for the moment.)

end-year	A	B	[A − B]
0	−99	−90	−9
1	10	50	−40
2	10	40	−30
3	10	29	−19
4	123	−	123

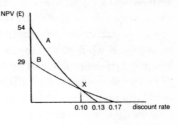

Project A has a lower IRR than project B (0.13 *versus* 0.17), but for discount rates of less than 0.10 its NPV exceeds that of B. Thus if the investing firm's cost of capital is lower than 0.10, the IRR and NPV measures of profitability give contradictory indications of the *relative* desirability of the two projects. (In the absence of mutual exclusiveness, both projects would presumably be accepted for any cost of capital up to 0.13.)

The possibility of a contradiction between the IRR and NPV criteria is due to the marked difference between the cash flow patterns of the two projects. The future cash flows of A have a more remote 'centre of gravity' than those of B, although as an undiscounted total A's net cash flow exceeds B's (£54 versus £29). A given increase in the discount rate must penalise the present value of A's cash flows more than that of B, and the possibility of a 'crossover', as at point x in our diagram, cannot be ruled out.

To illustrate the resolution of the contradiction between IRR and NPV in such a case, we assume that the investing firm's cost of capital in our example is 8 per cent per annum; that is, within the range in which the two criteria are in conflict. The NPVs of A and B for this discount rate are £17.175 and £5.932, respectively, and we can confirm the superiority of A *even in terms of the IRR criterion* by considering the 'project' [A − B] whose cash flows are shown alongside those of A and B above. The investment [A − B] represents the additional investment needed to switch from B to A on the assumption that B, the cheaper of the two projects, is acceptable on its own merits and as such has already been tentatively selected. Given the cost of capital, the NPV of [A − B] is obviously the difference between the NPVs of A and B, that is £11.243; but the IRR of the [A − B] cash flow series is found to be 0.0978, and this actually exceeds the firm's cost of capital. The fact that the NPV of [A − B] is positive, using the firm's cost of capital as discount rate, implies that the [A − B] cash flow pattern will have a zero NPV at a higher discount rate than the firm's cost of capital. In other words, the IRR measure of investment profitability, properly applied, confirms the recommendation given by the NPV approach.

A general word of warning should be added to our rather narrow treatment of the problem of mutual exclusiveness. The two projects in our example terminated at different dates, but because we assumed implicitly that neither project had any follow-up prospects or any differential effect of any kind on the remainder of the firm's present and future investment programme, it was appropriate to confine our comparison to the two projects themselves. But if projects are not 'self-contained' in this rather artificial way, a proper comparison demands that follow-up investments and any other differential effects of the immediate choice also be taken into account. The reader will recognise our treatment of replacement analysis in 9.2 as an illustration of this point. In general, however, uncertainty about future opportunities inevitably clouds the clarity of the choice that must be made immediately; and an explicit risk framework may seem a more appropriate context for decision making than the certainty model adopted here (see 9.4 (iv)).

Note

1. Serial correlation in this sense is present when the probability distribution of cash flow in a future period depends on the actual cash flow in an earlier period.

10 CAPITAL MARKET THEORY AND CAPITAL BUDGETING

Anyone who thinks there's safety in numbers hasn't looked at the stock market pages.

Irene Peter

10.1 Introduction

It would be a serious dereliction to conclude a book dealing with modern advances in various areas of business decision making without discussing the portfolio theory of capital market equilibrium and its relevance for firms' capital budgeting decisions. This entails a fairly lengthy introduction to the portfolio theory of capital market equilibrium – a subject, however, of great interest and importance in its own right. Out of this framework in recent years has grown a new school of capital budgeting theory, claiming in principle at least to offer a more complete and theoretically satisfactory basis for investment choice than the 'traditional' valuation model with its numerous limitations in the area of cost of capital theory.

10.2 The Capital Asset Pricing Model

10.2 (i) Properties of Portfolios of Risky Securities

Our first task is largely mechanical. We wish to identify the risk and return properties of portfolios of financial investments, confining our interest at first to portfolios made up exclusively of risky securities. (Outstanding expositions of the whole theory of capital market equilibrium, including the fundamental relationships discussed here, are contained in Sharpe, 1970 and 1978.) We simplify this task by defining the investor's holding period for securities, i.e. the length of time between decisions regarding his portfolio, as of fairly short duration – for example, a month or a quarter. The prospective one-period rate of return on any asset is given by the value of r in the following relationship:

$$P_0 = \frac{D_1 + P_1}{1 + r} \qquad \text{(i)}$$

231

where P_0 is the current price of the asset, P_1 is its price at the end of the period and D_1 is the amount of dividend (if any) to be received at the end of the period. When D_1 and/or P_1 is subject to risk, the value of r is also subject to risk. In this case the expected return on the asset, $\bar{r}$, is obtained from the expression

$$P_0 = \frac{\bar{D}_1 + \bar{P}_1}{1 + \bar{r}} \tag{ii}$$

in which $\bar{D}_1$ and $\bar{P}_1$ are the expected values of D_1 and P_1, respectively. The variability of the amount $(D_1 + P_1)$ obviously determines the variability of r, given P_0; and we employ the standard deviation of possible r values, denoted by σ_r, as a measure of this variability — the risk associated with holding the asset for one period.

Most investors purchase portfolios of securities — directly, or, through various institutions, indirectly — and we now require the risk and return properties of a portfolio of risky securities. The formulae given in 9.5 (i) are applicable here, suitably modified to allow for the fact that the investor can invest any proportion of his resources in any security. The actual rate of return on a portfolio, denoted by R, is given by

$$R = w_1 r_1 + w_2 r_2 \ldots w_n r_n = \sum_{i=1}^{n} w_i r_i \tag{iii}$$

where r_i is the rate of return obtained on an investment in security i $(i = 1 \ldots n)$, and w_i is the proportion of the investor's resources invested in i. Given that returns on securities $1 \ldots n$ are risky, we can state the investor's expected return as follows:

$$\bar{R} = w_1 \bar{r}_1 + w_2 \bar{r}_2 \ldots w_n \bar{r}_n = \sum_{i=1}^{n} w_i \bar{r}_i \tag{iv}$$

where $\bar{R}$ is the expected return on the portfolio and $\bar{r}_i$ is the expected rate of return on security i. The standard deviation of possible values of R, denoted by σ_R, is obtained as follows:

$$\sigma_R = \sqrt{\begin{aligned}(w_1\sigma_1)^2 + (w_2\sigma_2)^2 \ldots (w_n\sigma_n)^2 + 2w_1 w_2 \sigma_1 \sigma_2 c_{12} + \\ 2w_1 w_3 \sigma_1 \sigma_3 c_{13} \ldots 2w_{n-1} w_n \sigma_{n-1} \sigma_n c_{n,n-1}\end{aligned}} \tag{v}$$

or

$$\sigma_R = \sqrt{\sum_{i=1}^{n} (w_i\sigma_i)^2 + 2\sum_{i=1}^{n-1} \sum_{j=i+1}^{n} r_{ij} w_i w_j \sigma_i \sigma_j} \tag{vi}$$

In (v) and (vi) w_i again denotes the proportion of funds committed to security i, σ_i denotes the standard deviation of security i's rate of return, and c_{ij} is the coefficient of correlation between the probabilistic returns of securities i and j. It should be emphasised that c_{ij} is a conventional correlation coefficient, taking a value between -1.00 and $+1.00$ which indicates the strength and direction of association between the two variables r_i and r_j.

Given the necessary estimates of $\bar{r}_i$, σ_i and c_{ij} (i = 1 . . . n), these formulae can be employed quite mechanically to obtain the one-period risk and expected return properties of portfolios comprising any number of securities. To reduce the volume of estimation required, as well as to overcome the logical objection that investors may simply have no basis for estimating c values for many pairs of securities, Sharpe (1963) proposed that securities should be seen as being correlated with one another indirectly, through their probabilistic associations with one central indicator such as a general index of security prices. With each security's return linked probabilistically to the market index, we can dispense with the direct approach of estimating a correlation coefficient between the possible returns on each pair of securities, greatly reducing the amounts of estimation and computation required.

10.2 (ii) The Efficiency Frontier of Portfolios

Can we progress beyond the mechanics of identifying portfolio characteristics, and say anything definite about the portfolios investors are likely to favour? Just as we were able to identify 'efficient' com-binations of investment proposals in 9.5 (i) without introducing managerial preferences, so we can in principle identify a frontier of efficient portfolios of risky securities. The important difference between the two situations is that because each company's equity capital is assumed completely divisible, the frontier of efficient portfolios must be continuous.

Figure 10.1 illustrates the choices open to the typical purchaser of a portfolio of risky securities, each possible portfolio of securities being represented by a point on or below EE' showing its $\bar{R}$ and σ_R values. Portfolios differ not only in the securities they include, but also – as equations (iv) and (v) showed – in the proportions in which a given set of securities are combined. As we would expect, following our discussion in 9.5 (i), the investor faces a continuous frontier of 'efficient' portfolios, EE', such that at any point on EE' a higher value of $\bar{R}$ can only be attained by accepting a higher level of σ_R. The

Figure 10.1: Feasible Combinations of Portfolio Risk and Expected Return

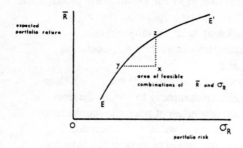

curvature of EE′ is perhaps not entirely self-evident, but we can appreciate the reason for it through a simple example involving just two securities (or portfolios), a and b, with the following characteristics:

$$\bar{r}_a = 0.04 \qquad \sigma_a = 0.03 \qquad c_{ab} = +1.0 \; or$$
$$+0.6 \; or$$
$$\bar{r}_b = 0.08 \qquad \sigma_b = 0.07 \qquad 0.0 \; or$$
$$-0.5$$

Figure 10.2 shows the portfolio choices open to the investor, given the basic data for each security, for each possible value of c_{ab} (the correlation coefficient between r_a and r_b). The two extreme points on the efficiency frontier are A (a portfolio consisting entirely of a) and B (a portfolio consisting entirely of b).

Each frontier is constructed by varying the proportions in which the two securities are combined, using equations (iv) and (v) with the appropriate value of c_{ab} and the stated data on each security. Only when r_a and r_b are perfectly and positively correlated does the locus of attainable $\bar{R}$ and σ_R combinations form a straight line between points A and B, and we can see that the lower the value of c_{ab}, the lower the level of risk associated with any given value of $\bar{R}$. This is the 'gain through portfolio diversification' that can be achieved when security returns are imperfectly correlated with one another.

In the case of the efficiency frontiers for $c_{ab} = 0.0$ and $c_{ab} = -0.5$, a part of the frontier in each case actually bends backwards and is shown by a dotted rather than a solid line. This is to indicate that

Figure 10.2: Alternative Efficiency Frontiers for Two-Security Portfolio

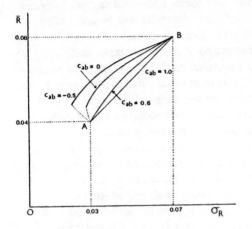

combinations of $\bar{R}$ and σ_R in such a range will not be chosen by the rational investor, whom we expect to prefer points on the same frontier vertically above those on the backward-bending section, i.e. 'more return for the same risk'. In fact, it is most unlikely that broad portfolios of securities will correlate negatively with one another, given that they will have many shares in common; and because returns on most individual securities are influenced in the same direction by general economic conditions, we expect most correlation coefficients between pairs of security returns to be positive. Thus the frontier of attainable combinations of $\bar{R}$ and σ_R is expected to have the general shape shown in Figure 10.1.

10.2 (iii) The Market Portfolio of Risky Securities

If we wish to expand our picture of individual portfolio choice into a theory of capital market equilibrium, we require a number of further assumptions. These may appear somewhat daunting, but they are in fact similar in nature and effect to those generally employed in the construction of general equilibrium models. We assume that all investors share the same estimates of the probability distributions of one-period returns of all securities, and of the correlation coefficients between all pairs of one-period returns. (Alternatively, we assume that all investors make the same estimates of the data required by Sharpe's index model approach.) Next we assume the existence of a completely risk-free asset, yielding a 'pure' interest rate, r_f, during the period in question. The value of r_f can change over time, but at the outset of each period its value is of course known for certain. Investors are able to lend or borrow freely at this interest rate. Supplies of all risky securities are given (this is a model of capital market equilibrium in the short period) and there are no transaction costs or taxes. All investors are price-takers in the capital market, each facing the same set of security prices. Finally, we must assume that each investor is actually motivated to behave in the way assumed in portfolio theory, i.e. he chooses the portfolio offering the combination of one-period expected return ($\bar{R}$) and risk (σ_R) that he most prefers.

An investor now has to make two choices: (1) how much to invest (or borrow) at the ruling risk-free interest rate, and (2) which (if any) portfolio of risky securities to purchase. We can show that the introduction of the risk-free asset alters the efficiency frontier confronting each investor in a crucial way, enabling us to predict the answer to question (2). In Figure 10.3 the efficiency frontier for portfolios of risky securities is shown as EE', and the risk-free interest rate is shown as r_f on the vertical axis.

An investor who places a fraction δ of his resources in the risk-free asset and fraction $(1 - \delta)$ in a particular efficient portfolio, k, of risky securities (shown by point k on EE') achieves the following expected one-period rate of return:

$$\bar{R}_p = \delta r_f + (1 - \delta)\bar{R}_k \tag{vii}$$

in which $\bar{R}_k$ is the expected return on portfolio k and $\bar{R}_p$ is the overall expected return on the investor's mixed portfolio (we use the term 'mixed' to denote a mixture of risky securities and a risk-free investment). Allowing for the facts that the standard deviation of the risk-free asset's return is zero and that the correlation coefficient between the risk-free return and R_k (the variable return on portfolio k) is also zero, equation (v) yields the following expression for σ_{R_p}, the standard deviation of the mixed portfolio:

$$\sigma_{R_p} = \sqrt{[(1 - \delta)\sigma_{R_k}]^2} = (1 - \delta)\sigma_{R_k} \tag{viii}$$

It is easy to show that the characteristics of all mixtures of the risk-free asset and portfolio k lie on the straight line joining r_f and point k in Figure 10.3. From (viii) we obtain

$$\delta = \left[1 - \frac{\sigma_{R_p}}{\sigma_{R_k}}\right] \tag{ix}$$

Figure 10.3: The Effect of the Risk-Free Asset on Rational Portfolio Choice

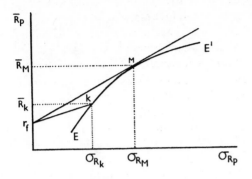

which we employ in (vii) to obtain

$$\bar{R}_p = r_f + \left[\frac{\bar{R}_k - r_f}{\sigma_{R_k}} \right] \sigma_{R_p} \tag{x}$$

This is in fact the relationship shown in Figure 10.3 as the line from r_f to k, having a vertical intercept of r_f and a slope given by $(\bar{R}_k - r_f) \div \sigma_{R_k}$. This slope describes the trade-off between expected return and risk in mixtures of portfolio k and the risk-free asset — a unit increase in the risk of the mixed portfolio increases its expected rate of return by $(\bar{R}_k - r_f) \div \sigma_{R_k}$ units. For any other efficient portfolio of risky securities the same applies; the straight line from r_f to the relevant point on EE' shows the properties of all mixtures of the risk-free asset and the risky portfolio in question.

In fact, Figure 10.3 makes it clear that the investor will *not* choose portfolio k as the basis of a mixed portfolio. However he balances expected return and risk in his own mind, we can be certain that the investor who wishes to hold a mixed portfolio will make his choice along the straight line joining r_f and point M on EE' (and extending beyond M in the case of an investor who borrows at the risk-free interest rate in order to invest more heavily in portfolio M). This line is obviously the most advantageous that can be attained, given that at point M the line from r_f is tangential to EE', and by making his choice in this way our investor secures a higher expected return for any given level of risk than he would obtain from any other mixed portfolio. Because all investors choose mixed portfolios based on risky portfolio M, this portfolio is known as the *market portfolio*, and the straight line

Figure 10.4: The Capital Market Line and Investors' Choices

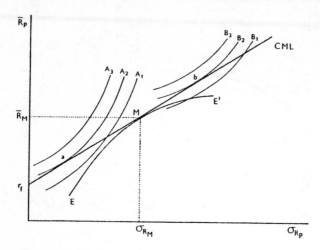

running through points r_f and M is termed the *capital market line* (CML).

$$\bar{R}_p = r_f + \left[\frac{\bar{R}_M - r_f}{\sigma_{R_M}} \right] \sigma_{R_p} \qquad \text{(xi)}$$

In Figure 10.4 we repeat the construction of Figure 10.3, but our attention now focuses on the capital market line and the choices of individual investors.

The slope of the CML is known as the *market price of risk* and is symbolised by λ:

$$\lambda = \frac{\bar{R}_M - r_f}{\sigma_{R_M}} \qquad \text{(xii)}$$

This is the standard trade-off at the margin between risk and expected return reflected in the decisions of countless individual investors, two of whom are represented by their respective indifference curve systems in Figure 10.4. These systems are drawn on the assumption that all investors are — in varying degrees — averse to risk, preferring a lower to a higher risk for a given expected return and a higher to a lower expected return for a given level of risk; and requiring an increasing increment in $\bar{R}_p$ for successive equal increments in σ_{R_p} at any given level of utility. Each investor maximises his utility by moving along the capital market line to the point of tangency between the CML and one of his indifference curves. Investor A chooses point a, dividing his own resources between the risk-free asset and the market portfolio; investor B chooses point b, committing his own resources and some funds borrowed at the risk-free interest rate to the market portfolio. For both A and B the marginal rate of substitution of expected return and risk is given by the slope of the CML.

We have now moved a considerable distance towards a theory of capital market equilibrium. What remains is to see how individual securities find their own equilibrium values within the picture of overall market equilibrium we have outlined.

10.2 (iv) Equilibrium Expected Returns on Risky Securities

Can we say anything specific about the market portfolio of risky securities which we expect all investors to hold as some proportion of their total resources? (We exclude investors whose aversion to risk is so strong that they invest only in the risk-free asset.) In particular, which securities form the market portfolio, and what are their prices? These two questions can be answered very briefly and then at greater length.

If the market portfolio is being held by all investors, to the exclusion of other possibilities, then *every* security must belong to it. Were it not so, an excluded security would command no price at all and would exist in a kind of limbo, held by no-one. Generalising this point, every security must occupy a place in the market portfolio at a price that makes it marginally attractive to all investors. Any higher price would result in its exclusion; any lower price would result in an excess demand which would lead to an increase in price. The formula for the critical expected return corresponding to this critical price will be introduced shortly, without proof. First, we introduce two statistical concepts which figured implicitly in our formulae for σ_R (equations (v) and (vi), page 232) but which now require formal definitions to enable us to follow the development of capital market equilibrium theory.

The *covariance* between two variables, x and y, is denoted by $\mathrm{Cov}(x, y)$ and can be defined as follows:

$$\mathrm{Cov}(x, y) = \sigma_x \sigma_y c_{xy} \qquad \text{(xiii)}$$

where σ_x and σ_y are the standard deviations of x and y, respectively, and c_{xy} is the coefficient of correlation between x and y. Evidently covariance is a measure of the strength and direction of association between the two variables, but its value is not confined to the range -1.00 to $+1.00$ as is the case with c_{xy}. The second concept we shall find useful is that of the *variance* of a variable, by which we mean simply the square of its standard deviation:

$$\text{Var}(z) = \sigma_z^2 \qquad \text{(xiv)}$$

The equilibrium level of expected return on an individual security, i.e. the critical value of $\bar{r}$ that just ensures its presence in the market portfolio, is defined in a number of equivalent ways. We employ $\bar{r}_i^*$ to denote the critical value of the expected return on security i:

$$\left.\begin{aligned}
\bar{r}_i^* &= r_f + c_{iM}\sigma_i \left[\frac{\bar{R}_M - r_f}{\sigma_M} \right] = r_f + c_{iM}\sigma_i \lambda \qquad \text{(a)} \\[2em]
\bar{r}_i^* &= r_f + \frac{\text{Cov}(i, M)}{\sigma_M^2}(\bar{R}_M - r_f) = r_f + \beta_i(\bar{R}_M - r_f) \quad \text{(b)}
\end{aligned}\right\} \quad \text{(xv)}$$

In version (a) of (xv) we see that $\bar{r}_i^*$ is a function of two constants, r_f and λ (the risk-free interest rate and the market price of risk, respectively) and two terms relating directly to security i. Given r_f and λ, the required expected return on security i is higher, the higher the value of c_{iM} (the correlation coefficient between r_i and R_M) and the higher the value of σ_i. This is much as we would expect; other things being equal, a security commands a higher market value — equivalent to a lower expected rate of return in equation (ii) — the lower its correlation with security returns in general (the security is valued for its portfolio risk-reducing effect) and the lower its individual risk. (The latter effect is reversed if c_{iM} is actually negative; the value of $\bar{r}_i^*$ will then actually be lower than r_f, and this advantage will be enhanced by a higher σ_i value.)

Version (b) of equation (xv), obtained by a straightforward manipulation of version (a), focuses on the relationship between the 'risk premium' on the market portfolio, i.e. the excess of its expected return over the risk-free interest rate, and the expected return on security i. The symbol β_i is used to denote the complex expression $\text{Cov}(i, M)/\sigma_M^2$, and it is in this final, much-simplified version that attempts to quantify the relationship of an individual security to the market are usually made.

10.2 (v) The Characteristic Line of a Risky Security

The picture of individual equilibrium valuation within a wider model of general equilibrium is known as the *capital asset pricing model* (CAPM). We shall find version (b) of equation (xv) extremely useful in discussing the implications of the CAPM for capital budgeting by

firms; but first we must explore the meaning and measurement of a
security's *beta coefficient*, i.e. β_i in equation (xv), version (b). By
a further small manipulation we can express β_i as the crucial linkage
between the excess return on the market portfolio, $(\bar{R}_M - r_f)$, and the
excess return on security i, $(\bar{r}_i{}^* - r_f)$:

$$(\bar{r}_i{}^* - r_f) = \beta_i(\bar{R}_M - r_f) \tag{xvi}$$

Given that our model relates to a holding period of short duration,
the expected return on a security or a portfolio is inevitably dominated
by expected price movements within the period. It follows that β_i
can be seen as a measure of the extent to which the expected price
movement of the security in question exceeds, matches or falls short
of the expected change in the price of the market portfolio. Thus, for
example, a beta coefficient that is positive but less than unity implies
that *on the average* the price of the security in question is expected
to fluctuate in the same direction but less widely than the price of the
market portfolio. Exactly analogous interpretations apply to beta
coefficients in other ranges.

In principle the value of β_i can be estimated by regression analysis,
if historical data on actual rates of return over a number of previous
periods are accepted as representative of the probabilistic relationship
between r_i and R_M likely to apply in the near future. Equation (xvi)
suggests a regression of the following form:

$$(r_i - r_f) = \alpha_i + \beta_i(R_M - r_f) + v_i \tag{xvii}$$

in which $(r_i - r_f)$ and $(R_M - r_f)$ are the actual excess returns on
security i and the market portfolio, respectively — one pair of
observations for each period covered by the regression; α_i is the
constant term in the regression equation; β_i is the regression coefficient;
and v_i represents the variation in $(r_i - r_f)$ that is due to factors other
than the influence of general conditions as represented by $(R_M - r_f)$.
(The expected value of v_i is zero.)

Each point in Figure 10.5 represents the observed combination of
excess returns $(r_i - r_f)$ and $(R_M - r_f)$ in one period, and the dashed
regression line is accepted as an estimate of the relationship between
the excess return on the market portfolio and the expected excess
return on security i — a relationship known as the *characteristic line*
of security i. The characteristic line is shown passing through the
origin, indicating $\alpha_i = 0$, as implied by equation (xvi). The logic of this
is that in an efficient market when the expected excess return on the
market portfolio is zero, no individual security can offer a lower

Figure 10.5: Characteristic Line of a Risky Security

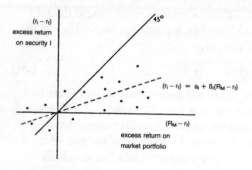

expected excess return; and since the expectation for the market portfolio is simply the weighted average for all securities, each security must have a zero alpha value (see Sharpe, 1978, pp. 104–19). In practice, if regression analysis reveals an alpha value significantly greater (less) than zero, analysts will respond by buying (selling) the security in question until its alpha value as perceived in the market is again equal to zero.

We turn now to the beta coefficient in the characteristic line of security i, estimated as the slope of the regression line shown in Figure 10.5. As stated, the value of β_i indicates the extent to which the return on security i is expected to move in line with the movement in the return on the market portfolio. In other words β_i measures the ith security's *systematic* or *undiversifiable* risk, the component of its risk which cannot be neutralised or offset by combining security i with a holding of the market portfolio. The characteristic line of security i in Figure 10.5 has a slope of less than 45 degrees, implying a beta coefficient of less than unity; as explained above this suggests that security i is, on the average, less volatile in its price movements than the market as a whole, and that it might therefore be a desirable security to hold during a general market downturn.

The remaining aspect of risk relating to security i is also shown in Figure 10.5. *Unsystematic* or *diversifiable* risk is illustrated by the scattering of the actual observations around the estimated regression line which we are accepting as an estimate of the security's characteristic line. The wider the dispersion of observations, the greater the potential for factors other than those reflected in the general movement of security prices to influence the price of (and return on) security i.

It is important to recall that the factors underlying the dispersion of actual r_i values are by definition unique to security i, and as such are assumed to have no correlation with the unsystematic risk factors of other securities. It follows that risk of this type *is* diversifiable, through the purchase of a sufficiently large number of risky securities; and as demonstrated in 10.2 (iii) this is exactly how risk-averse investors are expected to behave. (Numerous studies illustrate the dramatic reduction in diversifiable risk that can be achieved through the random selection of a fairly small number of securities; see Sharpe, 1978, pp. 113-17.) This helps us to understand why, in equation (xvi), the risk premium for security i depends only on its undiversifiable risk, as measured by β_i. Capital market theory holds that the market offers no premium for risks that the individual investor is perfectly capable of neutralising by his own actions in diversifying his portfolio (recall that we are still assuming that all transactions are costless).

10.2 (vi) Qualifications to the Capital Asset Pricing Model

Before we consider the strong implications of the CAPM for capital budgeting by firms, we should be aware of the aspects of the model that may cause us to question its practical relevance. The assumptions in this category are: (1) all investors hold the same expectations about all securities and all correlation coefficients, with information about securities' prospects being made available simultaneously and at zero cost to all investors; (2) all investors can lend or borrow freely at the same risk-free interest rate; (3) there are no transactions costs; (4) the absence of distorting effects of taxation, whether between dividend income and capital gains or between different groups of investors; (5) all investors are similarly motivated in the general nature of their utility functions and the one-period horizon they all observe in their portfolio decision making.

We cannot enter here into the considerable literature devoted to the measurement of capital market efficiency in the sense implied by these assumptions and to establishing the robustness of the CAPM under various types of departure from the ideal. (For a summary of various empirical tests of the CAPM, see Firth, 1977, pp. 96-8; a more detailed analysis of the model and of its statistical testing is contained in Jensen, 1972.) For our purpose it is sufficient to note that the presence of various imperfections may dilute the implications of the CAPM for capital budgeting, and we shall discuss our reservations in that context.

10.3 The CAPM and the Cost of Capital

10.3 (i) The Expected Rate of Return on Investment

At first glance the CAPM appears to offer little potential guidance to the firm in its investment decision making, if only because of the contrast between the short-period orientation of the CAPM and the much longer horizons involved in capital budgeting. But before we approach this obstacle we present the formal extension of our earlier analysis from the required rate of return on an individual security to the required rate of return on an individual investment project. A number of writers (e.g. Rubinstein, 1973, and Litzenberger and Budd, 1970) have demonstrated the applicability of the expression for the required return on risky security (equation (xv)) to the required return, or cost of capital, on an investment project which, initially at least, we shall assume to have a lifetime comparable to the short period assumed in the CAPM. For reasons of space our discussion in this section abstracts from considerations of capital structure and dividend policy.

Starting from the basic proposition that an investment's cost of capital is given by that rate of return (expected rate of return in this case) which results in an increase in the firm's market value just equal to the cost of the investment (8.3 (iv)), the following equation for the expected rate of return required on a project (j), denoted by $\bar{r}_j{}^*$, is obtained:

$$\bar{r}_j{}^* = r_f + \frac{\text{Cov}(j, M)}{\sigma_M{}^2}(\bar{R}_M - r_f) = r_f + \beta_j(\bar{R}_M - r_f) \qquad \text{(xviii)}$$

In (xviii) the terms used in version (b) of (xv) are repeated, the only difference being that the beta coefficient is that of *project* j, i.e. the relationship between the *project's* and the market's returns. If the rate of return required by an investor on an individual risky security depends on the probabilistic relationship between that security's return and the return on the market portfolio, it is appropriate and logical that the return on investment required by a firm *on behalf of investors* should be determined in the same way. Perhaps the most significant feature of the cost of capital condition given in (xviii) is the *absence* of any recognition of the importance of the investment's effect on the firm's own risk; an investment made on behalf of investors by a firm is subject to exactly the same test of acceptability as an investment made by an investor on his own account.

The relationship between a project's expected rate of return and its

Figure 10.6: Cost of Capital for Risky Projects

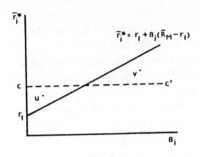

beta coefficient defined in (xviii) is illustrated in Figure 10.6 (based on Figure 3 in Rubinstein, 1973, p. 172).

Given the excess return on the market portfolio $(\bar{R}_M - r_f)$, a project's cost of capital depends on its beta coefficient in the way shown by the upward-sloping schedule in Figure 10.6. (The analogous relationship for a security's required rate of return in relation to its beta coefficient is known as the *security market line*.) Interpreting this line as a cost of capital line, we can see that it offers a solution to the problem posed but left unanswered in 9.4 (iii), i.e. the problem of identifying a non-arbitrary risk premium for a risky investment project. Given the characteristics of the market portfolio, the risk premium appropriate to project j, i.e. the value of $(\bar{r}_j{}^* - r_f)$, depends on the beta coefficient of project j *and on nothing else*.

This finding appears to contrast sharply with the traditional view of cost of capital which, as we saw in Chapter 8, focuses on the effect a project is expected to have on the *firm's* overall risk. In Figure 10.6 the dashed schedule cc' represents a firm's traditional cost of capital for investments that are expected to leave the firm's own risk unchanged. The comparison of CAPM and traditional cost of capital lines highlights two kinds of error to which the traditional approach may be subject. Figure 10.6 shows combinations of actual expected return and beta coefficient for two projects, u and v, both of which are assumed to have an insignificant effect on the firm's business risk. (The reader may confirm that projects with markedly different beta coefficients *may* nonetheless have similarly negligible effects on business risk.) By ignoring wider portfolio considerations the traditional approach will mistakenly reject u and accept v.

In essence, the contrast between the traditional and CAPM views of cost of capital is clear. According to the CAPM the significant aspect of an investment to an investor whose portfolio of risky securities is already well diversified is its probabilistic relationship to that portfolio – the effect on the business risk of the investing firm is of no particular significance. It follows that the desirability of undertaking a project should not depend on the capital budgeting procedures or business risk of the firm considering it.

In fairness to 'managerial' capital budgeting, it should be pointed out that the cost of capital line cc' in Figure 10.6 does *not* fully reflect the kind of managerial approach to risky investment appraisal discussed in Chapters 8 and 9. This point deserves some elaboration.

10.3 (ii) CAPM and 'Traditional' Risk Premiums

Given that management working within a broadly traditional cost of capital approach would attempt to fix a project's risk premium to reflect either its individual risk or, more probably, its effect on the firm's overall risk, we can be reasonably sure that if a cost of capital line reflecting managerial policy could be represented in Figure 10.6 it would actually have an upward slope. A reminder of the full definition of a project's beta coefficient (see equations (xiii) and (xviii)) will help to illustrate this point:

$$\beta_j = \frac{\text{Cov}(j, M)}{\sigma_M^{\,2}} = \frac{c_{jM}\,\sigma_j\sigma_M}{\sigma_M^{\,2}} \tag{xix}$$

in which c_{jM} denotes the correlation between the returns on project j and the market portfolio, and σ_j and σ_M are the standard deviations of returns on project j and the market portfolio, respectively. Given σ_M, the value of β_j depends on c_{jM} and σ_j; and it can be argued that management's arbitrary, self-centred and inevitably inexact fixing of a risk premium for project j produces the same kind of result as the more sophisticated apparatus of the market-oriented beta coefficient approach. For σ_j this point is obvious enough: assuming for the moment that project j correlates positively with the firm's other investments, management will set a target for $\bar{r}_j$ that rises as σ_j increases, thereby reflecting the adverse effect of the project on the firm's overall risk in the target return for the project.

The proposition that management's response to c_{jM} is more or less appropriate, albeit unconsciously so, is subject to rather more qualification. It rests on the likelihood that, given the value of σ_j, the higher the value of c_{jM} the more adverse is the effect of project j *on the firm's own risk*, and the higher therefore will be the risk premium fixed by management. It is easy to see why this should be so in the extreme case where the firm's own return correlates perfectly and positively with R_M; in this situation a low (or negative) value of c_{jM} would result in a lowering of the firm's overall risk and, presumably, a low risk premium for project j. Generally we expect a firm's return to correlate positively but less than perfectly with R_M, which has the effect of weakening but probably not completely destroying the linkage between a project's c_{jM} value and the direction of that project's effect on the firm's own risk.

Generalising these points, it is probably unfair to traditional cost of capital thinking to represent it as completely ignoring the relevance of the correlation between the firm's and the market's returns. Management is presumably aware of any significant association between a firm's cost of capital as described in Chapter 8 and the way in which the firm's earnings tend to move with or against the general movement in company performance. This point, taken together with the above arguments relating to σ_j and c_{jM}, suggests that the results of 'traditional' investment decision making are unlikely to differ as spectacularly from those emerging from the CAPM approach as the rather simplistic comparison in Figure 10.6 implies. (Weston, 1973, p. 27, concedes that the representation of 'traditional' decision making is oversimplified in Figure 10.6.)

10.3 (iii) Implications of the CAPM for Capital Budgeting

Accepting the CAPM for the purpose of this discussion as a true picture of capital market equilibrium, our foremost reservation about its relevance to capital budgeting stems from the contrast between its short-period horizon and the much longer life span of the typical 'real' investment proposal. This contrast by itself presents no insuperable theoretical problem. After all, financial securities as well as physical investments have extended lifetimes; and if markets in 'second hand' physical investments were as perfect and costless as we assume the securities market to be, it would be comparatively easy to accept the relevance of the CAPM to business investment decisions.

In practice, matters are very different. With few exceptions long-lived assets are *not* traded during their lifetimes in conditions approximating to those prevailing in securities markets, and such trading as does take place may be done at uneconomic prices and involve substantial costs (transfer of ownership and possibly location, delay, etc.). The calculation of a project's short-period rate of return and beta coefficient are thus likely to be distorted or made impossible by a species of market imperfection not present in securities markets.

Different ways of overcoming this incompatibility between portfolio decision making and capital budgeting have been suggested, but a completely satisfactory integration remains to be demonstrated. Bogue and Roll (1974) showed that a multi-period project can be evaluated in the short-period context of the CAPM if the decision maker can estimate (i) the probabilistic relationship between the anticipated cash flow of the project and the performance of the market portfolio in each future period, and (ii) the behaviour, in probabilistic terms, of the risk-free interest rate in future periods. These estimates enable the decision maker to identify the present value of the project's future prospects for comparison with its immediate cost. However, the intermediate conditional valuations defined under this approach are those valuations that fully reflect the project's prospects during the remainder of its economic life, with no allowance for the project's possible premature disposal at an uneconomic price.

Faced with major theoretical obstacles, a number of writers have suggested practical ways of employing the CAPM framework in capital budgeting (see Van Horne, 1977, pp. 172-9). One obvious approach is to employ as the beta coefficient in equation (xix) an average or representative estimate derived from market data relating to businesses engaged in activities similar to those of the project in question.

An alternative to seeking an external proxy is to estimate β_j directly, by one of several possible simulation approaches. In one such approach the analyst would 'forecast' the rate of return the project would have achieved in each year of its lifetime, supposing this to have occurred under the actual economic conditions experienced by the firm and the country over recent years. In principle this exercise would yield a time series of hypothetical excess returns on the project in question which could be regressed with the actual excess returns on the market portfolio to obtain the project's beta coefficient, as described earlier for an individual security. The exercise is likely to be bedevilled by the impossibility of making accurate conditional annual earnings 'forecasts' and, more seriously, by the likelihood that the hypothetical annual project rates of return obtained depend crucially on information about asset values at the beginning and end of each year which is either unobtainable or unreliable. (The procedure involved in obtaining each year's hypothetical rate of return is analogous to identifying a security's r value in equation (i), substituting the opening and closing market values of the project's assets for P_0 and P_1, respectively, and the project's earnings for D_1.)

An alternative means of estimating a project's beta value bypasses most of the above objections. Taking the project's anticipated lifetime as the 'period', the performances of the project and the market portfolio are forecast under a limited number of different assumptions about the 'state of the world' (Weston, 1973, p. 27), and by assigning probabilities to the latter a beta coefficient for the project is estimated. However, in bypassing the problems of the dubious measurement and significance of short-period r values, this method exposes the fundamental incompatibility between the frameworks for portfolio and capital budgeting decisions. In portfolio theory the active investor does *not* see the probabilistic relationship between project j's lifetime rate of return and the prospective return on the market portfolio over the same period as particularly significant.

Apart from doubts about the statistical reliability and theoretical validity of techniques for estimating project beta coefficients, there is an even more fundamental question regarding the appropriateness of the CAPM in capital budgeting. An implication of portfolio theory is that the firm need not and should not attempt to eliminate diversifiable risk *on behalf of investors* (need not, because investors diversify their own portfolios; should not, because businesses are probably much less efficient at achieving diversification than individual investors). While this logic is acceptable up to a point, shareholders may be reluctant to see management accepting investments which, in certain circumstances, might actually lead to the bankruptcy or liquidation of the firm. Implicit in our discussion thus far has been the assumption that the bankruptcy of a firm is a smooth and painless process — at least as far as investors are concerned. In a perfect market productive assets can be sold for their full economic values, i.e. values that fully reflect their future earnings prospects and risks, so investors are indifferent to the survival of the actual business units in which they invest. Putting the same point rather differently, the return to investors from project j in any year is not affected by the overall financial position of the firm investing in the project. Assets can always be transferred between firms at zero cost and with no delay.

The practical objections to this line of argument are obvious. If a perfect market in the assets of bankrupt firms does not exist, so that bankruptcy is not a costless event for investors, it may after all be advisable for a manager to choose projects with a view to reducing the firm's own diversifiable risk and that faced by its investors. This conclusion is strengthened if investors' portfolios are not in fact as well diversified as portfolio theory assumes.

Quite apart from the risk of business bankruptcy, the failure of investors to achieve full elimination of diversifiable risk constitutes a serious reservation in its own right about the validity of the CAPM in capital budgeting. Because of transactions costs, information costs, etc., investors may place additional value on the shares of firms that *have* undertaken the elimination of diversifiable risk on their behalf (see Douglas, 1969).

How significantly do the reservations we have mentioned affect the basic recommendation of the CAPM in the capital budgeting context — that a firm should disregard the impact of a project on its own risk and should concentrate on the relationship between the project's risk and the undiversifiable risk of the market portfolio? Our objections to the implications of the undiluted CAPM (bankruptcy risk and lack of portfolio diversification) may be dismissed as comparatively unimportant as far as most firms and investors are concerned; but our reservations on the actual identification of the crucial beta coefficient are much less easily dismissed. At the present stage of development of the CAPM a pragmatic approach is perhaps most appropriate. Investments should be appraised under the traditional *and* CAPM criteria, and any disagreements (see Figure 10.6 and related discussion) should be resolved in the light of such considerations as risk and cost of bankruptcy, the nature of the market for the firm's equity capital and the reliability of the data on which rival appraisals are based.

10.4 Conclusion

The reader may be forgiven for harbouring a lingering suspicion that portfolio theory and capital budgeting — theory and practice — do not, cannot and should not meet; that prospective short-period risks and returns in the securities market are not suitable criteria by which to measure the value of long-term benefits generated by investments. A feeling that purely 'speculative' considerations should not impinge upon 'real' investment decision making is entirely understandable, especially when it is expressed by businessmen actually enmeshed in difficult investment choices. Equally understandably, a businessman may feel more at home within the traditional framework described in Chapter 8, for two reasons: (1) the traditional framework's explicit acceptance of the long-term basis of valuation, and (2) its implicit confirmation of his inclination to adopt a partial or self-centred interpretation of the firm's market valuation (Mao, 1970, p. 352). It seems appropriate, therefore, to conclude our study of investment appraisal theory by briefly discussing possibilities for closing the gaps between rival valuation models and approaches to cost of capital measurement.

In what can be seen as an attempt to narrow the 'cost of capital gap', Weston (1973) suggested that a company's beta coefficient, estimated from historical data, might be used along with forecasts of average future values of r_f and R_M to yield an equity cost of capital estimate for the firm in question. For firm x the cost of equity, $\bar{k}_x^*$ — the required level of expected return on equity investment — would be estimated as follows:

$$\bar{k}_x^* = \bar{r}_f + \beta_x(\bar{R}_M - \bar{r}_f) \tag{xx}$$

in which $\bar{r}_f$ and $\bar{R}_M$ now represent, respectively, management's estimates of the average future values of the risk-free interest rate and the rate of return on the market portfolio, and β_x is the estimated beta coefficient for firm x. In two ways this represents a move towards the traditional approach to the cost of equity. First, the value of $\bar{k}_x^*$ is accepted as the cost of equity for *firm* x rather than for any single project, subject to the qualification that projects undertaken by the firm do not significantly affect its systematic risk, β_x. Second, the cost of capital is seen as influenced by the average anticipated performance of the market over a lengthy period of time, in much the same way as the traditional cost of equity can be interpreted as the rate of return equity investors can expect to earn over the long term (Merrett and Sykes, 1963, pp. 72–4, and 1963a). The attempt to link the return on each project to the performance of the market portfolio in the ultra-short period (or succession of short periods) gives way to a much-diluted compromise version of a CAPM criterion.

A more ambitious gap-bridging exercise is to try to narrow the differences between traditional and portfolio valuation models. We have referred earlier to such factors as transactions costs and bankruptcy costs as possible reasons for a firm's equity being valued *not only* on the basis of its systematic or undiversifiable risk; and these qualifications to the pure CAPM represent something of a move towards the traditional position. The two views can be brought even closer together by a determined effort to 'get behind' the expected end-period value of a risky security in the portfolio valuation model, i.e. $\bar{P}_1$ in equation (ii). It can be shown (Baker, 1978, pp. 29-38) that by repeatedly pushing forward the horizon of the single-period valuation model a standard valuation model along traditional lines is obtained, subject to the not unreasonable condition that investors assume unchanging future trends in interest rates, market returns and the systematic risk of the firm in question. The typical equity discount factor that emerges from this exercise turns out to be a probability-weighted average of the discount factors that are believed possible in each future short period.

By establishing conditions for the equivalence of the two super-ficially opposed valuation models we can at least answer the obvious criticism that unless portfolio theory can be shown to recognise the importance of long-term earnings expectations, it cannot be applied to capital budgeting. More positively, it becomes acceptable to cross-check cost of capital estimates derived in quite different ways from portfolio and traditional valuation models. This possibility is no less welcome for its emphasis on compromise — as we have shown, estimating beta coefficients for investment projects is far from being a straightforward mechanical exercise. Similarly, estimation of the cost of equity in the traditional framework is attended by numerous difficulties, both conceptual and practical (Baker, 1978, pp. 168-81).

We conclude by briefly summarising our findings on the applicability of the CAPM to capital budgeting. Long-lived investments, while theoretically amenable to appraisal within the CAPM framework, are subject to two kinds of special difficulty. (1) Their probabilistic relationships to the performance of the market portfolio over time are crucially important yet extremely difficult to estimate. In principle, all types of assets are alike in these respects, but most financial securities have the advantage of long (and presumably relevant) histories of relationships to the market portfolio. (2) The risk of business bankruptcy can be altered by the firm's choice of investment projects, and with imperfect markets for second-hand physical assets a proposal's required rate of return may depend on the circumstances of the firm carrying out the investment. Quite apart from questions about the validity of the CAPM, these factors are likely to continue to bedevil the full integration of capital budgeting with capital market theory.

BIBLIOGRAPHY

Allen, R.G.D. (1960) *Mathematical Economics*, 2nd ed., Macmillan, London.

Archer, S.H., Choate, G.M. and Racette, G. (1979) *Financial Management: An Introduction*, John Wiley, New York.

Baker, A.J. (1978) *Investment, Valuation and the Managerial Theory of the Firm*, Saxon House, Farnborough.

Baker, A.J. (1979) 'Growth and Valuation in "Managerial" Theory: An Alternative View', *Journal of Economic Studies*, vol. 6 (May), pp. 39-63.

Battersby, A. (1966) *Mathematics in Management*, Penguin, Harmondsworth.

Baumol, W.J. (1967) *Business Behaviour, Value and Growth*, rev. ed., Harcourt, Brace and World, New York.

Baumol, W.J. (1972) *Economic Theory and Operations Analysis*, 3rd ed., Prentice-Hall, Englewood Cliffs, N.J.

Baumol, W.J. (1977) *Economic Theory and Operations Analysis*, 4th ed., Prentice-Hall, Englewood Cliffs, N.J.

Berle, A.A. and Means, G.C. (1932) *The Modern Corporation and Private Property*, Macmillan, New York

Bierman, H. (1970) *Financial Policy Decisions*, Macmillan, London.

Bierman, H. and Hass, J.E. (1975) *An Introduction to Managerial Finance*, Pitman, London (first published in USA in 1973 by W.W. Norton).

Bogue, M.C. and Roll, R. (1974) 'Capital Budgeting of Risky Projects with "Imperfect" Markets for Physical Capital', *Journal of Finance*, vol. 29 (May), pp. 601-13.

Boulding, K.E. and Spivey, W.A. (1960) *Linear Programming and the Theory of the Firm*, Macmillan, New York.

Bridge, J. and Dodds, J.C. (1975) *Managerial Decision Making*, Croom Helm, London.

Brigham, E.F. (1979) *Financial Management, Theory and Practice*, 2nd ed., Dryden Press, Hinsdale, Ill.

Bromwich, M. (1976) *The Economics of Capital Budgeting*, Penguin, Harmondsworth.

Chamberlin, E.H. (1933) *The Theory of Monopolistic Competition*, Harvard U.P., Cambridge, Mass.

253

Charnes, A. and Cooper, W.W. (1959) 'Chance-Constrained Programming', *Management Science*, vol. 6 (October), pp. 73-9.

Crew, M.A. (1975) *Theory of the Firm*, Longman, Harlow, Essex.

Crew, M.A., Jones-Lee, M.W. and Rowley, C.K. (1971) 'X Theory *versus* Management Discretion Theory', *Southern Economic Journal*, vol. 38 (October), pp. 173-84.

Dantzig, D.G. (1963) *Linear Programming and Extensions*, Princeton U.P., Princeton, N.J.

Dorfman, R. (1953) 'Mathematical or "Linear" Programming: A Non-Mathematical Exposition', *American Economic Review*, vol. 43 (Dec.) pp. 797-825.

Dorfman, R., Samuelson, P. and Solow, R. (1958) *Linear Programming and Economic Analysis*, McGraw-Hill, New York.

Douglas, G. (1969) 'Risk in the Equity Markets', *Yale Economic Essays* (Spring).

Edwards, W. (1954) 'The Theory of Decision Making', *Psychological Bulletin*, vol. 51, no. 54, pp. 380-417. (Reprinted in Edwards, W. and Tversky, A.T. (eds.), *Decision Making*, Penguin, Harmondsworth, 1967.)

Elton, E.J. (1970) 'Capital Rationing and External Discount Rates', *Journal of Finance*, vol. 25 (June), pp. 573-84.

Firth, M. (1977) *The Valuation of Shares and Efficient Markets Theory*, Macmillan, London.

Frazer, J.R. (1968) *Applied Linear Programming*, Prentice-Hall, Englewood Cliffs, N.J.

Friedman, M. and Savage, L.J. (1948) 'The Utility Analysis of Choices Involving Risk', *Journal of Political Economy*, vol. 56 (August), pp. 279-304.

Garvin, W.W. (1960) *Introduction to Linear Programming*, McGraw-Hill, New York.

Gitman, L.J. and Forrester, J.R. (1977) 'A Survey of Capital Budgeting Techniques Used by Major U.S. Firms', *Financial Management* (Fall), pp. 66-71.

Gordon, M.J. (1962) 'The Savings, Investment and Valuation of a Corporation', *Review of Economics and Statistics*, vol. 44 (February), pp. 37-51.

Haley, K.B. (1967) *Mathematical Programming for Business and Industry*, Macmillan, London.

Hall, R.I. and Hitch, C.J. (1939) 'Price Theory and Business Behaviour', *Oxford Economic Papers* (May), pp. 12-45.

Hamburg, M. (1970) *Statistical Analysis for Decision Making*, Harcourt,

Brace and World, New York.

Hammond, J.S. (1967) 'Better Decisions with Preference Theory', *Harvard Business Review* (November-December, pp. 123-41).

Hawkins, C.J. (1973) *Theory of the Firm*, Macmillan, London.

Hawkins, C.J. and Pearce, D.W. (1971) *Capital Investment Appraisal*, Macmillan, London.

Helliwell, J.F. (1968) *Public Policies and Private Investment*, Clarendon Press, Oxford.

Henderson, A. and Schlaifer, R. (1965) 'Mathematical Programming; Better Information for Decision Making', in Bursk, E.C. and Chapman, J.F. (eds.), *New Decision Making Tools for Managers*, Mentor, New York.

Hertz, D.B. (1964) 'Risk Analysis in Capital Investment', *Harvard Business Review* (January-February, pp. 95-106).

Hespos, R. and Strassman, P. (1965) 'Stochastic Decision-Trees for the Analysis of Investment Decisions', *Management Science*, vol. 11 (August), pp. 244-59.

Hillier, F.S. (1963) 'The Derivation of Probabilistic Information for the Analysis of Risky Investments', *Management Science*, vol. 9 (April), pp. 443-57.

Horowitz, I. (1972) *An Introduction to Quantitative Business Analysis*, 2nd ed., McGraw-Hill, New York.

I.C.E. (Institution of Civil Engineers) (1969) *Engineering Economics*, Institution of Civil Engineers, London.

Jensen, M.C. (1972) 'Capital Markets: Theory and Evidence', *Bell Journal of Economics and Management Science*, vol. 3 (Autumn), pp. 363-91.

Jones, G.T. (1972) *Simulation and Business Decisions*, Penguin, Harmondsworth.

Kmietowicz, Z.W. and Yannoulis, Y. (1976) *Statistical and Financial Tables for the Social Sciences*, Longman, London.

Knight, F.H. (1921) *Risk, Uncertainty and Profit*, Houghton Mifflin, Boston.

Koutsoyiannis, A. (1979) *Modern Microeconomics*, 2nd ed., Macmillan, London.

Krekó, B. (1968) *Linear Programming*, English translation, Pitman, London.

Leibenstein, H. (1966) 'Allocative Efficiency *vs* X-Efficiency', *American Economic Review*, vol. 56 (June), pp. 392-415.

Lerner, E.M. and Carleton, W.T. (1966) *A Theory of Financial Analysis*, Harcourt, Brace and World, New York.

Levy, H. and Sarnat, M. (1978) *Capital Investment and Financial Decisions*, Prentice-Hall International, London.

Litzenberger, R.H. and Budd, A.P. (1970) 'Corporate Investment Criteria and the Evaluation of Investment Portfolios', *Journal of Financial and Quantitative Analysis*, vol. 5 (December), pp. 395-420.

Lorie, J.H. and Savage, L.J. (1955) 'Three Problems in Rationing Capital', *Journal of Business*, vol. 28 (October), pp. 229-39.

Machlup, M. (1967) 'Theories of the Firm: Marginalist, Behavioural, Managerial', *American Economic Review*, vol. 57 (March), pp. 1-33.

Madansky, A. (1963) 'Linear Programming under Uncertainty', in Graves, R.I. and Wolfe, P. (eds.), *Recent Advances in Mathematical Programming*, McGraw-Hill, New York.

Magee, J.F. (1964) 'Decision Trees for Decision Making', *Harvard Business Review* (July-August, pp. 126-38).

Magee, J.F. (1964a) 'How to Use Decision Trees in Capital Investment', *Harvard Business Review* (September-October, pp. 79-96).

Mao, J.C.T. (1969) *Quantitative Analysis of Financial Decisions*, Macmillan, London.

Mao, J.C.T. (1970) 'Survey of Capital Budgeting: Theory and Practice', *Journal of Finance*, vol. 25 (May), pp. 349-60.

Marris, R.L. (1964) *The Economic Theory of Managerial Capitalism*, Macmillan, London.

Merrett, A.J. and Sykes, A. (1963) *The Finance and Analysis of Capital Projects*, Longman, London.

Merrett, A.J. and Sykes, A. (1963a) 'Incomes Policy and Company Profitability', *District Bank Review* (September), pp. 18-30.

Modigliani, F. and Miller, M.H. (1958) 'The Cost of Capital, Corporation Finance and the Theory of Investment', *American Economic Review*, vol. 48 (June), pp. 261-97.

Modigliani, F. and Miller, M.H. (1959) 'The Cost of Capital, Corporation Finance and the Theory of Investment: Reply', *American Economic Review*, vol. 49 (September), pp. 655-69.

Modigliani, F. and Miller, M.H. (1961) 'Dividend Policy, Growth and the Valuation of Shares', *Journal of Business*, vol. 34 (October), pp. 411-33.

Modigliani, F. and Miller, M.H. (1963) 'Corporate Income Taxes and the Cost of Capital: A Correction', *American Economic Review*, vol. 53 (June), pp. 433-42.

Moore, P.G. (1972) *Risk in Business Decision*, Longman, London.

Moore, P.G. and Thomas, H. (1976) *The Anatomy of Decisions*,

Penguin, Harmondsworth.

Morgan, B.W. (1968) *An Introduction to Bayesian Statistical Decision Processes*, Prentice-Hall, Englewood Cliffs, N.J.

Myers, S.C. (1972) 'A Note on Linear Programming and Capital Rationing', *Journal of Finance*, vol. 27 (March), pp. 89–92.

Naylor, T.H. and Vernon, J.M. (1969) *Microeconomics and Decision Models of the Firm*, Harcourt, Brace and World, New York.

Niland, P. (1970) *Production Planning, Scheduling, and Inventory Control*, Collier Macmillan, London.

Penrose, E.T. (1959) *The Theory of the Growth of the Firm*, Basil Blackwell, Oxford.

Porterfield, J.T.S. (1963) *Investment Decisions and Capital Costs*, Prentice-Hall, Englewood Cliffs, N.J.

Quirin, G.D. (1967) *The Capital Expenditure Decision*, Richard D. Irwin, Homewood, Ill.

Robichek, A.A. and Myers, S.C. (1965) *Optimal Financing Decisions*, Prentice-Hall, Englwood Cliffs, N.J.

Robichek, A.A. and Myers, S.C. (1966) 'Conceptual Problems in the Use of Risk-Adjusted Discount Rates', *Journal of Finance*, vol. 21 (December), pp. 727–30.

Robinson, J. (1933) *The Economics of Imperfect Competition*, Macmillan, London.

Rubinstein, M.E. (1973) 'A Mean-Variance Synthesis of Corporate Financial Theory', *Journal of Finance*, vol. 28 (March), pp. 167–81.

Samuels, J.M. and Wilkes, F.M. (1975) *Management of Company Finance*, 2nd ed., Nelson, London.

Sasaki, K. (1970) *Introduction to Finite Mathematics and Linear Programming*, Wadsworth, Belmont, California.

Sasieni, M., Yaspan, A. and Friedman, L. (1959) *Operations Research: Methods and Problems*, John Wiley, New York.

Scitovsky, T. (1943) 'A Note on Profit Maximisation and its Implications', *Review of Economic Studies*, vol. 11 (Winter), pp. 57–60.

Sharpe, W.F. (1963) 'A Simplified Model for Portfolio Analysis', *Management Science*, vol. 9 (January), pp. 277–93.

Sharpe, W.F. (1970) *Portfolio Theory and Capital Markets*, McGraw-Hill, New York.

Sharpe, W.F. (1978) *Investments*, Prentice-Hall, Englewood Cliffs, N.J.

Smythe, W.R. and Johnson, L.A. (1966) *Introduction to Linear Programming, with Applications*, Prentice-Hall, Englewood Cliffs, N.J.

Solomon, E. (1963) *The Theory of Financial Management*, Columbia U.P., New York.

Solomon, E. and Pringle, J.J. (1977) *An Introduction to Financial Management*, Goodyear Publishing Company, Santa Monica.

Swalm, R.O. (1966) 'Utility Theory — Insights into Risk Taking', *Harvard Business Review* (November–December), pp. 123-36.

Van de Panne, C. (1971) *Linear Programming and Related Techniques*, North Holland, Amsterdam.

Van Horne, J.C. (1966) 'Capital Budgeting Decisions Involving Combinations of Risky Investments', *Management Science*, vol. 13 (October), pp. 84-92.

Van Horne, J.C. (1977) *Financial Management and Policy*, 4th ed., Prentice-Hall, Englewood Cliffs, N.J.

Von Neumann, J. and Morgenstern, O. (1944) *Theory of Games and Economic Behaviour*, Princeton U.P., Princeton, N.J.

Weaver, W. (1977) *Lady Luck, The Theory of Probability*, Penguin, Harmondsworth (first published in 1963).

Weingartner, H.M. (1963) *Mathematical Programming and the Analysis of Capital Budgeting Problems*, Prentice-Hall, Englewood Cliffs, N.J.

Weston, J.F. (1973) 'Investment Decisions Using the Capital Asset Pricing Model', *Financial Management* (Spring), pp. 25-33.

Weston, J.F. and Brigham, E.F. (1979) *Managerial Finance*, 1st British edition adapted from the 6th American edition by Boyle, J. and Limmack, R.J., Holt, Rinehart and Winston, Eastbourne.

Wildsmith, J.R. (1973) *Managerial Theories of the Firm*, Martin-Robertson, London.

Wilkes, F.M. (1977) *Capital Budgeting Techniques*, John Wiley, London.

Williams, J.D. (1966) *The Compleat Strategyst*, McGraw-Hill, New York.

Williamson, J.H. (1966) 'Profit, Growth and Sales Maximisation', *Economica*, vol. 33 (February), pp. 1-16.

Williamson, O.E. (1963) 'Managerial Discretion and the Theory of the Firm', *American Economic Review*, vol. 53 (December), pp. 1032-57.

Williamson, O.E. (1964) *The Economics of Discretionary Behaviour: Managerial Objectives in a Theory of the Firm*, Prentice-Hall, Englewood Cliffs, N.J.

Williamson, O.E. (1970) *Corporate Control and Business Behaviour*, Prentice-Hall, Englewood Cliffs, N.J.

Yamane, T. (1967) *Statistics: An Introductory Analysis*, Harper and Row, New York.

INDEX